CW01281442

New Approaches in Sociology
Studies in Social Inequality, Social Change, and Social Justice

Edited by
Nancy A. Naples
University of Connecticut

A Routledge Series

New Approaches in Sociology
Studies in Social Inequality, Social Change, and Social Justice
Nancy A. Naples, *General Editor*

Talking Back to Psychiatry
The Psychiatric Consumer/Survivor/Ex-Patient Movement
Linda J. Morrison

Contextualizing Homelessness
Critical Theory, Homelessness, and Federal Policy Addressing the Homeless
Ken Kyle

Linking Activism
Ecology, Social Justice, and Education for Social Change
Morgan Gardner

The Everyday Lives of Sex Workers in the Netherlands
Katherine Gregory

Striving and Surviving
A Daily Life Analysis of Honduran Transnational Families
Leah Schmalzbauer

Unequal Partnerships
Beyond the Rhetoric of Philanthropic Collaboration
Ira Silver

Domestic Democracy
At Home in South Africa
Jennifer Natalie Fish

Praxis and Politics
Knowledge Production in Social Movements
Janet M. Conway

The Suppression of Dissent
How the State and Mass Media Squelch USAmerican Social Movements
Jules Boykoff

Are We Thinking Straight?
The Politics of Straightness in a Lesbian and Gay Social Movement Organization
Daniel K. Cortese

"Rice Plus"
Widows and Economic Survival in Rural Cambodia
Susan Hagood Lee

"Between Worlds"
Deaf Women, Work, and Intersections of Gender and Ability
Cheryl G. Najarian

If I Only Had a Brain
Deconstructing Brain Injury
Mark Sherry

Minority within a Minority
Black Francophone Immigrants and the Dynamics of Power and Resistance
Amal I. Madibbo

Gender Trouble Makers
Education and Empowerment in Nepal
Jennifer Rothchild

No Place Like Home
Organizing Home-Based Labor in the Era of Structural Adjustment
David E. Staples

Negotiating Decolonization in the United Nations
Politics of Space, Identity, and International Community
Vrushali Patil

Negotiating Decolonization in the United Nations
Politics of Space, Identity, and International Community

Vrushali Patil

Routledge
New York & London

First published 2008
by Routledge
270 Madison Ave, New York, NY 10016

Simultaneously published in the UK
by Routledge
2 Park Square, Milton Park, Abingdon, Oxon OX14 4RN

Routledge is an imprint of the Taylor & Francis Group, an informa business

© 2008 Vrushali Patil

Typeset in Sabon by IBT Global
Printed and bound in the United States of America on acid-free paper by IBT Global

All rights reserved. No part of this book may be reprinted or reproduced or utilised in any form or by any electronic, mechanical, or other means, now known or hereafter invented, including photocopying and recording, or in any information storage or retrieval system, without permission in writing from the publishers.

Trademark Notice: Product or corporate names may be trademarks or registered trademarks, and are used only for identification and explanation without intent to infringe.

Library of Congress Cataloging in Publication Data
Patil, Vrushali.
Negotiating decolonization in the United Nations: politics of space, identity, and international community / by Vrushali Patil.
p. cm. —(New approaches in sociology)
Includes bibliographical references and index.
ISBN 0-415-95856-3
1. Decolonization. 2. Colonies (International law). 3. United Nations. 4. Afro-Asian politics. I. Title. II. Series.

JV185.P37 2007
341.2'8—dc22   2007018049

ISBN10: 0-415-95856-3 (hbk)
ISBN10: 0-203-93505-5 (ebk)

ISBN13: 978-0-415-95856-1 (hbk)
ISBN13: 978-0-203-93505-7 (ebk)

To Edward

Contents

Acknowledgments ix

Introduction 1

Chapter One
Kinship Politics and Space, Identity and International Community Prior to Legal Decolonization: The Problem and the Query 5

Chapter Two
(Re)negotiating the Colonial Problematic: The UN Charter, the Emergence of Asia-Africa, and the Anti-Colonial Challenge to Kinship 39

Chapter Three
The Limits of the Anti-Colonial Critique: Anti-Colonialists' Visions and Divisions 69

Chapter Four
Contending Perspectives?: The Overlap between Colonialist and Anti-Colonialist Narratives on Dependency and Sovereignty 95

Chapter Five
Masculinity, Time and Brotherhood: Resolving the Colonial Problematic 113

Chapter Six
Conclusion: Twentieth Century Transformations of Space, Identity and International Community 137

Appendix
Tables and Figures 149

Notes 167

Bibliography 175

Index 189

Acknowledgments

This project could not have been completed without the tireless efforts and support of Patricio Korzeniewicz, nor the invaluable advice of Deborah Rosenfelt, Richard Brown, Laura Mamo, Meyer Kestnbaum, Claire Moses and Katie King. I would also like to thank the Driskell Center/CRGE Writing Group, Na-young Lee, Robyn Epstein, Gwyn Weathers, Emily Mann, Kelly Ryan, and Nancy Forsythe for the fabulous conversations along the way. This research was partially supported by the University of Maryland. Finally, thanks to Mom, Dad and Prachi, to my "second" parents, Marcia and Gary, and to Edward.

Introduction

Sociological work on difference and inequality has proceeded at multiple levels of analysis, each of which speaks to the others only rarely. At the "macro" level, for example, this work has been preoccupied with terms such as modernity, development and rationalization, and sociologists here have compared states at different stages of the so-called modernity-development-rationalization continuum, concerning themselves with delineating the factors that determine advancement or stagnation on this front. At the "micro" level, on the other hand, work on difference and inequality has examined experiences of racism, classism, and sexism; and in recent years, intersectional work has also focused on how these different dimensions of inequality intersect and interact. Additionally, some studies also exist at the "meso" level of institutions and organizations. Yet, despite this plethora of work on difference and inequality, the attempt to bring together these multiple levels of analysis and indeed, to speak to these levels simultaneously, is rare. From such a multi-level perspective, for example, what might a state's comparative position on this modernity-development-rationalization continuum have to do with decidedly local but globalized constructions of racial or cultural or sexual inequality? Otherwise stated, how do we broaden our understanding of the intersections of racial, cultural and sexual hierarchy within the largely United States-focused literature to incorporate broader histories of globalization? Moving one step back from experiences of racial, cultural or sexual inequality, as well as from determinants of modernity or development or rationalization, I am interested in the processes of racialization and sexualization—in the power-laden processes of differentiation—that help constitute categories of difference and inequality across multiple levels of analysis in the first place.

I am especially interested in exploring these multi-level processes of differentiation within the histories of Euro-American imperialism, colonialism and decolonization that have been so integral to the contemporary shape of the modern world—an analytical space that has rarely been examined by sociological work at any level. For example, how have these histories of colonialism in Asia, Africa and the Americas, in their various manifestations, shaped not just modern notions of racial, or sexual or cultural difference, but also of the statuses of development and underdevelopment—all identity constructs through which colonialism denied the spatial and identity claims of its various others? Regarding this denial of spatial and identity claims, according to Michael Shapiro, "to be an object of moral solicitude and a subject with eligibility to act within the domain of the political, one must occupy space and have an identity that commands a recognition of that occupation (See, for example, 1999: 74–75)." Thus, the identity/spatial order of the colonial era—a world map dotted by metropoles and their dependent territories—relied on granting "moral solicitude" only to some while denying it to others. In doing so, it relied on what I call a "differential personhood" or "differential subjectivity," thereby helping to construct an international community based on affirming the personhood of some while denying personhood to others.

Beyond these hierarchies of colonialism, I am also interested in how anti-colonialists related to, negotiated with, and ultimately challenged these constructions of space, identity and international community in their efforts at decolonization. Specifically, in this process, I am interested in how anti-colonialists addressed the colonialist construction of differential personhood, and the racial, cultural and sexual politics on which it relied.

In this study, I address these questions in several parts. First, I examine colonialist discourses prior to legal decolonization in order to develop a theory about space, identity and international community in the colonial era. I start here with an examination of the development of the nation-state system as the advance of imperial models of space and identity over alternative, non-state models. I argue that this process is driven in part by what I call a "politics of embodiment," or the deployment of the developing modernist hierarchy of rational/irrational. Also manifesting as a gender (masculine/feminine) and an age (parent/child) hierarchy, the politics of embodiment ultimately becomes a key component in colonial theories of racial, cultural and gender inequality. For example, colonialist discourse often constructed its others as insufficiently masculine men or as children, thereby denying them full personhood and providing a key step in the ultimate take-over of their lands. But this differential personhood via embodiment politics is only one piece of a broader kinship politics, which, I argue, is the key to understanding international community, or relations of power across these (differentially ordered) territories and peoples, in the colonial era. That is, a central way in which colonialist discourse imagined the nature of its authority in colonial relationships was on the model of authority within kinship relations, particularly the western European family. Thus, this rule positioned itself as the rational/masculine/paternal, which possessed a natural and legitimate right to rule, much like the father within the family, in relation to a number of irrational/feminine/childlike others. I argue, moreover, that this kinship politics was a moving politics, providing a range of imagery for constructing naturalized, hierarchical association across peoples and territories, from the absolute authority of the father within classic patriarchy—concomitant with the ideology of absolute authority within colonial rule—to "softer" notions of parenting for the benefit or "development" of children, which loosely correlates with notions of colonial rule for the beneficence and development of dependent peoples.

How did anti-colonialists address this differential personhood—this irrationalization, effiminization, infantilization—which served to deny their spatial and identity claims? How did they contend with the politics of embodiment and kinship? How did they negotiate decolonization? In this study, I explore these questions by examining a particular "macro-micro," local-global event: the discursive and institutional negotiation within the United Nations General Assembly (UNGA), between the years of 1946–1960, of the 1960 UN Declaration on the Granting of Independence to Colonial Countries and Peoples, a new legal instrument which would initiate legal decolonization. The GA is the main deliberative organ of the UN, and each session is organized as a general debate in which Member States express their views on matters of international concern. I argue that institutionally, the GA brings together more diverse, competing, and submerged voices than ever before (including European colonial interests, newly independent Asian and African anti-colonial interests, and colonial moderates). Thus, the GA meetings are the ideal location in which to observe the polyvocal, local-global negotiation of the movement away from the old geopolitical order to the new—from the old politics of differential personhood and hierarchical international community to something new. In the GA, then, I examine archival records to explore how the previous spatial/identity order is defended, challenged, and ultimately reworked via the renegotiation of the associated embodiment and kinship politics.

In brief, I argue that the racialized, sexualized embodiment and kinship politics of the colonial era re-crystallize in the GA debates in a particular way. For their part, colonialist powers and sympathizers largely resort to the kinship politics of paternal rule on the part of developed, rational, mature, and competent territories, the purpose of which is to teach and guide childlike, underdeveloped peoples so that they are prepared for (eventual) political independence. Interestingly, for anti-colonialists in the GA, such infantilization amounts to an emasculation. Thus, anti-colonialists argue, colonial rule is an illegitimate rule that serves to emasculate already grown men; and political independence is a prerequisite for the return of masculine dignity. Rather than international relations being modeled on the image of parents and children, thus, anti-colonialists argue that they should instead be modeled on the image of brotherhood.

Ultimately, then, within this "macro-micro," local-global space of the UNGA debates, we see the utility of transnationalizing the current intersectional perspective within Sociology. To the racialized, sexualized construction of space, identity and international community in the colonial era, anti-colonialists ask for a new, "more equitable" masculine international community thereafter. Thus, though they contest the racial and cultural hierarchies of the colonial era, in this moment, often represented as a "global advance of democracy," anti-colonialists reaffirm gender hierarchy. In doing so, they provide a window onto the emerging masculinization of "postcolonial" states as well as "postcolonial" international community.

Chapter One
Kinship Politics and Space, Identity and International Community Prior to Legal Decolonization: The Problem and the Query

In this chapter, I first introduce the theoretical approach for thinking about space, identity and international community prior to legal decolonization, what I term *kinship politics*. I begin with a review of the emergence of a particular geopolitical organization of space, the modern nation-state system. I argue that in its confrontations with alternative models of space over time, this particular ordering denies the ontological validity of other organizations of space (for example, nomadic and other non-Westphalian models outside of the post-17th century European state-system). Next, I explore how the modern geopolitical order constructs identity as well as identity distinctions (including racial, sexual and cultural distinctions) through a process of what I term *embodiment politics*. I argue that such politics becomes a central mechanism for the exercise of power, as it constructs some identities as subjects while simultaneously producing others as less than subjects. Even more, I make the case that it is in this process of *other-ization* that emerge colonial constructions of race, gender and culture. Next, I articulate how this racialized, sexualized embodiment politics becomes deployed as part of a larger kinship politics in the development of the modern state-system to construct hierarchical structures of trans-territorial community. I end the discussion of kinship politics with a brief review of some historical connections between images of kinship and ideologies of colonial rule.

After introducing the theoretical approach of kinship politics, I then outline the research methodology employed. I discuss the sources and nature of the data, the general research strategy used, and specific procedures for analysis.

ON SPACE AND TERRITORY

In this section, I discuss the ordering of space as a variable cultural and political construction. More specifically, I focus on shifting constructions of territory, which may be understood as *bounded space associated with formal political structures* (Cox 2002; Gottman 1975). First, I outline a number of different organizations of space that have existed historically, each of which implies a particular construction of territory. Second, I discuss modern forms of territory in particular, highlighting how, as these developed, meaning and identity themselves became "territorialized" in some particular ways. Finally, I explore how forms of territoriality that are considered modern confronted and contested alternative forms, often denying these others ontological validity in their advancement.

Work on space and spatiality in general explores how the spatial is a thoroughly social, cultural and historical phenomenon, shifting in both form and meaning in different locations and indeed, even functioning as a medium through which the social is produced and reproduced (Soja 1989; Lefebvre 1991; Gottdiener 1993; Abbott 1997; Gieryn 2000; Matias 1999; Gregory and Urry 1985; Cox 2002). Considering political space, Agnew (1999) argues that political power has a different spatiality over time, and identifies four models of the "spatiality of power," which he associates with different historical epochs. Prior to the 16th century, he argues that human groups live in separate cultural areas with limited communication and interaction between them, and there is a strongly physical conception of space as distance to be overcome or circulation to be managed. From the 16th century, the state emerges as a rigidly defined territorial unit, and the dominant spatiality becomes that of state-territory, in which political boundaries provide the containers for the majority of social, economic, and political activities. After 1945, the spatial structure of the world economy, in which cores, peripheries, and semi-peripheries are linked together by flows of goods, people and investment, produce a series of spatial networks joining together a hierarchy of nodes and areas. Finally, an integrated world society has been somewhat in ascendance in the last ten years. Agnew (1999) argues that there is overlap between these models, with the former two models somewhat in eclipse since 1945 and the latter two in ascendance.

While a number of authors may disagree with the details of this periodization,[1] nevertheless, Agnew's argument is useful for its overall historical approach. The medieval system of rule was legitimated by common bodies of law, religion, and custom that expressed inclusive natural rights. These inclusive legitimations posed no threat to the integrity of the constituent political units because these units viewed themselves as municipal embodiments of a universal moral community. Territorially, these political units were divided through "frontiers" or large "zones of transition" rather than by clearly demarcated boundaries. There were also plural allegiances, asymmetrical suzerainties, and anomalous enclaves. Hence, the political map was an inextricably superimposed and tangled one, in which different juridical instances were geographically interwoven (Anderson 1974; Ruggie 1993; Gottman 1975; Spruyt 1994).

Gottman (1975) argues that from the 14th century, there began to emerge an understanding of sovereignty over national territory as an essential component of political power, and from the 15th through the 17th centuries, the doctrine of space partitioning matured in Europe, the Treaty of Westphalia (1648) being a critical moment in this development. All these changes prefigured what Ruggie (1993: 144) calls "the central attribute of modernity in international politics . . . an peculiar and historically unique configuration of territorial space." In the modern form, states are mutually exclusive and functionally similar. The chief characteristic is the consolidation of all parcelized and personalized authority into one public realm, which entails two fundamental spatial demarcations: the first between the public and the private within the state and the second between the internal and the external to the state. In terms of power, internally, legitimate power is fused with the provision of public order and externally, legitimate power is fused with statecraft. Reciprocal sovereignty becomes the basis of the new international order as well as the new principle of international legitimacy (Ruggie 1993). Perhaps most significant in terms of the political dimension of modern notions of territory, however, is what Taylor (1994) calls "the state's capture of politics (Taylor 1994: 151)." That is, he argues that with the linkage of "the political" to the state, anything that is perceived to be exterior to the state—whether the "private" realm within states or that nebulous dimension "above" states—is seen as somehow outside of politics.

With these shifting meanings of territory, a particularly interesting line of work has focused on how the meaning of territorial space within different kinds of political orders depends on particular kinds of bounding. For example, as mentioned above, while political identity in medieval Europe may have crossed "territorial boundaries" in numerous and complicated ways (Ruggie 1993; Anderson 1974; Gottman 1975), modern states territorialized meaning by manipulating languages, education systems, myths, symbols and narratives (Paasi 1999; Hobsbawn 1990; Anderson 1991). The American and French Revolutions not only helped to construct a "people," but also established a direct relationship between people and territory (Gottman 1975). An additional element was the imagination of horizontal as opposed to hierarchical relationships with members of one's particular territory (Cerwonka 1999; Anderson 1991). Such projects of the territorialization of meaning in turn changed the very meaning of territory. Now, the community became indissolubly linked to the land. No longer parcels of land transferable between states as the outcome of wars, all territory, including borderlands, became inviolate. Hence, as migration from villages to towns increased, "national culture" still gave people a continued identity with their land as the land became sacred (Taylor 1994).

Since 1945, several authors identify what they see as important shifts in the characteristics of political space and territory in the modern world. According to Ruggie (1993), for certain kinds of issues, an "institutional negation of territoriality serves as a means of dealing with those dimensions of collective existence that territorial rulers recognize to be irreducibly trans-territorial in character . . . [and this is] where international society is anchored (Ruggie 1993: 165)." Matias (1999) argues that in some locations, we are seeing the emergence of a "new medievalism," or an overlapping of various authorities on the same territory, giving rise to "empire-like" structures in some parts of the world (such as western Europe).

Political space and territory, then, are variable objects of historical and cultural construction. Likewise, they have also historically been mechanisms for the exercise of power. Indeed, Paasi (1999) uses a second noun form of the term territory, *territoriality*, to denote a spatial strategy which can be employed to affect, influence or control resources and people by controlling area. What is interesting about the emerging states of western Europe, from the perspective of power relations, is that modern, European statehood rendered to the political entities that could claim its mantle a particular form of territorial *subjecthood*, which, when confronted with alternative, particularly "non-European,"[2] "non-state," territorial forms, tended to deny other possible territorial subjectivities, or at least their viability. Delanty (1995: 6–10) suggests that just the idea of Europe, grafted on as it was to notions of Christianity and civilization in opposition to others, itself served as a kind of legitimation for the politics of the territorial state. Certainly, Westphalia created a system of states that were to be equal to each other, but even a cursory consideration of imperial and colonial practices demonstrates that the status of legitimate territoriality and equality was not extended to all territories (Eva 1999; Theodoropoulos 1988). Moreover, celebrated as an evolutionary achievement, European state power, when confronted with other political entities and alternative forms of territoriality, did not hesitate to impose its preferred models of space (Shapiro 1999; Edney 2003; McClintock 1995).

Discussing the spatial politics of the colonial project, McClintock (1995) argues that during the colonial period, scientists invented two things:

panoptical time and anachronistic space. In terms of the first, as social evolutionists attempted to read from a discontinuous natural record a single pedigree of evolving world history, they collected, assembled and mapped not only natural space but also historical time. They sought to break the hold of Biblical chronology and to instead secularize time. Their solution, hence, was to spatialize time, where the axis of time was projected onto the axis of space. Or to put it another way, perceived geographical difference across space was figured as historical difference across time. Hence (European) travelers that sailed to distant lands actually traveled "back in time." Particularly when applied to cultural history, then, time became a geography of social power, a map from which to read a global allegory of "natural" social difference. In terms of spatial politics, consequently, the agency of various "others" was disavowed and projected onto anachronistic space. These others were hence rendered somehow prehistoric, atavistic, irrational—inherently *out-of-place* in the historical time of modernity (McClintock 1995).

CONSTRUCTING DIFFERENTIAL PERSONHOOD: THE ROLE OF EMBODIMENT POLITICS

But what are the precise mechanisms of this removal of various "others" onto anachronistic space and from the historical time of modernity? How is geographical difference constructed as historical difference? In this section, I explore how the modern geopolitical order constructs identity as well as identity distinctions through a process of what I term *embodiment politics*. By the term *embodiment politics*, I mean to indicate a particular cultural and political construction of the body as a metaphor for disorder.[3] That is, particularly in the "west," historically what we term the body or the bodily has alternatively signified the uncontrollable, the irrational, the emotional, the uncivilized, the savage and the barbaric in some pervasive and systematic ways. Below, I explore this particular figuration of the body as well as its role in the modern exercise of power. First, I examine how the object of "the body" has been constructed through a number of western narratives. Second, I use the work of Haraway, Bourdieu and a number of others on the politics of classification to explore the politics of what becomes classified as "the body." That is, once the body is figured as that which requires control, how do different objects become *embodied*? How do they become categorized as "the body" or "the bodily?" How do they come to qualify as requiring control? Finally, I argue that such processes of embodiment are mechanisms for the exercise of power, serving to simultaneously define the subjectivity and agency of those that are somehow "disembodied" (dissociated from the bodily and thus disorder) while denying these to the "embodied" (overly associated with the bodily and thus disorder). This distinction between the "disembodied" and the "embodied," I argue, is central to understanding the colonial construction of space and identity within modernity.

Donna Haraway (2000) begins from the notion that there is no place in the world outside of stories. As objects are frozen stories, our own bodies become "objects" only through metaphor. Embedded in "physical, semiotic, fleshy, bloody existence (Haraway and Goodeve 2000)," then, despite its "physicality," the body is a particular kind of physical, material object only from inside of stories. Similarly, Turner (1997) writes that the body is plastic; instead of a closed, sealed entity, Harvey (2000) adds, rather a relational "thing" that is created, bounded, sustained, and ultimately dissolved in a spatiotemporal flux of multiple processes. As a relational yet frozen object, then, the thing-i-fi-cation of the mutable body is accomplished through reification.

A number of scholars have elaborated the scientific, religious, capitalist and other narratives in the west that have frozen "the body" into an object of concern. Perhaps the most pervasive metaphor for the body has been that of the non-rational or the barbaric (Berman 1989; Patterson 2002; Turner 1992; Turner 1996; Elias 2000; Johnson 1987; Horkheimer and Adorno 1973), and multiple authors have traced the processes in modernity which have consequently sought to discipline or civilize the body (Foucault 1978; Elias 2000; Foucault 1988a; Foucault 1977). Although the focus has typically been on the shift from the medieval to the modern and the sacred to the secular, writers have repeatedly pinpointed one critical historical moment in this construction of the body as disorder: the rise of mechanical philosophy (Berman 1989; Holliday and Hassard 2001; Turner 1996).[4] As Berman (1989) argues, in mechanical philosophy, everything in the world, from atoms to animals to galaxies, was thought to be comprised of material particles and to operate on the model of a machine. With regard to the body, Descartes drew a distinction between the soul and the body as well, with the body also conceptualized as a machine that received its instructions from the soul (Turner 1996). Such reasoning clearly subordinated "the body" or "the bodily" to "the soul" or "the mind." Effectively, then, the ideology of Cartesianism served to exclude the irrational and the magical, and to regulate emotions, sexuality and affective life through the regulated and disciplined body (Turner 1996).[5] As a worldview, Turner argues that Cartesianism became a basic principle of Protestant individualism, scientific rationalism, and the Protestant spirit.[6] The principal feature in all of these was thus the separation of mind and body, with the subordination of body

Kinship Politics and Space, Identity and International Community 11

to mind, and the associated dominance of cognitive rationalization. In the following centuries, there was a further elaboration of this ascetic attitude towards the body. The body was seen as a threatening, difficult and dangerous phenomenon—a conduit for unruly, ungovernable, irrational passions, emotions and desires. As such, it had to be controlled and regulated by cultural processes. While the flesh stood in the same sphere as sub-human animality, the soul became the carrier and symbol of all forms of spirituality and rationality. Turner connects this will to control the body in Christianity, ultimately, with the ethic of world mastery which was central to the rationalization processes that Weber traces, as well as the new epistemological philosophies of empiricism, positivism, and Cartesian rationalism (Turner 1996; Turner 1992). From the perspective of the body, then, Berman (1989) argues that the shift from the medieval to the modern was key; while oral cultures had strong somatic bases, with participation being highly sensuous in nature and its immediate, visceral quality valued as a mode of knowing, the emerging philosophy instead prioritized psychic distance. Consequently, new formulations of "objectivity" now required the removal of the body from analysis, the essential feature becoming "psychic distance, the existence of a rigid barrier between observer and observed (Berman 1989; See also Elias 2000)." Likewise, the "emotional," associated as it was with the body, now became the "unreliable (Berman 1989)."

From the perspective of power, Donna Haraway makes a critical gesture here. She asks: what is at stake in boundary making? What is at stake in maintaining the boundaries between what gets called nature and what gets called culture (Haraway and Goodeve 2000)? Similarly, we may think of classification systems as "historical and political artifacts (Bowker and Star 2000)," ways of seeing the world or "principles of vision and division (Bourdieu 1984)," through the acquisition of which people learn the hierarchies embedded within the social system prior to and outside of any conscious intention. Hence the consequent naturalization of hierarchy makes various forms of appropriation appear legitimate, even to those who stand to lose from these arrangements. For the oppressed, consequently, this is a form of symbolic violence. Misrecognized and naturalized, it is a "gentle, invisible form of violence (Bourdieu 1977)," and thus, what we learn to bound as the "body" is a technology of power . . . the effect and instrument of complex power relations (Foucault 1977; 1988b).

A critical example of this "gentle, invisible violence"—this "technology of power"—is the notion of what Nancy Stephan terms the "disembodied individual." She writes that starting in the 1600s, and culminating in the writings of the new social contract philosophers of the 1700s, there developed the concept of the political individual, an imagined, universal individual who was the bearer of equal political rights. In the theoretical imagination, this person was to be someone who could be imagined stripped of individual substantiation and specification so that he could stand for everyman. Unmarked by specificities such as wealth, rank, education, age, and sex, he expressed a common psyche and political humanity. The contract philosophers used the notion of the universal individual to establish a theoretical ground for moral autonomy and democracy. However, the historical counterpart to this "disembodiment" of the universal individual of modernity was the ontologizing via *embodiment* of sexual and racial difference, a rendering of certain racialized and sexualized groups as somehow closer to their bodies than the disembodied individual. These groups were thus distinguished in their biology and differentiated from an implicit white (European), male norm. By being embodied as qualitatively different in their substantial natures, communities of individuals were placed outside the liberal universe of freedom, equality and rights. In effect, a theory of politics and rights was articulated as an argument about the nature of particular racial(ized) and sexual(ized) groups (Stephan 2000). For Descartes, then, "pure mind" meant the rational, sovereign individual (Holliday and Hassard 2001). It follows that if the essence of humanity was defined as a set of qualities of "mind," such as reason, intelligible language, religion, culture, or manners, anyone who was deemed to not fully possess those qualities was considered subhuman (Patterson 2002), outside of sociality (Witz 2000), with their subjectivity rendered a non-subjectivity (Holliday and Hassard 2001). Thus, from the 1500s, non-Europeans were imagined in various ways as savage, barbaric, cannibalistic, sexually aberrant, and lacking history (Patterson 2002; Augstein 1996). For example, some groups of Africans were thought to be animalistic and brutish, with a beast-like, excessive sexuality, while particularly in the nineteenth century, Asians came to be seen as weak and lacking of virility (Patterson 2002; Aldrich 1996). Indeed, by the 1800s, European scientists were using the disembodiment-embodiment hierarchy in various ways to construct theories of racial, sexual, cultural and even class inequality. These emerging constructions of inequality set white, European males above non-Europeans, women, and Jews in multiple ways. Women, non-whites, Jews, and the working classes within "superior" races were all considered to be lower forms of humans (Patterson 2002; Witz 2000; McClintock 1995; Roberts 1997; Dyer 1997; Turner 1996). Such embodiment discourses, which constructed Jews as animalistic and insect-like, also informed the logic that sought to legitimate the Holocaust (Horkheimer and Adorno 1973; Perry 1983).

That it was the politics of embodiment that was an important, common mechanism of subordination in all these instances also becomes clear when we consider a number of things. First, with regard to race and gender, there were important connections between the treatment of women and of non-Europeans in the language, experience, and imaginations of western men. For both race and gender, existing philosophical and religious ideas combined with new natural and social science theories of classification, and there were a number of comparable ways in which difference was constructed and used to justify subordination for women and ethnic others. Differences between sexes as well as between races were seen as essential, or understood as inherent in their *bodies*. For groups marked by gender (women) or race (non-whites or non-Europeans), both kinds of categories were inferior in relation to one category: European men (de Groot 2000).

More important than mere similarities in mechanisms of subordination, however, is that despite the diversity of working-class groups, women, and non-white, racial-ethnic groups, the embodiment of a particular group was nevertheless available as a resource in the cultural repertoire for the embodiment of another through analogy. For example, because European women, as a sexually marked group, were embodied in relation to European men, the main symbols through which the feminine was constructed— lack of virility, lack of masculinity, irrationality, emotionality—could all be deployed as signifying mechanisms to embody different racial-ethnic groups.[7] In this way, for example, the Orient, South Asia, and Africa were all, at different times, imagined as irrational and emotional—as feminine— and therefore in need of (masculine/European) control and authority (de Groot 2000; Ramamurthy 2003: 119; Staum 2003). Ashis Nandy argues that from the early nineteenth century in India, British colonial culture marginalized local androgynous traditions, arguing that Indian men were insufficiently masculine and therefore in need of colonial rule (Nandy 1988; See also Sinha 1995). In this way, thus, the imperial social order created a "hierarchy of masculinities (Connell 2000:48)."

Similarly, in addition to these groups being "not masculine enough" or "like women," women in turn were seen to be like them as well. Thus, French scholars in the nineteenth century constructed European women as "like blacks, predominantly sensitive and affective, incapable of the highest exercise of reflective faculties (Staum 2003)." In this vein, working-class European women who transgressed the norm of the housebound wife were particularly racialized, as they violated even the expectations of civilized, European womanhood (McClintock 1995).

Such processes of feminization and racialization intersected in various and complex ways. For example, in the "global" eighteenth century, the globe itself was imagined as four distinct quadrants, represented iconographically as female figures:

America was represented as bare breasted, with a feathered headdress, carrying arrows and a bow; Asia bore incense and was veiled against a backdrop of desert and camel, or the harem; Africa, naked except for an elephant headdress, sat on a lion, and was flanked by a cornucopia signifying its natural riches; and Europe was represented as a muse surrounded by arts and letters as well as the signs of military victory (Nussbaum 2003: 2).

In this representation, we see an example of the intersection of racialization and feminization processes in the imagination of different spaces across the globe. This representation particularly demonstrates how the feminization of Asia, Africa and America was racialized in particular ways in opposition to the feminization of Europe. Such contrasting feminizations played a key role in constructing distinctions between civilized and uncivilized peoples. Indeed, comparative constructions of gender and sexuality in general were often central in creating such distinctions between peoples. As demonstrated in the example of India above, colonialists deployed such comparative constructions of masculinity to build racial and/or cultural hierarchies, though comparative constructions of femininity seemed to be even more central in such classificatory schemes. In nineteenth century French scholarly discourse, for example, the so-called

> status of women often signaled the degree of civilization attributed to a people. Heavy manual agricultural labor or brutal treatment of women was sufficient to label a group barbaric . . . there was also revulsion at the apparent absence in indigenous males of the stereotypical politeness and delicacy approved for European interaction with middle- and upper-class European women (Staum 2003: 102).

Considering British colonial discourse on India, there was similar concern regarding the practice of sati. The "traditional Indian practice of sati," however, has itself been shown to be a socially and politically constructed reification (Mani 1987; Narayan 1997). Moreover, as Cynthia Enloe points out, such concern for "native" women was ultimately hollow and hypocritical, for at the same time that British officials passed legislation to prohibit these "barbaric practices," they enacted laws which imposed prison sentences on wives who refused to fulfill sexual obligations to their husbands and imposed a system of prostitution that provided Indian women to sexually service British soldiers stationed in India (Enloe 1989: 49).

Thus, the politics of embodiment is significant for helping to build theories of human inequality on multiple levels. Given its seeming omnipresence, particularly from the early modern period, how do we understand the relationship between this politics and the spatial project of European colonialism? Bryan Turner (1996) writes of the complex relationship between developing ideas of rationality, difference, and colonial expansion:

> The emergence of the ethic of world mastery corresponded with the philosophical project whereby the external world could be understood by rational inquiry. The expansion of European colonialism created especially at the political level the origins of a global society within which philosophical universalism could flourish. It was on the basis of the colonial world that the Enlightenment philosophers could, with a sense of security and confidence, philosophically speculate about the essential and fundamental questions about truth, irrationality and beauty. Truth had become universal because the world had become a global environment. Societies which diverged from these central notions of truth, reason and beauty were understood as deviations from a rational culture, otherness and difference. There existed a complex relationship [therefore] between the notion of subordinate and free peoples on the one hand and the subordination of the body to the mind on the other (Turner 1996: 13).

Thus, the developing binary of rationality and irrationality, centered on a politics of embodiment, was critical to constructions of cultural, racial, and other kinds of difference within the colonial project. Such distinctions helped to define European civilization itself. "Natural man, envisioned variously as the bestial Hottentot, the noble American native or even the wild and solitary European, figured centrally into Enlightenment classificatory schemes . . . 'Seductive' financiers, 'immodest' clerics, 'infamous courtesans,' 'vile prostitutes,' unnatural nuns, sinful celibates, and 'lusty nègres (Colwill 1998: 200–201)'" were the "transgressive bodies" against which (European, male) civilization gained its meaning. Indeed, this concept of civilization "summed up everything in which Western society of the last two to three centuries believes itself superior . . . [it summed up] the self-consciousness of the West (Elias 2000: 5; See also, Mosse 1985)." As such, then, the politics of embodiment met the needs of the European colonial project precisely. Thus, in the late seventeenth century, John Locke advanced his theory of property rights, in which he argued that while rational individuals can trust and enter into contracts to acquire property, non-rational people cannot trust or be trusted because they live outside of contracts in a state of nature, by anarchy, and by the rule of force

(Grovogui 1988). The logic of embodiment, particularly as it relates to the spatial politics of colonialism, culminated in the nineteenth century in the argument of the liberal John Stuart Mill, who argued that because savages do not have society, actual societies do not have to recognize them as either coherent collectivities or on the basis of their land use. Because savages fail to exercise a notion of property in the European legalist sense, they have no basis for nationhood, and therefore no rights as a nation (Shapiro 1999).

It is critical to note here that while certain bodily codes also served to legitimate the position of those in power, these were of the disembodied and so were not recognized as such. That is, the bodily codes of the disembodied were somehow outside of the scope of what counted as embodiment—what mattered for purposes of subordination. Rather, the bodily codes of the disembodied signified their superiority. For example, when Bourbon absolutism painted the monarch as a strong, virile, self-sufficient father, it was certainly manipulating bodily codes, just not those that rendered him embodied. Theorists of Bourbon absolutism linked personal order in the male self with public order in the state, comparing the king to a male head of household who ruled over a potentially unruly extended family. That only certain bodily codes were deemed problematic is apparent in that while this patriarchal image was important to the king's legitimacy, it's lack could undermine this authority. If he failed to live up to his position, he was then vulnerable to charges of effeminacy, irrationality, and lust (Merrick 1998)—that is, embodiment. It is of little surprise, then, that when Louis XIV took power, royal propagandists laid particular stress on the virile, masculine nature of his person. Particularly when the young king's rule was unstable, between the years of 1658–1659, his propaganda apparatus strove to create images of virility (Zanger 1998).[8]

KINSHIP POLITICS: THEORIZING HIERARCHICAL CONSTRUCTIONS OF SPACE, IDENTITY AND INTERNATIONAL COMMUNITY BEFORE LEGAL DECOLONIZATION

In the first section of this chapter, I argued that a particular politics of space becomes a critical mechanism of power relations in the modern world. Such a spatial strategy privileges the modern, statist form of territoriality as opposed to alternative forms by granting ontological validity only to the former. In the second section, I identified a central, recurring mechanism for denying the personhood of various groups, that of embodiment politics. As a device of power relations, embodiment politics figures only some as the embodied, irrational objects of control, while others become the disembodied, rational subjects of control. In this manner, embodiment politics in the modern period have marked particular bodies as racial, sexual, and savage, culminating in colonialist projects that used these multiple dimensions of embodiment in conjunction. In this section, I bring together both of the above in order to explore one question: *how do colonialist discourses bring a particular kind of identity politics to their spatial politics, enabling colonialist rulers to justify their presence in and conquest over foreign peoples and lands in the legitimated language of natural hierarchy?* My answer here is what I term "kinship politics," a politics that brings together the notion of natural *association* across peoples and territories, with the notion of natural *hierarchy* within this association. As I will discuss below, particularly important in the "west" for naturalizing not only association but also hierarchy-within-association in this way, have been the nature metaphors of the body and the family. Thus, within colonialist discourse, I define kinship politics as a politics that uses these metaphors of the body and family in order to construct such association as well as hierarchy-within-association. That is, kinship politics uses the metaphors of the body and family in order to naturalize 1) trans-territorial association across distinct lands and peoples and 2) a radically differential recognition of subjectivity, based on theories of racial, cultural and gender inequality, within this trans-territorial association.

In what follows, I develop this theory of kinship politics further. First, I discuss the metaphors of the body and family within kinship politics, and particularly how these metaphors work to naturalize differential personhood and hierarchy within political association. Next, I move on to an exploration of the connection between kinship politics and such hierarchical association across peoples and territories within ideologies of colonial rule. I also pay some attention to how this relationship is expressed within international law, enabling hierarchical, colonialist constructions of space, identity, and international community prior to legal decolonization.

The Body and Family: Nature Metaphors, Hierarchical Metaphors

That the body and the family are metaphors of association is evident. We may speak of the total "body of work" on anorexia to indicate psychological, biological and popular work on the condition. Similarly, we may speak of the "family of Marxist theories" to indicate that dependency, world-systems, post-colonial and other theories are all thought to be influenced by the work of Karl Marx. Regarding political association, Felstiner argues that political metaphors work by connecting something new with something already commonly accepted (Felstiner 1983). In this vein, Bryan Turner (1992) writes of the historical use of the image of the body specifically as a metaphor for *political* association. Thus for Christian philosophers, according to Turner (1992), the balance of the human body provided a metaphor for the balance of political life, while disturbances in political life were thought to produce disease in the human body. Similarly, as medicine was closely aligned with government, in medicine too, the doctrine of the four humors provided a rich source for political theorizing about the intimate connections between the dietary management of the body and the political regulation of the body politic. It also provided a related set of theories about the necessity for personal government, if the government of the entire community were to be preserved. In early Christianity, then, there was a close relationship between diet, sexual asceticism, and the social order. The regulation of desire was seen as a precondition for orderly community, and this remained a fundamental feature of Christian teaching. Turner (1992) continues that the Christian concept of the body politic paved the way for the medieval idea of the king's two bodies, namely a division between the body natural and the body political . . . his earthly and corruptible body and his mystical and sacred, incorruptible body. The notion that the king had a definite authority to rule, rather like the father in the household, was challenged by individualistic and utilitarian political theories. Hence the struggle for representation in 18th century France was a struggle against the idea of the king's monopolistic embodiment of power.

With modernity, a number of parallel treatments of the "modern state" and the body of the "individual" are also especially compelling here. Historically, for instance, there is the similar figuration of both in the narrative of modernity. Hence one may note that the linear, modernist narrative of the "emergence" of the body from kinship systems within lineage societies to "autonomous" individuals bears strong resemblance to the "emergence" of the modern state from overlapping, nonexclusive territories to "sovereign" nation-states. What is important here is not the facticity of this so-called emergence, but its prominence in understandings of modernity. Likewise in modernity, both "the state" and "the body" are imagined through container metaphors (Chilton and Ilyin 1993). Such connections are evident even in the foundation of international law, such that Grotius based his writings on the idea that agreements between states were to be analogous to agreements in private law (Prott 1991).

Likewise, the metaphor of the family may also be deployed to invoke a sense of political association. Thus, connections have been made between images of motherhood, fatherhood, and fraternity and the French Revolution (Hunt 1992), family, motherhood, and the Fascist national project (Berezin 1999), and motherhood, fatherhood, and the Turkish national project (Delaney 1995). Regarding independence movements in the Spanish and

British colonies, too, which sought to dissociate any political association from the metropole and construct alternative political collectivities, these movements also used the language of family. For example, in their bid for independence, Chilean nationalists spoke of Spain as a cruel mother and Chile as a loving mother (1983). Beyond such national projects, the "family of nations" also invokes global or international association (Grewal 1998).

But even more than providing a language for political association, the metaphors of the body and family are important for articulating power within this discourse. This is the case, first, because both operate as what I call *nature metaphors*; that is, both are almost always invoked as emergent from nature. Second, as such nature metaphors, both contain deeply rooted, naturalized notions of hierarchy. Thus, feminist anthropologists write that particularly within "Euro-American" discourses, images of nature (alternatively, biology or god) function to naturalize power (Yanagisako and Delaney 2001). For the body, specifically in modern, western narratives, this naturalization of power is evident within discourses that proceed from the notion that as a "natural" state of affairs, the brain/head/mind must control or restrain the "rest of the body (Berman 1989; Turner 1992; Turner 1996)." As discussed above, if the elite, European male is disembodied in modern narratives while bodies marked by race, gender, sexuality, and class become embodied, then the former become the "mind" in Descartes' famous binary—rendering the elite, European male a modern, necessary, natural right to rule (Holliday and Hassard 2001; Patterson 2002; Witz 2000).

Similarly, the image of the family, too, sanctions social hierarchy in this way (McClintock 1995; Collins 2000; de Groot 2000). That is, the metaphor of the family in "Euro-American" discourse constructs specifically gendered but potentially also other kinds of hierarchies, such as by age, as natural (Schneider 1980; Yanagisako and Delaney 2001; Franklin and McKinnon 2001; Nandy 1988; Nandy 1987). However, although composed of different bodies, we should note that the image of the family itself incorporates the body as that which requires control. Hence the "head" of the body becomes within the family the "head" of the family (Turner 1992; Felstiner 1983; McClintock 1995). Embodied others on the other hand occupy different locations (on the body). In the European colonial project, for example, Europeans imagined a physical geography of the body in which the brain was the European male, the heart was the European female and together, they were the forces of civilization which were to hold the (black) nether regions in check (Colwill 1998).

Kinship Politics and Colonial Rule: Naturalizing Hierarchical Association

Given this role of the metaphors of the body and family in theories of unequal political association, how has kinship politics historically informed colonial projects? As an image that alternatively naturalizes the hierarchy of the rational over the irrational, the masculine over the feminine, and parents over children, the metaphor of kinship has multiple points of entry. It is a flexible politics, it bends, and it expands and contracts, enabling multiple logics and languages for colonial rule. It may permit the harshest of legitimations, as in arguments that view colonialism as the natural extension of human supremacy over the "animal kingdom (Patterson 2002)," or as the natural authority of masters over servants or of parents over children (de Groot 2000), or just the natural exercise of European or American masculinity and virility over insufficiently masculine groups (Doty 1996: 31; McClintock 1995). Alternatively, kinship politics also offers "softer" legitimations, such as the argument that those possessing greater amounts of rationality or masculine competency or maturity have the obligation to offer guidance to irrational/insufficiently masculine/immature others, and that such tutelage is for the latter's own benefit.

In the necessarily exploratory discussion that follows, I suggest that one of the most important determining factors of ideologies of colonial rule historically has been the nature of family or kinship itself within the metropolitan or colonial culture in question. I start with the periodization of European empires provided by Anthony Pagden (1995) in his comparative study of Spanish, British and French colonialist practices. In this work, Pagden argues that there have been two distinctive phases in the history of modern, European empire-building, dating the first from the end of the fifteenth century through the early nineteenth, and the second from the early nineteenth. Even more relevant for my purposes, Pagden makes some connections between notions of authority and rule within the family and ideologies of colonial rule, particularly for the first period of empire-building. Nevertheless, his commentary on this question is brief and undertheorized. Examining the historical record from the early modern period, I suggest that his two historical eras connect to changing ideas of kinship in Western Europe in some interesting ways. In the former, I argue that harsher, "classical" or "traditional" patriarchal models of family offer "hasher" metaphors for imagining, theorizing and speaking about the nature of authority within colonial rule. In the latter, "softer" models of family emerge, which have important implications for changing ways of imagining and thinking and speaking about colonial rule. Thus, in the first period, while images of absolute authority, honor, rights and rule offered by the classical patriarchal family are available for legitimating colonial rule, in the second, these are eclipsed by—though by no means entirely replaced by—images of the beneficence of colonial rule for the colonized.

In the first period of empire offered by Pagden, the focus is on European empires in the Americas. He argues that despite differences in Spanish, British and French ideologies and practices of colonial rule, there are important continuities, including a legacy of absolute authority, honor, and right to rule, which comes from the Roman Empire. Moreover, he argues that the source of this model of authority and right comes from the model of the Roman family, which grants parents absolute power over children (he seems to ignore the gender dimension of the patriarchal Roman family) (Pagden 1995: 145). In British political thinking in particular, a second important source of such ideologies of rule is also the seventeenth century work of Robert Filmer, who argued that the absolute rule of fathers within the patriarchal family should be the model for all authority relations in society.[9] In the early modern period, this image of absolute authority and rule based on the metaphor of the traditional patriarchal family underpinned not only the ideology of colonial rule but also of absolute monarchies in Europe (Pateman 1988; Adams 2005; Pagden 1995).

Such notions of absolute authority and rule, and particularly their complete denial of the spatial and identity claims of various "others," are especially evident in the development of international law over this period. For example, Grovogui (1996; 1988) reviews the development of international law over a number of "regimes" since the fifteenth century, and claims that from the beginning, the subjects of each of these have been Europeans. Theodoropoulos (1988: 6) writes furthermore that this law, because it excluded from its subjects colonized peoples, was not really an international law but rather, a "regional" law of European or so-called civilized nations. The first regime of this regional international law began with the papal bulls of Alexander VI, when the Pope ordered Spain and Portugal to conquer heathen lands for Christianity. This period also saw the development of the foundation of modern international law, as the desire of industrializing Netherlands and Britain for colonies of their own posed a problem for Spain and Portugal: how would all these different parties justify their monopoly over their overseas ventures? Hugo Grotius, whom we may perhaps consider "the father" of international law, asked why only some Christian countries were allowed to be sovereigns over non-Christians. Thus developed the *Jus Gentilis*, the body of law governing relations between the separate political groups in Christendom. This law made critical distinctions between different kinds of subjects. Based on the premise that there were three distinct kinds of humanity, civilized, barbaric, and savage, the law gave a different kind of political recognition to each: plenary recognition for the first, partial for the second (which included Turkey, China, Siam and Japan)[10], and mere human recognition to the rest.

It was up to civilized man to determine the conditions under which the non-civilized should be recognized. As concerns with property relationships started to dominate in legal theory, territories that belonged to the "other" were treated as if vacant, without title or ownership, and ownership was defined as the retention of titles. This regime was further biased towards "others" in that not only did this law constitute rules of evidence "others" were unfamiliar with to determine the status of property, but it also failed to recognize that most other signatory parties lacked the authority to enter the subject's legal agreements, if their own laws and customs were considered. In the foundations of modern international law, ultimately, the property and sovereignty of Europeans was distinctly privileged over other kinds of concerns (Grovogui 1988; 1996).

Interestingly, an important component of such differential subjectivity within international law was the way in which sovereignty came to be defined. Theodoropoulos (1988) argues that while the basis of the relations of production was ownership of land and partial ownership of serf by landlord, as in feudalism, no distinction was made between *imperium* (rule over the territory) and *dominium* (land ownership). Hence the landlord exercised both, and sovereignty was the landlord's absolute supremacy within the country (his feud). As power began to concentrate in the hands of absolute monarchs against landlords, however, kings and monarchs struggled for recognition against emperors and popes. With the success of the former, the principle of state sovereignty was recognized in the Westphalia Peace of 1648, which consisted of the Treaties of Munster and Osnarbruck, and this event marked the birth of the feudal-absolutist state as the final stage of feudalism. Here, the principle of sovereignty was transformed into a new weapon for the protection and strengthening of the state, the rationale of which was also then revised. Thus arose a new theory of the nature of states, the doctrine of sovereignty. As capitalism continued to develop and the feudal-absolutist state came to be replaced with the capitalist state, the old concept of the sovereignty of the feudal monarch was replaced by the concept of the sovereignty of the people, as well as the recognition of the sovereign equality of all states and the prohibition of interference with their internal affairs. Such agreements were codified in the Draft Declaration on the Rights of Nations submitted to the Convention in Paris on the 23rd of April, 1795. Eventually, however, such a notion of sovereignty came to be equated with the power to exercise it, with the "right to wage war" and the "right of the victor." As European colonialism intensified, the major legal technique under international law used to do so was the denial of sovereignty to "other" lands. Similar to the mechanisms cited by Grovogui (1988; 1996) above, Theodoropoulos (1988) writes that colonialism also advanced through a series of unequal treaties in a number of ways "forced" upon people. All of these actions violated the principles of sovereignty, and hence while the system formally recognized the principle of the respect for sovereignty, it also regulated institutions such as vassalages, colonial protectorates, capitulation regimes, mandates, and the like.

Given these harsh ideologies of colonial rule, as well as how they shape international law, how do these move to the "softer" conceptions of rule identified by Pagden? I argue that from the early eighteenth and nineteenth centuries and on, a number of ongoing transformations contribute to shifts in traditional patriarchal conceptions of the family, which in turn contribute to "softer" ways for imagining, thinking about and speaking about authority within colonial rule. First, according to Philip Ariès' study of France, there are central transformations in the idea of family as well as of childhood from the medieval era to the modern. In the former, he argues that "the idea of childhood did not exist (Aries 1962)." Over the course of centuries, developing in particular ways in the seventeenth and eighteenth centuries and culminating in the nineteenth, however, he argues that not only does the notion of "childhood" emerge, but that the parent comes to develop an interest in the child and in childhood. Thus, the parent now becomes concerned with every aspect of "his child's life, from 'coddling' to education; he watches closely over their health and even their hygiene. [Now] everything to do with children and family life has become a matter worthy of attention. Not only the child's future but his presence and his very existence are of concern: the child has taken a central place in the family (Aries 1962: 133)." Hence, from the medieval to the modern period, there is a shift from the notion that childhood is not a distinct state to the idea that not only is childhood a distinct state, but that it requires in a number of ways, active parenting. Exploring this shift in Britain, one author terms this new call to parents "responsible parenthood (Johansson 1991)." From the eighteenth century, this call to parenting is also accompanied by new ideas about privacy and domesticity, about intimacy between spouses and between parents and children, and about love and reason as the basis for relationships rather than absolute authority and right (Coontz 2004; Aries 1962; Johansson 1991; Coontz 2005: 148–49).[11] Thus, from the first period of empire to the second, there are ongoing transformations in the meaning of family and in the nature of relationships within the family.

These changing notions of the family are concomitant with some parallel changes on other levels. From the period of the Enlightenment, intellectuals and secularists develop unilinear theories of civilization as well as the notion that progress is the gradual triumph of human reason and freedom over unreason and necessity (Todorov 1993; Staum 2003). It is important to note that these understandings incorporate the rational/irrational dichotomy of embodiment politics in particular ways. For example, in Hegel's teleological view, something exists by virtue of its rationality and similarly ceases to exist by virtue of its irrationality. As theories of human classification emerge, then, they seek to classify different lands and peoples according to their supposed "stages of development" along this unilinear path to civilization (Wesseling 1997: 35). For example, for Adam Smith, societies are classified on the scale of development based on their mode of subsistence, with the most primitive societies being "gathering societies," which are superceded by "hunting societies," then pastoral, agricultural, and at the most advanced stage, commercial and manufacturing societies (Staum 2003: 8).

Thus, these evolving notions of family and childhood, the theory of progress, and this conception of "stages of development" intersect in emerging theories of colonial rule in the second period of empire-building. According to Ashis Nandy,

> colonialism dutifully picked up these [emerging] ideas of growth and development and drew a new parallel between primitivism and childhood. Thus, the theory of social progress was telescoped not merely into the individual's life cycle in Europe but also into the area of cultural differences in the colonies. What was the childlikeness of the child and childishness of immature adults now also became the lovable and unlovable savagery of primitives and the primitivism of subject societies (Nandy 1988: 15–16).

Thus, if Pagden is correct in his argument that the legitimating languages of empire shift in the second period from the absolute rule, rights and honor of colonialists to the welfare and benefits of the colonized,[12] this shift may have a connection with the aforementioned transformations in family, childhood, and understandings of patriarchal authority. Ultimately, these shifts are concordant with changing meanings of racial difference as they inform legitimations of colonialism. Thus, older understandings of racial inferiority as inherent and fixed also begin to move from the 1800s to more "historicist" notions of the capacity for change and especially, for guided maturation via colonial tutelage (Goldberg 2002: 74–75).

I do not want to suggest that this change is entirely unidirectional or universal; it is rather, fractured, incomplete, and continually subject to challenge. Indeed, the two poles of "harsher" and "softer" legitimations are never that far from each other. For example, while the latter, emergent in the eighteenth century (Staum 2003), became prominent in the wake of abolition (Hall 1999: 79; Goldberg 2002), such sentiment retreated in the following decades with the biological determinism of racial science (Hall 1999; Goldberg 2002: 77; Staum 2003). The two logics could even exist simultaneously within one state, as evidenced by the United States' attempts between the late 1880s and early 1900s to assimilate Native Americans while African Americans were deemed incapable of change (Goldberg 2002: 76). While France and Britain seemed especially—though not always—to adopt softer legitimations of colonial rule, this was typically not the case with Belgium, Germany, or apartheid South Africa (ibid).

Writing on France, for example, Martin Staum (2003: 9) argues that the emerging theories of classification, which placed individuals and peoples on the same life cycle toward greater development, were especially embraced in the wake of the French Revolution and the declining legitimacy of aristocratic modes of differentiation. In the French Republican civilizing mission, it was the duty—and the right—of the Third Republic to develop these peoples (Conklin 1999; Thompson and Aldoff 1975); and the benevolence of this tutelage negated any potential contradiction between professed ideas of self-determination and colonial practice (Brunschwig 1978:118; Conklin 1999:66). Thus, according to Robert Aldrich, colonial theorists envisioned the role of France as

> the mother country offering itself to these young peoples, these children in an act of "association, mutual comprehension, mutual respect, and common labor among children of the same family." France was the country known universally as liberator; wherever France had passed, "the indigene found himself at peace, fed, reared, healed and multiplied by French presence (Aldrich 1996: 4)."

Focusing particularly on North Africa, where the French exercised different levels of control over Algeria, Tunisia, and Morocco over the course of the 19th century (Sluglett 2005: 248), Orlando(2001) points out that this French colonial discourse infantilized and emasculated Arab men, constructing them at once as sexual deviants, which possessed a "masculine weakness and childlike behavior" and as barbaric in their excessive domination of the Arab woman. The feminist historian Joanna de Groot emphasizes especially the feminization of the Orient, as French and other European colonialists imagined it as emotional and irrational (de Groot 2000). Such discourse authorized "a *carte blanche* for Europeans' tutelage . . . It was [thus the French man's] duty to show these 'Arab despots' the way to civilization (Orlando 2001: 181)." Focusing particularly on Algeria, Gosnell (2001: 162) argues that the "mother country" was seen as offering "just and protective action" and the colonial literature of the day produced titles such as *Algeria, Daughter of France (1935)* and *Our Child Algeria (1949)*.

Such theories of the capacity of inferior peoples to change and develop competed in the 1800s with organic views of a global society in which the globe was likened to a body and different groups within to different tissues, each with their own organic function. This organic view made "bloodthirsty" Africans and "indolent" Asians inherently incapable of rising to the level of Europeans (Staum 2003: 20). In her fascinating discussion of a slave rebellion on the colony of Saint Domingue a mere two years after 1789, Colwill (1998) discusses how pro and anti-slavery perspectives moved back and forth between the two poles of inherent difference and capacity for change, as proslavery opinion insisted on the "eternal childhood" of Africans, while antislavery groups argued that freedmen would only require "enlightened 'guides' on the road to emancipation, just as a 'necessary passage' existed between 'youth to manhood (virilité)(Colwill 1998).'"

Surveying peoples from west and North Africa to Southeast Asia, the Caribbean, and the Pacific, then, French colonial legitimation moved back and forth between the two poles of colonial thought, deeming some groups capable of development and civilization, while others were inevitably stuck in a state of savagery. The notion that Europeans could help mature these peoples into a more adult stage loosely mapped onto the French colonial policy of assimilation prominent in the nineteenth century, as well as association from 1914 (Conklin 1999: 66; Brunschwig 1978: 118; Staum 2003).

Considering Britain, scholars argue that beginning in the 19th century, British colonialist discourse also began to see the role of the metropole as that of providing benevolent, parental tutelage to children (Mengara 2001). Victorian ideals of manliness and gentlemanliness especially shaped colonial strategies of rule, as administrators conceived themselves as "fathers" to "childlike natives (Conklin 1999: 97)." To be a supporter of the weak and the dependent—women, children, slaves and animals—constituted the "independence" of middle-class masculinity. Thus, in the 1830s, respectable English middle-class men also supported the anti-slavery movement and emancipation (Hall 1999: 103). This logic made itself felt in particular and varying ways within legitimations of colonial rule in South Australia, parts of the Caribbean, India, the Middle East and southern and North Africa.

Considering masculine protection and tutelage in India, for example, Nandy points to the colonialist writing of James Mill:

> The nineteenth-century liberal and Utilitarian thinker's view of this private responsibility as a father meshed with his view of Britain's responsibility to the societies under its Patriarchal suzerainty. Mill chose to

provide, almost single-handed, an intellectual framework for civilizing India under British rule . . . he saw Britain as the elder society guiding the young, the immature, and hence, primitive Indian society towards adulthood or maturity (Nandy 1987: 57–8).

In South Australia, too, colonial administrators saw "Aboriginal savages [as] children of the wild [that] needed to be protected from their own savagery and made anew (Hall 1999: 100–110)."

Once again, however, this emerging "softer" logic of colonial rule competed with notions of fixed incapacity. For example, in Jamaica after emancipation, the pro-slavery plantocracy continued to insist that Africans were fundamentally different in their inferiority, while anti-slavery groups argued of their capacity for change and growth (Hall 2002: 100–108). As scientific racism began to solidify in the mid-1800s and especially in the wake of Jamaica's Morant Bay rebellion, Hall argues that the latter quickly lost ground.

And yet, despite such inconsistencies, as the nineteenth century moved on, British colonial discourse continued to advance the idea that the empire was "part of a disordered universe which was being put right by British skill, technology and moral superiority (Finkelstein 2003: 100)." "Treat them as children; make them do what we know is for their benefit, robustly advised one 'China hand' in 1860 as British entrepreneurial and strategic interests tried to push into Chinese markets: he was echoed in numerous other uses of the 'child' metaphor for Africans, Tibetans, Tahitians, or the Indians (de Groot 2000: 44)." Thus, in places like Afghanistan in the early 1880s, Egypt in 1882 and the African colonies in the 1890s, this discourse argued that it was the duty of empire to provide good, sound government. Corresponding to the height of European colonialism within Africa, in the late 1800s, this discourse especially imagined southern Africa as at the earliest stages of evolution (Diallo 2001). In its territories in Africa, thus, particularly from 1895, the Colonial Office began to explicitly espouse the idea that the African territories were underdeveloped and that they must be developed to a "higher level of civilization," resulting in a number of development policies in the areas of science, health, medicine, agriculture, and so forth (Pedler 1975). These policies were put in place decades before the first British Colonial Development Act of 1929 (Christopher 1984: 62).

An initial impact of this "softer" conception of authority within colonial rule on international law is evident in Grovogui's discussion of the Berlin Conference of 1885. She argues that in this conference, Africans were selectively granted limited juridical capacity. Here, colonialist powers also decided to introduce commerce into these lands and claimed "spheres of influence" and "spheres of interest" within the lands, asserting a concern for bringing civilization and well-being to these peoples. However, Africans' subjectivity continued to be negated, as they were not consulted about these decisions. Moreover, their newly granted juridical capacity served only to enable them to transfer their sovereign and territorial rights to European powers, so providing colonialists with legal documents with which to justify their presence in foreign territories, and to ward off rival claims (Grovogui 1988).

After World War I, this new paternalistic language of colonial rule was institutionalized on a transnational basis. Given the problem of what to do with the dependent territories of the enemy, the Allies institutionalized softer familial notions of the childlike incompetency of dependent territories and their own responsibility regarding these territories through the League of Nations Mandates System:

> [for] peoples not yet able to stand by themselves under the strenuous conditions of the modern world, there should be applied the principle that the well-being and development of such peoples form a sacred trust of civilization . . . the tutelage of such peoples should be entrusted to advanced nations who by reason of their resources, their experience or their geographical position can best undertake this responsibility, and who are willing to accept it, and that this tutelage should be exercised by them as Mandatories on behalf of the League (Article 22, Covenant of League of Nations. 1919).

While this obligation has of course often been critiqued as ethnocentric and racist (Grovogui 1988; Lauren 1998; Obadele 1996; Reus-Smit 2001; Rajagopal 2003), some have nevertheless also pointed out that the mandate

> introduced the novel concept of *international responsibility* regarding the peoples in non-autonomous countries . . . [and contributed to] a new type of relationship between nations which was markedly different from the idea of timeless domination which had characterized the previous period: the mandate was not a definitive but an evolutionary arrangement which one day would come to an end (Grimal 1978: 16–17).

In this vein, it also introduced a new actor into the relationship between European and non-European peoples: the international institution (Rajagopal 2003: 51).

Nevertheless, it is interesting to note here that in accordance with the differential recognition granted to different categories of humanity in earlier colonialist discourse and practice, as well as the two poles of colonial legitimation, the mandates system similarly made a distinction between different kinds of territories using the language of "stages of development." Based on these "stages," the system created three different classes of mandates, classes A, B, and C (see Table 1). Within these classes, class A consisted of the former Turkish territories, while B and C were comprised of territories from Africa and the Pacific. While the mandates system may have contributed to a "new type of relationship between nations," only the first were "to be brought to" (eventual) independence, while the second two differed little from other colonies (Grimal 1978). With regard to the discussion of French and British colonial rule above, under this system, France was to "bring Syria and Lebanon to independence" while Britain was to do the same for Iraq, Transjordan, and Palestine. The rest of the territories, in Africa and the Pacific, were thought to be inevitably and permanently stuck in their lower stage of development.

With the emergence of the United Nations after 1945, the League's prior mandate system was transformed into the UN Trusteeship System, in which territories designated as Trusts were to be moved to (eventual) independence if so chosen, while those designated as Non Self-Governing Territories (NSGTs) were not.

In a sense, the shift from "harsher" notions of colonial rule to "softer" notions may imply a narrative of linear progress from the absolute authority and rule of colonialist powers to the welfare of dependent peoples. Indeed, the shift has been enabled in part by an ongoing dialogue between colonial rule and anti-slavery and anti-colonial movements from the eighteenth century and on. I have to emphasize, however, that even the softer imagery of welfare, beneficence and obligation is a controlling imagery that serves to maintain differential subjectivity and personhood. For example, in her research on counterinsurgency politics in the fifties, Doty discusses how the British seized on the imagery of Mau Mau rebels as insane, excessively passionate, children in order to legitimate their counterinsurgency policies. Likewise, in the newly sovereign Philippines, the United States dealt similarly with the Huk rebels, constructing them not only as excessively passionate and childlike, but as "bad children" as opposed to more cooperative Third World "good children (Doty 1996)."

Considering constructions of space, identity and international community prior to legal decolonization, then, the argument here is that colonial discourses—despite variation over space and time—have over the centuries engaged in a kinship politics, which constructs proximity and indeed association, as well as hierarchy, between otherwise distinct or far-flung groups. I want to emphasize that I am not making a universal argument here for either embodiment or kinship politics. By no means am I arguing that these were the only mechanisms of the colonial construction of hierarchy, or always the central ones. Nor am I denying that the hierarchical categories of embodiment and kinship politics could be turned on their head and used anti-systemically. Moreover, kinship politics in particular is a moving politics, shifting over time and space, and traversing between a softer imagery of benevolence and care to harsher notions of absolute authority and right. Such contrasting images might exist in conjunction within a particular era or a particular set of practices of colonial rule as well. Whatever the case, however, from a world-historical perspective, the politics of kinship draws from naturalized assumptions about hierarchical relations between different body parts and/or family members. Moreover, inescapably related to emerging values of order, reason, and rationality in modernity, kinship politics renders superior entities within the collectivity the right to rule by virtue of their greater ability to reason, while lesser entities are made incapable or less capable of reason. In this manner, the discourses of embodiment—in variable, complex and intersecting processes—have targeted women, "lower" classes, "other" races, and "other" cultures. Even more, they have been critical to defining the very *meaning* of civilization, race, culture and gender in the colonial era, as they helped to construct notions of the west, whiteness, black, woman, and man (among others).

THE QUERY: NEGOTIATING DECOLONIZATION IN THE UNITED NATIONS

Given the significance of this kinship politics in the hierarchical construction of space, identity and international community in the formal colonial era, what happens to this politics with legal decolonization in the UN? Is it dismantled? Is it reconfigured? And what happens to the racial, sexual and cultural inequalities on which it relies (and also perpetuates)? In the remainder of this chapter, I outline the strategy for exploring these questions. I first introduce the UN and anti-colonial efforts regarding legal decolonization in the UN. Then, I discuss the sources and nature of the materials used for analysis. Finally, I situate my research design and strategy of inquiry within broader approaches to discourse and communication research, ending with specific procedures for analysis.

The UN is an international organization in which member states can come together and consider matters of "international concern." The

Kinship Politics and Space, Identity and International Community

General Assembly (GA) of the UN is the main deliberative organ of the UN. It is also the most democratic, as all UN members are also members of the GA and have an equal vote within the GA. Thus, the GA is the ideal location in which to explore how contending and differentially situated perspectives negotiate matters of "international concern." Moreover, a number of member states that participate within these debates are formerly dependent, newly independent, anti-colonialist states themselves. Thus, the conversations in the GA provide an official forum for the dependent territory "perspective"—and indeed, for a *dialogue* between this perspective and others.

In the UNGA, these newly independent, anti-colonial states provide the main push for legal decolonization. These states opposed the initial institutionalization of dependent territories as Trusts and NSGTs within the UN system in 1945; they were unsuccessful, however, in overturning this system at that time. Over the years, nevertheless, they launch a number of institutional-discursive maneuvers to do so. In the GA, they introduce various measures and initiate rigorous debate on extending the norms of human rights and self-determination to the dependent territories, increasing the binding nature of the principles of human rights and self-determination articulated in the UN Charter, increasing their own oversight in the way dependent territories are handled in the UN, and giving dependent territories the means for voicing their concerns to the GA. (Their specific moves regarding both Trusts and NSGTs will be discussed more fully in the next chapter). While in 1946, these newly independent, anti-colonialist states comprise only a handful of member states within the UN, over the years their numbers continue to grow so that by 1960, they are able to introduce and pass a draft resolution that becomes the UN Declaration on the Granting of Independence to Colonial Countries and Peoples.

Sources and Nature of Materials for Analysis

Given my interest in the contentions in the GA, my main source of materials for analysis is the General Assembly Official Records for the years 1946–1960. These records are public documents and are available at the United Nations Information Centre of Washington, DC (United Nations 2003). The GA, as mentioned above, is the main deliberative organ of the UN. It meets annually for regular sessions, as well as for special and emergency special sessions. Each session is organized as a general debate, in which Member States, represented by their diplomatic delegations, express their views on a wide range of matters of international concern. Included are required reports submitted by the Secretary-General, as well as by a number of other bodies. Because of the great number of questions that the

GA is called upon to consider, the GA allocates most questions to its six Main Committees. Some questions are considered directly in plenary meetings, rather than in one of the Main Committees. All questions are voted on in plenary meetings, usually towards the end of the regular session, after the committees have completed their consideration of them and submitted draft resolutions to the plenary Assembly.

The Official Records of the GA consist, thus, of the meeting records, committee reports, and resolutions. The records of specific interest to me are the *Verbatim Records*, or the meeting records of the statements/speeches made and actions taken during GA meetings. These include discussion of any submitted committee reports and draft resolutions, as well as votes on draft resolutions and explanations of particular votes. The Verbatim Records, thus, provide a full, first-person account of the proceedings of a meeting, and are particularly useful for discourse analysis.

Finding Materials for Analysis

The Verbatim Records are published as bound volumes, one (or two) for each annual session. The front matter of each volume includes a Table of Contents with a listing of the agenda for that session, as well as what was discussed. I selected records for analysis by the subject headings that were listed on the agenda. Specifically, I chose anything that mentioned the terms: NSGT Territories, Trust Territories, and colonialism.[13] I fully recognize that such a strategy may leave out important debates on the problem of colonialism that are not captured by this terminology. However, I adopted this strategy as a way of reducing and managing information. Also, as the agenda terminology guides the topic of discussion, I believe my focus on NSGTs, Trusts and colonialism will sufficiently capture the material that I require for my purposes.

Debates of interest on particular agenda items sometimes spanned several meetings. One meeting could also contain several debates of interest. Hence, there is no direct relationship between the number of debates examined and the number of meetings covered. In total, I examined the speeches/statements that transpired in almost 100 debates on Trusts, NSGTs or colonialism, spanning 100 meetings over a 15-year period.

A Note on What These Records Do Not Tell

One important caveat that must be made is that although these records are one window onto the negotiation of legal decolonization in the UN, they of course do not and cannot represent a "pure" or "authentic" or "unmarked" negotiation of legal decolonization or of any of the other issues that will be discussed. The most basic reason for the unavoidable partiality is inherent in the nature of my sources. That is, we must problematize the degree to which the delegates that officially represent their countries actually represent the multiple social groups differentially situated within a particular delimitation of territorial borders. The delegates examined here are overwhelmingly educated, male, and elite. Their actions, discursive and otherwise, most directly represent the official policies of their governments and have little to say about the national populace in general, differentially situated social classes, women, and so forth. This partiality, however, does not make my material less "legitimate" for my purposes, but only highlights the relations of power which undergrid, shape and produce changing constructs of space, identity and international community.

RESEARCH STRATEGY

According to Guba and Lincoln (in Denzin and Lincoln 1998b: 195–219), both constructivism and critical theory[14] are alternatives to positivist approaches to qualitative research, the key distinguishing factor of the first being its ontological relativism and the second being its stress on the always value-laden, always political nature of inquiry. In this work, I draw from the anti-essentialist insights of constructivism (Schwandt in Denzin and Lincoln 1998b: 221–259) but especially from the critical stress on power relationships, aiming to offer "*simultaneously* an account of radical historical contingency for all knowledge claims . . . *and* a no-nonsense commitment to faithful accounts of a 'real' world (Haraway 1988: 579)."[15]

Within this general approach, my specific strategy of inquiry consists of a discourse analysis, broadly speaking, of the statements of different delegates to the General Assembly, where the notion of documents as cultural texts subject to discursive analysis (Tuchman in Denzin and Lincoln 1998c: 244–248) is key. (I also pay some attention to their voting and other procedure-related practices that transpire in the context of these debates, but the bulk of the analysis focuses on the arguments exchanged). The statements/speeches made by diplomats in the GA can be seen as constituting a particular genre of discourse, with its own distinctive features. First, made in this international forum in the context of not just the delegates of other countries but also countless news media, the audience for this discourse goes beyond the immediate gathering and can be assumed to be "universal." Second, the statements made have a particular format, comprised of a series of monologues in which the head of each delegation takes a "tour d'horizon" of the current state of the world's problems as seen in light of the policy of her/his government. Third, certain features are repeated in this discourse, including congratulation to the President of the

GA, an affirmation of the importance and necessity of the UN, and the use of highly formal and polite language (Donahue and Prosser 1997: 65). At the end of a monologue each speaker also takes a stance on a particular draft resolution that has been submitted for discussion and adoption (which ends with a yes, no or abstention vote on the draft resolution under consideration).

First, then, I examine these debates as *persuasive* discourse, aimed at justifying a speaker's own stance on a draft resolution and also of convincing others to take on a similar stance (and ultimately, to vote similarly). Thus, I pay particular attention to each speaker's "tour d'horizon" of the current state of the world's problems from the perspective of the government that speaker represents, and I use Walter Fisher's narrative approach to persuasive communication to do so. Extending Kenneth Burke's argument that the individual is above all a symbol-user, Fisher argues that human beings are above all story-telling creatures. Human communication, then, should be viewed as stories/accounts competing with other stories/accounts, purportedly constituted by "good reasons," acceptable to an audience when they satisfy certain requirements of narrative probability and fidelity, with the central goal of identification with the audience and inevitably, functioning *as moral inducements*. The term "good reasons" here is central, as he considers these "the paradigmatic mode of human decision-making and communication," varying in form among situations, genres and media of communication and the production and practice of which is ruled by matters of history, biography, culture and character (Fisher 1987: 58–59). In short, individuals are adequately persuaded by a story when they perceive it as offering "good reasons (also, appeals)."[16]

The narrative approach is particularly appropriate for my analysis of GA statements as persuasive discourse because of how the approach situates itself in relation to Cartesian conceptions of knowledge and rationality. In his work, Fisher is explicitly in debate with the traditional rhetorical perspective on rhetorical argument, which assumes that such argument must "be marked by clearly identifiable modes of inference and implication, and that the norms of evaluation of rhetorical communication must be rational standards taken exclusively from informal or formal logic (Fisher 1987: 58–59)." With the narrative approach, he means to expand the meaning of rationality from the notion of formal and informal logic to narrative rationality, or rationality as constituted in narrative. "Rationality is determined by the nature of persons as narrative beings—their inherent awareness of narrative probability, what constitutes a coherent story, and their constant habit of testing narrative fidelity . . . whether or not the stories they experience ring true with the stories they know to be true in their lives (Fisher 1987: 64–65)."

This expanded conception of rationality is particularly appropriate because as discussed earlier, the crux of differential personhood in kinship politics is the construction of the embodied, irrational other in contrast to a disembodied, rational self; hence, the world of kinship politics systematically denies subjectivity to those considered incapable of rationality. Narrative rationality, on the other hand,

> is inimical to the hierarchical idea that some people are qualified to be rational and others are not . . . [That is, it *begins* with the acknowledgement that] denials of fundamental rationality have appeared repeatedly—in slave states, in monarchic states, in fascist states, in communist states, and even in democratic states . . . [It seeks to move beyond] the dualisms of modernism: fact-value, intellect-imagination, reason-emotion . . . [and embrace] non-Cartesian concepts (Fisher 1987: 67–68).

Thus, from the perspective that the GA debates serve as *persuasive* discourse aimed at justifying a speaker's own stance on a draft resolution and of convincing others to take on a similar stance, I am particularly interested in these debates as competing stories/accounts of the world which themselves embed contending appeals/good reasons.

Beyond examining these debates as *persuasive* discourse, I also examine them as *constitutive* discourse. That is, the stories/accounts of the world offered by speakers do not merely offer contending appeals for a particular stance on an issue—the stories themselves constitute alternative visions of the world. Following Tischer, Meyer, Wodak and Vetter (2000: 149), these stories[17] are simultaneously constitutive of *different social identities* (or distinctions between different categories of identity), the *relations between* these categories of identity, and *systems of knowledge and beliefs* about these identities. We may apply this approach to the hierarchical discourse of kinship itself. Regarding identity distinctions or categories of identities, for example, this discourse is constitutive of the distinctions of the "rational" versus the "irrational," the "paternal" versus the "childlike," and the "masculine" versus the "feminine." Additionally, this discourse naturalizes hierarchical relations within each binary, with the first term having the natural right to master, rule over, or guide the second. Finally, certain knowledge is also created about these identities in the process of defining these identities and relating them to each other, for example, that the irrational, childlike or feminine require such tutelage or rule from the rational, paternal or masculine.

In order to explore how the stories/accounts provided by different speakers might constitute alternative visions of the world, I begin with a specific technique for comparing the speech and ultimately the worldviews of different speakers, known as the cluster-agon method of analysis. Cluster-agon analysis was initially formulated by Kenneth Burke (1973; 1984), who argues that every work produced by a rhetor contains a set of implicit equations, or "associational clusters." The meanings that key symbols or terms (also known as god terms) have for the rhetor can be discovered by charting the symbols that cluster around those key symbols in the rhetorical artifact. In cluster-agon analysis, key symbols or terms are first identified by their frequency or intensity within a text. After the key terms/symbols have been identified, the words that cluster (i.e., appear in close proximity to the key term, or are joined by a conjunction to the key term, or are connected by a cause-and-effect relationship to the key term, and so on) around those key terms are charted. Next, any patterns that might appear within the clusters are charted. For example, is a particular word or symbol always associated with a key term? Next, one may perform an agon analysis, where opposing terms (also known as devil terms) are examined. Here, the goal is to discover what terms/symbols oppose or contradict the key terms/symbols. The final step is to use the pattern that emerges in the analysis to identify the speaker's motive (Burke 1973; Burke 1984; Foss 1989).[18]

Cluster-agon analysis is particularly useful for comparing the rhetoric of several speakers (Berthold 1976). Through the comparison of different speakers' key term clusters and opposing term clusters, one may compare structures of binary logic that undergrid and constitute varying meaning systems. In the case of this study, I use cluster-agon analysis to compare the meaning systems of not only different speakers but also different groups of speakers.

Considering these groupings, though one might expect certain patterns of discourse based on political perspective, particular groups were not identified *a priori*. Rather, groupings of speakers (and the countries that they represented) that tended to make similar kinds of arguments, to base their arguments on similar kinds of appeals, and to support one another against others, were allowed to emerge from the data. In this fashion, two fairly distinct, overarching groupings emerged: first, that of former and contemporary European colonialist powers, and second, that of former dependent, newly independent territories, what I term as the entity of Asia-Africa.[19] The United States and a number of former dependent territories in the Americas (such as Argentina, Peru, and Columbia) tended to side with the first group. The Soviet Union, and its associated bloc of countries,

Kinship Politics and Space, Identity and International Community 37

along with a number of different former dependent territories in the Americas (such as Mexico and Guatemala), tended to side with the second. As the first group tended to prioritize the perspective of the colonialist powers, I term this group the "colonialist" view. As the second group did the same for former and contemporary dependent territories, I term this group the "anti-colonialist" view.[20]

Given both the persuasive and constitutive approaches employed here, then, the central question under investigation becomes one of understanding *how colonialist and anti-colonialist groups in the General Assembly attempt to advance different stories/accounts of the world in order to negotiate alternative visions of different categories of identities, the relationships between these identities, and knowledge about them.* These (re)negotiations of identity are integrally part of the larger anti-colonialist project of the renegotiation of space.

OUTLINE OF THE CHAPTERS

In general, I examine two sets of debates within the UNGA that are related to my questions about colonialism and decolonization. One set consists of technical and other issues concerning NSGTs and Trusts within the UN system, and the second concerns the general problematic of colonialism within and beyond the UN system. The first occurs largely over the first fourteen years of interest, while the second occurs in the final year examined.

In Chapter Two, I examine the debates on Trusts and NSGTs. I begin by discussing the dependent status of Trusts and NSGTs within the UN Charter and the emergence of an anti-colonialist collective identity whose goal is to challenge this status. Then, I examine debate on Trusts and NSGTs between anti-colonialists and colonialists. In these debates, for each speaker, I take note of 1) their vote/stance on the matter under debate and 2) the central appeals or "good reasons" they offer to justify this stance. I argue that while colonialist speakers, continuous with earlier kinship discourse, appeal especially to the *rational* in justifying the status quo, anti-colonialists seek to disrupt this binary by appealing to the *moral*. In Chapter Three, I explore some of the ambiguities and complexities of these debates, particularly within the anti-kinship arguments of anti-colonialists. I argue that anti-colonialists' critiques of colonialist practices are inconsistent, of narrow scope, and sometimes entirely plastic. In Chapter Four, I seek to examine these contradictions of anti-colonialist discourse further. Thus, I perform a cluster-agon analysis of the debates of both colonialists and anti-colonialists. Based on this analysis, I argue that most anti-colonialists are actually in agreement with key tenets of colonialist kinship politics.

In Chapter Five, I examine how all of this is resolved in the debates on the general problematic of colonialism, which occurs in the final year. I argue that anti-colonialists' ambiguities in relation to colonialist kinship politics results in a partial challenge to kinship politics that fails to challenge its major elements. Additionally, I argue that this challenge is profoundly gendered and has important implications for gender and (hetero)sexuality in the "postcolonial" world. In Chapter Six, I end with some concluding remarks on how colonialists and anti-colonialists renegotiate the kinship politics of the colonial era, with particular focus on three dimensions of this negotiation: its temporality, its gendering and (hetero)sexuality, and what it tells us about resistance.

Chapter Two

(Re)negotiating the "Colonial" Problematic: The UN Charter, the Emergence of Asia-Africa, and the Anti-Colonial Challenge to Kinship

> *Our political referents and priorities—the people, the community, class struggle, anti-racism, gender difference, the assertion of an anti-imperialist, black or third perspective—are not there in some primordial, naturalistic sense. Nor do they reflect a unity or homogenous political object. They make sense as they come to be constructed in the discourses of feminism or Marxism or the Third Cinema or whatever, whose objects of priority—class, or sexuality or "the new ethnicity"— are always in historical and philosophical tension, or cross-reference with other objectives.*
>
> -Homi Bhabha, 1994

This study concerns legal decolonization specifically, but also resistance more generally. As argued in the above text, resistance is of course never in and of itself, never pure, nor authentic (Bhabha 1994a; See also Cooper 1996: 6–12). Rather, resistance is inescapably shaped by the multiple, often-heterogeneous conditions of its possibility, including circuits of capital, technology, and given institutional infrastructures. In the world-historical space and time of the post-war UNGA, then, what are the conditions of possibility for anti-colonialist resistance? In the nineteenth century, the politics of kinship imparted to the term "colonial" a number of positive connotations, which in various ways became embedded in and disseminated through emerging fields such as the biological sciences and ethnology, specific institutions such as colonial medicine and colonial development projects, as well as elaborate colonial bureaucracies (See, for example, Pedler 1975; Thompson and Aldoff 1975; Mengara 2001b; Conklin 1999). As discussed in Chapter One, this politics deployed especially the binary of the rational/irrational, which also manifested as the paternal/childlike and the masculine/feminine, in order to construct transnational hierarchies of space, identity and international community. In the twentieth century, however, two sets of developments served to disturb these conditions of possibility, helping to open up new space in which to (re)negotiate colonialist kinship and its hierarchies. First, from the mid-1800s and on, anti-colonialists advanced new theories of democracy and self-determination as part of a building global movement which sought to contend with older, colonialist meanings of the "colonial," and by the mid-1900s, this movement had succeeded in de-legitimizing the "western imperial project (Parrott 1997; Winant 2001)." Second, with the emergence of the purportedly universal UN after WWII, these anti-colonialist efforts were incorporated into the institutions of global knowledge production in a particular manner. That is, the UN incorporated on a formally equal basis newly independent, "postcolonial," anti-colonialist states, with elite, mostly male leaders representing (elite blocks within) these states within its apparatus. In the UNGA, then, these "postcolonial" states provided the central locus of anti-colonialist resistance and social change, pushing for legal decolonization against the reactionary politics of colonialist sympathizers. In this process, how did this anti-colonialist resistance challenge the politics of kinship, its construction of the "colonial," and its rational/irrational and other hierarchies? Critically, how did the conditions of possibility for this resistance, particularly its articulation by elite men representing "sovereign," if sui generis,[1] nation-states determine its shape? In this chapter, I argue that in the post-war moment in the UNGA, while colonialist speakers continued to legitimate their positions with the politics of kinship and particularly its distinct deployment of the *rational*, anti-colonialist speakers responded with recourse to the *moral*.

In what follows, I explore this (re)negotiation of kinship politics and the colonialist bounding of the "colonial," as well as the contention between the rational versus the moral, under the rubric of the "(re)bounding of the colonial problematic." By the term "colonial problematic," I intend to designate a particular apprehension of the colonial, including definition of its boundaries and parameters and assessment of its content. In the UNGA, debate on legal decolonization falls into two broad categories, a set of discussions on specific dependent territories under the purview of the UN as institutionalized in the Charter and a set of discussions on the general problematic of colonialism, beyond the particulars of the Charter. The first takes place during the first fourteen years of debate, and is comprised primarily of colonialist and anti-colonialist attempts to negotiate the colonial as it is institutionalized within the Charter. The second, which takes place in the fifteenth and final year of debate, moves beyond the particularities of the Charter to the general problem of colonialism, ultimately initiating the onset of legal decolonization. I characterize this first category of discussions,

(Re)negotiating the "Colonial" Problematic

thus, as fundamentally concerned with the (re)bounding of the colonial problematic, while the second is concerned more with the resolution of the colonial problematic. In this chapter, then, I turn to this first set of discussions, treating the second in a separate chapter.

Specifically, I examine three overlapping moments in this (re)bounding of the colonial problematic. I begin with an initial moment of this bounding, largely from the perspective of colonialist powers, within the UN Charter in 1945. Interestingly, we see in this bounding in the Charter the instantiation of a colonialist identity at the transnational level, one that collectively constructs itself as the rational/paternal/masculine in opposition to its colonial others. While this is certainly not the first or only manifestation of such a transnational identity,[2] it is significant in this instance in that it becomes incorporated into the institutional infrastructure of a new and enduring global organization. Next, I move outside of the UN to examine the emergence of the central source of challenge to this bounding of the colonial problematic: the crystallization of the also transnational, anti-colonialist, counter-identity of "Asia-Africa." This identity, in response to its designation as irrational, infantile and effeminate within the discourses of kinship politics, constructs itself instead in terms of masculine unity, or brotherhood, and morality. How do these two identities (re)negotiate the colonial? To explore this question, finally, I move to the UNGA debates. Here, I argue that the central contention in these conversations is inextricably linked to these two transnational formations of colonialist and anti-colonialist identity. While colonialist speakers continue to legitimate hierarchical relations between territories and identities with the logic of kinship, particularly the rational/irrational binary within this logic, Asia-Africa responds to this insistence on *the rational* with an emphasis on *the moral*. Indeed, with this focus on the moral, Asia-Africa especially seeks to disrupt the binary of the rational/irrational, also addressing the paternal/childlike binary to some extent. On the binary of the masculine/feminine, however, it remains silent.

These anti-colonialist interventions do not necessarily displace or replace colonialist knowledge, its politics of kinship, or its production of the colonial. Rather, they introduce competing narratives of kinship and colonialism, rationality and irrationality, paternalism, race, culture and democracy. Their challenge to especially the binary of the rational/irrational but also the paternal/childlike constitutes an important disruption of the colonialist politics of kinship. Their silence on the masculine/feminine binary, however, foreshadows a profoundly gendered anti-colonialist politics that will become more fully evident during the final year of debate and the "resolution" of the colonial problematic.

THE INITIAL MOMENT OF THE BOUNDING OF THE COLONIAL PROBLEMATIC: THE INSTITUTIONAL-DISCURSIVE STRUCTURE OF THE CHARTER

How is the colonial problematic bound within the UN Charter? How does the Charter betray a transnational colonialist identity constructed in opposition to a colonialist other? As a document, the Charter symbolizes both the conflict and the cooperation of the post-World War II period, bringing together conflicting perspectives, values and agendas in unity and hierarchy. This conflict is evident from the initial moment of the emergence of the UN, the signing of the Atlantic Charter (1941) and the Declaration of the United Nations (1942). The Atlantic Charter, in particular, emphasized the principles of seeking "no aggrandizement, territorial or other . . . no territorial changes that do not accord with the freely expressed wishes of the peoples concerned . . . the right of all peoples to choose the form of government under which they will live . . . sovereign rights and self government restored to those who have been forcibly deprived of them (Atlantic Charter, 1941)." While these principles may have been directed to the "Nazi tyranny (Atlantic Charter, 1941)," they nevertheless gave anti-colonialist groups hope that the Allies might support the cause of decolonization. However, any such hopes were thwarted as the Allies insisted that their principles were merely declarations, not legal obligations. According to Lauren (1998), these disagreements persisted through the decision to erect a new international organization and over the series of meetings held on the design of this new organization. While anti-colonialist groups (which by the last meeting in San Francisco included the Soviets, as opposed to the first meeting) wanted to address issues of race, sovereignty for all territories, an international standard of conduct, repudiation of territorial conquest, support for the principles of democracy, justice, and a number of rights, and a Trusteeship Committee to compel the process of decolonization,[3] the western powers, above all, wanted to protect their sovereignty and state's rights.

On one level, the Charter is of course a symbol of the cooperation of the post-World War II period. The final document includes a central identification of the exigencies of the moment as well as the "solution" to these exigencies. In just the Preamble (below), the exigencies identified are given in the first two passages and the solution to them is given in the third passage:

WE THE PEOPLES OF THE UNITED NATIONS DETERMINED

to save succeeding generations from the scourge of war, which twice in our lifetime has brought untold sorrow to mankind, and to reaffirm faith in fundamental human rights, in the dignity and worth of the human person, in the equal rights of men and women and of nations large and small, and to establish conditions under which justice and respect for the obligations arising from treaties and other sources of international law can be maintained, and to promote social progress and better standards of life in larger freedom,

AND FOR THESE ENDS

to practice tolerance and live together in peace with one another as good neighbours, and
to unite our strength to maintain international peace and security, and
to ensure, by the acceptance of principles and the institution of methods, that armed force shall not be used, save in the common interest, and
to employ international machinery for the promotion of the economic and social advancement of all peoples,

HAVE RESOLVED TO COMBINE OUR EFFORTS TO ACCOMPLISH THESE AIMS

Accordingly, our respective Governments, through representatives assembled in the city of San Francisco, who have exhibited their full powers found to be in good and due form, have agreed to the present Charter of the United Nations and do hereby establish an international organization to be known as the United Nations.

Hence, the Charter lays down a univocal series of justifications for the existence of the UN, supported by the central principle of peace and accompanied by the additional principles of human rights, international law and cooperation, and freedom.

On another level, the Charter also inevitably encompasses the ongoing and unevenly matched tension between state sovereignty/rights and self-determination. Hence, though both principles are articulated within the document—and at fairly similar levels, with state sovereignty mentioned a total of three times and self-determination mentioned a total of two times—by no means are both of equal importance. That is, the relative importance of both within the text is highlighted by the uneven level of forcefulness in their respective articulations. For example, while the first is mentioned only three times (in Article 2, Paragraph 1; in Article 2, Paragraph 7; and in Article 80), in each instance it appears as a master principle, overriding all other principles within the text. Thus Article 2, Paragraph 1 states: The Organization is based on the principle of the sovereign equality of all its members. Likewise, Article 2, Paragraph 7 states, "Nothing contained in the present Charter shall authorize the United Nations to intervene in matters which are essentially within the domestic jurisdiction of any state." Similarly, Article 80 states, "nothing in this Chapter shall be construed in or of itself to alter in any manner the rights whatsoever of any states or any peoples or the terms of existing international instruments to which Members of the United Nations may respectively be parties." The purpose of Article 2 is to outline the principles upon which the new organization will be built. The placement of the issue of sovereignty in Article 2, then, does the work of limiting the scope of the new international organization (i.e., this "international" organization may only intrude into the domain of sovereign states to a limited extent). Similarly, Article 80 is located within the Chapter concerned with the International Trusteeship System (Chapter XII), the locus of UN provision for legal decolonization. It is telling, then, that the second affirmation of the fundamental and prior principle of sovereignty is made in the context of the consideration of justice for dependent territories. This second mention, hence, does the work of constructing state's rights (read: the rights of territories which are at present considered sovereign, which include colonial powers and exclude dependent territories) as prior to the rights of dependent territories.

Consequently, despite the stated purpose in the Preamble of the maintenance of peace, human rights, international law and cooperation and freedom within the new organization of the United Nations, state sovereignty actually supercedes all other principles. As such, this hierarchy of values within the Charter renders the UN provision for legal decolonization problematic and incomplete and is most evident in the Charter distinction between Non Self-Governing Territories (NSGTs) and Trust Territories (Trusts) and in the Trusteeship System. First, the Charter makes a critical distinction between NSGTs and Trusts, where only Trusts are to be brought to independence, with definite obligations to be undertaken by administering powers in a framework of international accountability based on specific agreements, while the provisions for NSGTs consist of an unenforceable "Declaration (El-Ayouty 1971)." Moreover, only former League of Nations mandates and enemy territories are to be put into Trust status, while the dependent territories of Allies are to remain in the status quo of the ongoing dependence of NSGTs (Obadele 1996). Needless to say, most dependent territories actually fall into the NSGT category (see Table 2); moreover, any territory that qualifies as a Trust can nevertheless be designated as "strategic" and so retained, hence allowing colonialist countries to hold on to any territories they wish.

Beyond the distinction between NSGTs and Trusts, Lauren (1998) points out that the UN provision for decolonization via the Trust status is further handicapped by the watering down of the sole avenue provided for (eventual) self-determination. Hence, only vague terms such as "human rights," "fundamental freedoms," and "just treatment" are used to describe the powers of the Trusteeship Council that is to oversee the progress of the Trusts, while more active words such as "facilitate," "make recommendations," and "initiate studies" are excluded.

Ultimately, the unevenly matched goals of the sovereign rights of (especially western and colonialist powers) versus the self-determination of dependent peoples is evident in the way the process of legal decolonization is institutionally and discursively constructed within the Charter. For example, Article 73, applying to NSGTs, states:

> Members of the United Nations which have or assume responsibilities for the administration of territories whose peoples have not yet attained a full measure of self-government recognize the principle that the interests of the inhabitants of these territories are paramount, and accept as a sacred trust the obligation to promote to the utmost . . . the wellbeing of the inhabitants of these territories, and, to this end . . . to ensure . . . their political, economic, social, and educational advancement . . . to develop self-government, to take due account of the political aspirations of the peoples, and to assist them in the progressive development of their free political institutions, according to the particular circumstances of each territory and its peoples and their varying stages of advancement.

Similarly, in relation to Trusts, Article 76 states:

> The basic objectives of the trusteeship system . . . shall be . . . to promote the political, economic, social, and educational advancement of the inhabitants of the trust territories, and their progressive development towards self-government or independence as may be appropriate to the particular circumstances of each territory and its peoples and the freely expressed wishes of the peoples concerned, and as may be provided by the terms of each trusteeship agreement.

For both NSGTs and Trusts, then, the Charter constructs dependent territories as requiring guidance in "political, economic, social and educational advancement" and "progressive development." Trusts, to be brought to independence, are positioned as requiring such advancement and development before they can achieve independence, while the indefinitely dependent status of the NSGT is a "sacred trust." Such language continues themes from the Mandates system of the League of Nations, where any anti-colonialist voice was even more muted.

Thus, such logic betrays the reliance on a politics of kinship, embodiment and disembodiment, where more advanced, developed, rational and ultimately, disembodied administering authorities are to assist in the "development" and "advancement" of less developed, less advanced and less rational, embodied dependent territories. At the very least, such is the case for those territories that qualify as Trusts and so are designated for eventual independence. For NSGTs, however, defined outside of even this (eventual) possibility, the rights of the disembodied unconditionally trump the rights of the embodied.

Ultimately, then, despite the greater emphasis on global cooperation in the immediate post-war era, the UN Charter nevertheless bounds the colonial problematic from the perspective of colonialist kinship politics. Moreover, that this document with global reach relies on a politics of kinship to distinguish between transnational categories of subjects, most clearly "more advanced" administering authorities versus "less advanced" dependent territories, demonstrates something else. That is, kinship politics did more than just provide specific colonialist powers the logic for colonialist constructions of self and other; more importantly, it operated in this particular world-historical moment at a critical transnational level, helping to construct distinct and hierarchically ordered—if unsettled—transnational collectivities, including a *transnational colonialist identity* in opposition to a putative underdeveloped other.

THE EMERGENCE OF ASIA-AFRICA

If colonialist groups bound the colonial problematic in the Charter through the logic of kinship politics, the central challenge to this bounding emerged in the subsequent years with the gradual crystallization of the collective identity of Asia-Africa.[4] Beginning with the idea that collective identity is an achievement, end-point or result of a process (Melucci 1995), in what follows I examine the process of the construction of Asia-Africa. But first, I give a brief review of the larger global political context within which this identity negotiated its emergence.

The recent encounters with the horrors of Nazism and Fascism, the development of the most destructive weapons technology to date, the accelerated decline of the older European colonial powers and growing challenges to the "imperial idea," and finally, the seemingly sudden rise of the two new superpowers all pointed to the multiple possibilities, both hopeful and dangerous, for the post-war world. As newly politicized[5] Asian and African dependent territories became increasingly vocal and visible in their demands for democracy and political independence, European colonial powers like

(Re)negotiating the "Colonial" Problematic

Britain and France sought to appear progressive on the one hand, while devising new mechanisms with which to maintain their influence on the other. For the British, a central way of maintaining power was to encourage lost colonies to become members of the Commonwealth and to remain in the sterling area. For its part, France formed the French Union, eventually the French Community, to do the same and recast its language of "colonies" to that of "overseas départements." The Dutch also "incorporated" their Caribbean territories into the Kingdom of the Netherlands. Of course, not all European powers recognized or accepted the shifting ideological climate—Portugal, for example, refused to renegotiate the status of its possessions.

As Cold War tensions rose between the Soviet Union and the United States, various forms of overt and covert political pressure, economic aid, and military alliances divided Europe into two blocs. Perhaps the struggle was felt most intensely in the Third World, however, for just as the territories of Asia and Africa launched their struggles for independence, the Soviet Union and the United States sought to draw them into their economic, political and military struggles. Between the years of 1945–1990, the Third World was the theatre of over one hundred wars that had to do with the Cold War, and most of the crises that threatened to escalate into nuclear war also occurred in the Third World (Painter 1999; Mortimer 1984; Bell 2001).

Hence, the newly politicized subjects of Asian and African dependent territories struggled for independence over their own territories and identities in a climate where multiple groups sought power over them for a variety of reasons. Particularly with the emergence of the Cold War, former and contemporary dependent territories largely sought to shield themselves from the crossfire of battles that, though would often entangle them, did not necessarily originate from them. It is in this context, then, that we must examine the "awakening" of Asia-Africa. In what follows, I examine a series of governmental and non-governmental conferences convened by this group that took place outside of the UN throughout the late forties and fifties. I begin with a formative period, which I identify from 1945 through 1950, examining the decade of the fifties as the heyday of Asia-Africa. Regarding these conferences, I examine opening speeches, closing speeches, declarations and so on to explore the process of the building of Asia-Africa. What was the language of this process? How did it define a collective "we?" How did it define Asia-Africa's location in the world and its purpose? Did it address the kinship politics of European colonialism that was institutionalized in the UN Charter? I end with a consideration of the implications of this "we" for the ongoing debates on the colonial problematic within the UN.

In 1945, the governments of Egypt, Iraq, Lebanon, Saudi Arabia, Syria, Transjordan (Jordan, as of 1950), and Yemen formed the League of Arab States in order to "strengthen the ties between the participant States, to co-ordinate their political programmes in such a way as to effect real collaboration between them, to preserve their independence and sovereignty, and to consider in general the affairs and interests of the Arab countries (Covenant of the League of Arab States, 1945)." Two years later, the non-governmental Indian Council of World Affairs convened the first non-official Asian Conference in New Delhi in order to consider "the common problems which all Asian countries had to face in the post-war era (Asian Relations Organization 1955)." This new "awakening of Asia" was institutionalized with the founding of the Asian Relations Organization. In January 1949, when the Dutch took "police action" against Indonesia, the response of 15 Asian and African governments of meeting in New Delhi to publicly denounce this action (Asian Relations Organization 1955) signaled the awakening of not merely Asia, and not even Africa in addition to Asia, but of a nascent entity that I term "Asia-Africa." According to Indonesian President Susilo Bambang Yudhoyono, "that crucial demonstration of Asian-African solidarity helped ensure the survival of our young Republic. Indonesia may therefore be regarded as the first child of Asian-African solidarity (Presidential Speech delivered at 50th Anniversary Celebration, April, 2005)." Indeed, this was a new moment in the building of a "deep sense of kinship among Asian and African nations (ibid)." With the action of 1949, these countries began to consult each other and coordinate their actions in international forums, forming the basis of the emergence in the UN of what has been termed the "Afro-Asia bloc (Asian Relations Organization1955)."

Such a sense of connection was further developed and solidified in the fifties with the Baguio (1950), Colombo (1954), Bogor (1954), Bandung (1955), Cairo (1958), and Accra (1958) Conferences, among others. Discussing the three most globally visible ones, Bandung, Cairo and Accra, one author argues that the conferences' major accomplishment was in giving self-determination for all peoples a recognition, validity and respectability—at least to more liberal elements. He argues that the pre-World War II question associated with decolonization, one of *"whether,"* had now become one of *"when* (Lloyd 1959)."

But was a transnational, Asian-African identity really being built here? Such a question is important as countries were divided by varying attitudes toward the "West," on the particular issue of non-alignment, and by the myriad more local and complex identities they carried with them (i.e., Asia, Africa, the in-betweenness of "Arabia" in the middle of Asia and Africa, the

(Re)negotiating the "Colonial" Problematic 49

distinguishing of "Asia" from something called the Soviet Union, Animism, Christianity, and Buddhism, to name just a few). And yet, especially from the Bandung Conference, there was an important sense that there was an entity termed Asia-Africa, which perhaps contained smaller identities such as Buddhists, Africans and Communists, but which nevertheless was coming together in this particular historical moment to finally respond to their collective designation as the "Mysterious East" and the "Dark Continent."[6]

In my examination, hence, I first begin with the Bandung Conference of 1955. This conference was organized by the governments of Indonesia, Ceylon, India and Pakistan, firstly, "as a result of their frustration with the political logjam surrounding new membership in the United Nations. By 1953–54 no new members had been inducted into the organization since the acceptance of Indonesia in 1950 (Berger 2004: 11–12)." Secondly, the conference was a reaction to the colonization of the UN arena by Cold War rivalries (Lyon 1984). Beyond this immediate political context, however, the conference was notable for bringing together the first generation of "postcolonial" nationalist leaders. As such, it was a central event in the emerging "political renaissance of Asia and Africa (ibid)" and helped to create an "unprecedented sentiment of Third World change and potential . . . [indeed, a new] Third World consciousness (Mortimer 1984)." This new consciousness may be understood simultaneously as a transnational identity and movement—what some have termed "Third Worldism (Malley 1996; Berger 2004)." In his study of the Algerian independence movement, for example, Robert Malley defines Third Worldism as "an anti-imperialist ideology of national self-determination . . . [a call for] Third World solidarity" which was a curious and shifting crossbreed of three different philosophical stances, assimilationism (equality between colony and metropolis via cooptation), traditionalism (separation between colony and metropolis and affirmation of the former's "tradition"), and socialism (transcending the dichotomy between colony and metropolis through a universal working class revolution) (Malley 1996). Furthermore, this nascent consciousness inspired the emergence of new actors on the international stage. The radical African-Asian People's Solidarity Organization (AAPSO), for example, was such a "Third Worldist" organization; and it convened the second conference I examine, the First Afro-Asian Peoples Solidarity Conference in Cairo (December, 1957-January, 1958) to reiterate the "solidarity" of Asia-Africa (Berger 2004).[7] Finally, the third of these highly visible conferences, the Conference of Independent African States held in April 1958, focused especially on the unique issues of Africa but still within the larger collectivity of Asia-Africa.[8] It is to the documents of these three conferences to which I now turn.

In my examination of the conference documents, I found that participants constructed the "we" of Asia-Africa in three ways. First, they posited an essential *similarity* across these different territories, particularly the notion that what tied them together was what they had suffered and continued to suffer at the hands of the "imperialist west." Second, they largely seemed to work within the logic of kinship—particularly the parent/child binary—deployed by colonialist powers, simultaneously invoking a sense of *unity* between themselves and distinction between themselves and "the parents" by using the masculinized language of brotherhood. Finally, they crafted a *unique set of qualities* that were to distinguish Asia-Africa from the "materialist" and "aggressive" west and indelibly bind them to each other: their "common cultural, moral and spiritual heritage."

The *similarity* between the peoples of Asia and Africa was imagined, first, as the result of centuries of connection between different groups. For example, according to Nepal, "The contacts which we are seeking to revive and foster through this Conference among the nations of Asia and Africa are not at all new historically . . . The ties of history and geography, culture and religion, which bind together the countries represented here at this Conference, are very profound (Nepal, Text circulated during Opening Session, Bandung Conference, 1955)." A central element of this similarity was the common status of "underdevelopment," resultant of the unifying experience of colonialism:

> We, the nations of the new Asia and Africa, whatever our language, whatever our faiths, whatever our form of government, whatever the colour of our skins—black, brown or yellow—have one thing in common: we are all poor and underdeveloped. Centuries of servitude and stagnation have left their mark, a dire heritage of poverty and ignorance, upon the masses of our peoples (Ceylon, Text circulated during Opening Session, Bandung Conference, 1955)

Within Asia-Africa, the Accra Conference constructed a unified Africa. Interestingly, it did so with a new distinction—the "African Personality:"

> The former imperialist powers were fond of talking about "Arab Africa" and "Black Africa;" about "Islamic Africa" and "Non-Islamic Africa;" about "Mediterranean Africa" and "Tropical Africa." These were all artificial descriptions which tended to divide us. At this Accra Conference these tendentious and discriminating epithets are no longer valid. Today, the *Sahara is a bridge uniting us* [italics in original]. We are one, an entity symbolized by our united African Personality (K.

Nkrumah, Prime Minister of Ghana, Speech given at Closing Session, Accra Conference, 1958).

Behind and beyond this notion of *similarity* was a powerful, naturalized sense of *unity* between the peoples of Asia and Africa. The colonialist politics of kinship first invoked such a naturalized sense of connection, but fused with a naturalized sense of hierarchy in the relationships between colonialist powers and their dependent peoples. Specifically, as metaphors for trans-territorial community, images of the body and the family brought together a naturalized sense of unity (i.e., we are all part of one body/family) with a naturalized sense of hierarchy (i.e., the head must rule the rest of the body/the family head must rule the rest of the family) in colonial relationships. In these conferences, then, Asian and African speakers spoke of *disordered kinship*. Hence, peoples continuing to suffer under colonial rule were "diseased organs in the body of Asia and Africa. [This disease required eradicating, as] a body cannot continue to exist with half of its structure safe and sound while the other half is diseased and decayed (A. E. Sadat, President of Conference, Inaugural Address, Cairo Conference, 1958)." In this example, the body symbolized not the hierarchical colonialist community of metropole and dependent territory, but the entity of Asia-Africa. Similarly, in the following description of the experience of dependent peoples is another image of disordered kinship: "they suffered many years of torture, isolation and deprivation. They were surrounded by an atmosphere of injustice and treachery. They felt like orphans in the midst of a malicious community (Permanent Secretariat, Organization for Afro-Asian Peoples Solidarity, Cairo, 1958)."

This disordering of the kinship relations of the body and the family posited by a colonialist logic, moreover, could be followed by a refashioning of this kinship into something new: "Little by little these orphans began to realize that they were not alone in the world, that within the very same walls where they had been kept imprisoned, millions of other orphans were sharing their sorrows and fate (Permanent Secretariat, Organization for Afro-Asian Peoples Solidarity, Cairo, 1958)." Such reordering gave rise to a new imagery, an imagery of birth and a new kind of kinship. For example, at the Closing Session of the Bandung Conference, the representative of Iran stated, "the Africa-Asian Conference is proud, after a week of hard labour, to have given birth to a most cherished child: a child of a future with no special name, no special colour, no special race but with certain specific features in which we all, more or less, recognize ourselves (Delegation of Iran, Speech given at Closing Session, Bandung Conference, 1955)." Indeed, speakers insisted that "Asia and Africa have been reborn (President Sukarno, Speech Given at Opening Ceremony, Bandung Conference,

1955)," that "Africa is born (Delegation of Morocco, Speech given at Closing Session, Accra Conference, 1958)," and that "we are all united here by the ties of this brotherhood (Delegation of Lebanon, Bandung Conference, 1955)." Indeed, this reordering of paternalist kinship as rebirth and as fraternal kinship was to be the new kinship politics, *the resistance politics*, of Asia-Africa. Hence, speakers addressed audiences as "Brothers," "Brethren," and "Sons of Asia and Africa."[9] Most importantly, a sense of connection between these now formerly dependent territories and still dependent territories was forged through this new kinship:

> For thirty-five years we have been appealing to the Great Powers to do us justice . . . It is for the Afro-Asiatic nations and States now to see that justice is done . . . For in North Africa we have dear brethren who suffer indescribable agonies and injustices . . . the existing reign of terror in that part of the world does not allow our brethren there to be represented at this Conference (Delegation of Jordan, Speech given at Opening Session, Bandung Conference, 1955).

Similarly, at the Accra Conference, Libya added, "Libya hopes that we shall not be only eight at future meetings, but we hope to see around the same table as ourselves, the representatives of our brothers from Algeria, Cameroons, Nigeria, Somalia, and other African territories (Delegation of Libya, Speech given at Closing Session, Accra Conference, 1958)."

Finally, in addition to *similarity* and (masculine) *unity*, Asia-Africa also sought to distinguish a particular kind of identity for itself as a whole and in distinction from the "west." Repeatedly, in every conference, this identity was articulated as a sense of *cultural, moral, and spiritual heritage*: "The sense of moral and spiritual values in life is ingrained in our nature: it is part of ourselves, it is our essential way of life. Even people of the West admit this, for do they not say Ex Oriente Lux, Ex Occidente Lex: Out of the East Light, Out of the West Law? (Delegation of Thailand, Bandung Conference, 1955)." Similarly,

> Asia and Africa are the classic birthplaces of faiths and ideas, which have spread all over the world. Therefore, it behooves us to take particular care to ensure that the principle which is usually called the "Live and let live" principle—mark, I do not say the principle of "Laissez faire, laissez passer" of Liberalism which is obsolete—is first of all applied by us most completely within our own Asian and African frontiers (Sukarno, President of Indonesia, Speech given at Opening Session, Bandung Conference, 1955).

(Re)negotiating the "Colonial" Problematic

> It is not strange that such a loving, unbiased spirit should evolve out of Asia and Africa. Our peoples never enjoyed at any time oppressing other peoples; on the contrary, they were oppressed themselves. It is because of this that they are preaching now the message of love, justice and equality in this troubled world. We do not excel others in force or in the ability to manufacture arms, but we do excel them in the ability to sense the horrors of injustice and in the ability to comprehend the dangers to which the world is exposed (A. E. Sadat, President of Conference, Speech given at Closing Session, Cairo Conference, 1958).

Some authors have argued that this notion of unique spiritual and moral qualities was an important element of the discourse of specific anti-colonial writers such as Ho Chi Minh, Nehru, Fanon, and Nkrumah, as well (Duara 2004; Chatterjee 1986; Sartori 2005; Duara 2001). In India, for example, "a nationalist political discourse that pitted a developmentalist national state grounded in the ethical and spiritual practices of Indian culture against the shallow materialism of Western civilization (Sartori 2005)" flourished throughout the twentieth century. In a study on Asia as a whole, one author argues that after World War I, new nations throughout Asia produced multiple articulations of such difference of Asian or Chinese or Japanese civilization from the "imperial Civilization of the west." Though varying, each involved, in different ways,

> combining elements that are a) identical to and b) the binary opposite of the constituents of [imperial] Civilization. [For example,] one strategy is to rediscover elements identical to Civilized society within the suppressed traditions of civilization: Confucian rationality, Buddhist humanism, Hindu logic, and so on. Another strategy identifies the opposite of the West in Asian civilizations: "peaceful" as opposed to "warlike," "spiritual" as opposed to "material," "ethical" as opposed to "decadent," "natural" as opposed to "rational," "timeless" as opposed to "temporal," and more. Finally, the [new Asian] nation authorizes its opposition to imperialist Civilization by synthesizing or harmonizing the binaries after the equivalence has been established. Thus Western materialism will be balanced by Eastern spirituality and modernity redeemed (Duara 2001).

Hence, such difference from the "west" was expressed in complex and varying ways by intellectuals, nationalists, statesmen, and a variety of popular social movements in multiple governmental, academic and artistic spaces outside of the conferences of interest here. What we see in these conferences, then, is *a particular transnational elaboration of such uniqueness*, in which, either due to their "spiritual values" or through their experience of the "horrors of injustice," the collectivity of Asia-Africa distinguished itself from the putative "material west" as being able to offer a uniquely moral and spiritual perspective on the world.

Differences between speakers did emerge from the conferences on issues such as non-alignment, how to define colonialism, the appropriate sort of attitude towards the "west," and to what extent Asia-Africa should cooperate with the west in its post-independence efforts at development. For example, a number of states at Bandung were allied in some sense with one superpower or the other. Pakistan, Iraq, Iran and the Philippines all had relationships with the United States, while North Vietnam was linked to the USSR (Mortimer 1984). At Bandung, the debate on how to define a colonialist aggressor also erupted, where some wanted to target Soviet aggression in addition to European colonialism. In this vein, Ceylon, Iran, Iraq, Japan, Lebanon, Liberia, Libya, Pakistan, the Philippines, Sudan and Turkey submitted a draft resolution to condemn "all types of colonialism." However, China and India opposed this definition, and India's Nehru argued that members of the UN could not be colonies, thus excluding Eastern bloc countries that were members of the UN from being defined as such. Eventually, the conference settled on condemning colonialism without actually defining it (Bell 2001). On attitudes toward and cooperation with the "west," too, there were divisions between more pro-western countries such as Nkrumah's Ghana and the radical United Arab Republic.

Nevertheless, in these very visible, very public conferences, Asia-Africa endeavored to "speak with a concerted voice" and passed most of it resolutions with unanimity. In the rest of this project, I discuss the first major impact in world politics of this new construction of Asian-African brotherhood, the moral argument for the political independence of still dependent "brothers" in the United Nations General Assembly.[10] Over the years, this identity would also argue for peace and non-alignment in the Cold War, materializing in the Non-Aligned Movement in the sixties. It would call for more UN and World Bank assistance for Asian and African development and help to form what would become the Group of 77 (G-77). It would form the foundation for the argument for international community itself, specifically calling for more cooperation in the economic, cultural, and technical fields between not just Asian and African "brothers" but also between "the human family."

It was French demographer and economic historian Alfred Sauvy who first used the term "Third World" in his article "Three Worlds, One Planet" in the magazine *The Observer* on August 14, 1952. The article drew on the discussion of the French writer Sieyes on the Third Estate during the French Revolution, where Sieyes spoke of how against the First Estate (the clergy) and Second Estate (the nobility), the Third Estate (the "rest" of society—the bourgeoisie, petit-bourgeoisie, artisans, peasants and workers), which was ignored and despised, sought to "become something." Sauvy wrote that like the Third Estate, the Third World also sought to become something.[11] In the local-global space of politics in the United Nations General Assembly, this nascent Third World would make itself felt in particular ways. And from the "other side," it would invoke a fairly concerted response as well.

(RE)NEGOTIATING THE COLONIAL PROBLEMATIC: DEBATE ON NSGTS AND TRUSTS

Having delineated the bounding of the colonial problematic in the Charter, as well as the emergence of Asia-Africa, the central source of challenge to this bounding, I now turn to the renegotiation of the colonial problematic in the debates on decolonization within the UN. I specifically examine here a total of 54 debates, with 20 focused on NSGTs and 34 on Trusts. The debates consisted of speakers supporting, opposing, or abstaining on a particular item under consideration with one or a series of appeals. Focusing on the central appeals made to justify a position in a debate, eight appeals emerged as most prevalent in the period examined. Speakers appealed to *Peace*, the master principle articulated in the Charter for the existence of the UN; *International Cooperation (United Nations)*, the stated central avenue to Peace, with the UN, international cooperation, the Charter, and international community often used interchangeably; *Independence/Representation*, a norm that increasingly began to be applied to dependent territories by anti-colonialists after World War I and especially World War II; *Interests of Inhabitants*, the welfare and well-being of the inhabitants of dependent territories; *Colonialism not negative*, the basic logic of kinship politics that colonized peoples required and benefited from colonial rule; *Sovereignty*, the principle, as enshrined in the Charter, that state rights are paramount; *Proceduralism/Practicalism*, the argument that matters should proceed according to sound and agreed upon procedure or what was most commonsense or practical in a particular situation; and *Legalism*, the principle of adherence to the codes of national and international law.

Debate on NSGTs

My examination of the debates on NSGTs in the General Assembly points to specific sets of concerns regarding NSGTs for speakers. As mentioned earlier, the UN Charter made a central distinction between NSGTs and Trusts, requiring specific obligations from administering authorities for Trusts with the explicit goal of bringing these territories to political independence. This was not the case for NSGTs. The only significant obligation that the Charter placed on the administering authorities of NSGTs was to provide information regarding their territories to the UN on a regular basis. Specifically, the Charter required them

> to transmit regularly to the Secretary-General for information purposes, subject to such limitation as security and constitutional considerations may require, statistical and other information of a technical nature relating to economic, social, and educational conditions in the territories for which they are respectively responsible other than those territories to which Chapters XII and XIII apply (UN Charter, Chapter XI, Article 73).

Significantly, this Article specifically excluded the provision of information of "a political nature." This relative lack of UN supervision regarding NSGTs compared to Trusts was also estimated to affect far more people than the Trust status. For example, only a handful of territories were placed under trusteeship in the first couple of years. Indeed, between the years of 1945–1999, slightly over 100 dependent territories came under the purview of the UN, and of these, only about one tenth were placed into Trust status (see Table 2 for information on different dependent territories). A major component of the anti-colonialist presence had thus always opposed the distinction between Trusts and NSGTs, and once established, anti-colonialists consistently attempted to read (the conservative provisions of) Article 73 of Chapter XI, which were intended for the NSGTs, in light of (the more generous) Charter provisions, including those of Chapters XII and XIII, which were intended for the Trust Territories (El-Ayouty 1971). Specifically, my examination of the debates indicates that they sought to convene conferences where representatives from the NSGTs could air their aspirations and concerns—could in a sense, "represent themselves;" they developed a "list of factors" to determine precisely when a territory came under the purview of the United Nations and qualified as an NSGT, requiring the colonialist power it was associated with to comply with the obligations that resulted; and they proposed a resolution that NSGTs should be put into Trust status. By far the biggest move that this group made was to establish a Committee on Information, which would oversee the information that administering authorities were to provide to the Secretary-General on a regular basis. Particularly after 1948,

(Re)negotiating the "Colonial" Problematic 57

after the passage of the Universal Declaration of Human Rights (UDHR), anti-colonialists used the new rhetorical resources made available by the UDHR to press for the committee (El-Ayouty 1971). The power, scope, membership, and permanent or temporary status of this committee comprised the bulk of the debates on NSGTs in the General Assembly. While many of these proposals were rejected, many were also accepted, if in amended form. The central contention was that under the legal machinery of the UN, the NSGTs were not to be brought to independence, and hence, as El-Ayouty (ibid) argues, the goal of anti-colonialist groups was to try to extend the UN's competence to include the supervision of the NSGTs toward self-rule.

In my examination of these documents, I found that the most significant anti-colonialist appeals for social change for NSGTs were *Independence/Representation* and *International Cooperation (United Nations)*. Speakers argued that the ultimate goal for NSGTs, as for Trusts, should be independence:

> There should be constant endeavor to liberalize the working of the Charter in order that the millions of people outside of the direct supervision of the United Nations might achieve full self-government in the shortest possible period and qualify for direct membership. [These are] the legitimate functions of the General Assembly which it [can] not afford to surrender (Mr. Rao, India, Sess 4, 1949: 460).

Colonialist countries often claimed that the legal status of NSGTs was not problematic, that these territories did not lack political representation and indeed, that the metropolitan authorities themselves provided such representation. Anti-colonialist groups questioned the legitimacy of the notion that the administering authorities actually represented either dependent territories in general or NSGTs more specifically and argued that only the people within the NSGTs themselves could represent their own concerns and interests:

> However valuable the information provided by the metropolitan Powers may prove to be, the Philippine delegation believes it to be none the less essential that the Non Self-Governing Peoples be given an opportunity to submit facts on their own lands as they know them, to voice their own aspirations . . . We are asking, for the Non Self-Governing Peoples today, exactly the same opportunity for self-expression that we Filipinos enjoyed for forty years, in our relations with the United States of America (Mr. Romulo, Philippines, Sess 1, 1946: 1328–1329).

The profound significance of international community and of the United Nations as an institutional framework for the establishment of a more democratic international community was also an important appeal, and argued as a precondition for the other appeals:

> Just as individuals should be prompted in their mutual relations by a sense of human solidarity, so nations must assist each other to advance . . . it is necessary to encourage the political education of the peoples . . . prepare the ground for them so that they might shape their own future and direct their own affairs. All these things are impossible, except in an organization like the United Nations, in which the nations come together to study, considering the world as a whole—of which this institution is the true symbol—and examine common problems in a noble and generous spirit based on a community of ideas and ideals with the end of promoting the advancement and well-being of all peoples without exception . . . The United Nations is a democratic forum in which the peoples may come together and discuss matters freely not in order to widen the differences between them but in order to discover the common denominators that permit them to harmonize their efforts for the greater good of each of them and of all mankind (Mr. De Oliveira, Brazil, Sess 12, 1957: 518).

Beyond these two appeals, anti-colonialists also appealed to *Legalism* and *Proceduralism/Practicalism* in the debates on NSGTs. However, while the first two were central in explaining and justifying voting behavior, the latter two were most often in the form of rebuttal to legalist or proceduralist argument from colonialist speakers.

In response to such arguments on NSGTs from anti-colonialist speakers, former and contemporary colonial powers also seemed to come together to form a more or less cohesive response. The most important appeals structuring this discourse were *Legalism, International Cooperation (United Nations), Sovereignty*, and *Proceduralism/Practicalism*. Indeed, because NSGTs were legally outside of the purview of the UN for the most part, the colonialist appeal to *Legalism*, that the attempt to bring them more fully into the competence of the UN was legally problematic, was more significant for the NSGT discussion than for any other. Thus, in response to an impassioned appeal from the representative of the Philippines regarding the need for people from within the NSGTs to be able to circumvent administering authorities and represent themselves, one speaker claimed:

(Re)negotiating the "Colonial" Problematic 59

> I am wholly in accord with everything that has been said by the . . . representative of the Philippine Republic. [But we oppose this resolution because it seems to] clearly violate the basic provisions of the Charter. It ignores the basic distinction between the Trust Territories dealt with by Chapter XII and the non-trust territories that are dealt with by Chapter XI . . . the United Nations has no authority to intervene in such territories. That authority remains with their own national government (Mr. Dulles, United States, Sess 1, 1946: 1331–34).

Moreover, this appeal to *Legalism* was intimately tied to the appeal to *Sovereignty/State's Rights*:

> We are dealing with the fundamental issue of whether this organization can assert, within Member States, a political authority equal to that of the national governments themselves. If it can do so once, it can do so again. And no one can predict the consequences of the precedent we are here invited to set. We can, however, assert with confidence that constitutional limitations are, in the long run, the only defense of a minority against the passions of a majority and the emotions of the moment (Mr. Dulles, United States, Sess 1, 1946: 1334).

Entangled in colonialist appeals to legalism and state sovereignty were also appeals to proper procedure (i.e., *Proceduralism/Practicalism*) and an insistence that while colonialist powers were not necessarily opposed to the *ends* of a particular resolution, that they were rather opposed to the *means*: "We therefore ask this Assembly to reject this resolution, not because we do not agree with its purpose, but because the means chosen violate the Charter and disrupt the basic tie which holds us together (ibid.)."

Finally, colonialist speakers also appealed to *International Cooperation (United Nations)*, though their arguments here were *not* the same as the *International Cooperation (United Nations)* appeals of anti-colonialist speakers. For example, in the following example, a colonialist speaker reacts to some resolutions asking for political information on NSGTs, information not directly authorized by the Charter: "The information demanded by the resolutions under question is very different from that specified in the Charter, which in the case of NSGTs specifically excludes political information . . . The Charter is being violated under the pretext of interpreting it . . . it was a very careful compromise (Mr. Ryckmans, Belgium, Sess 2, 1947: 671–75)." Here, Belgium appeals to *International Cooperation (Untied Nations)* by arguing that resolutions passed by the

General Assembly must remain within the boundaries of the UN Charter. Contrast this appeal to the anti-colonialist appeal to *International Cooperation (United Nations)* made by Brazil above. While Brazil's anti-colonialist appeal seeks to advance the cause of social justice and social change, Belgium's colonialist appeal is a conservative appeal that in effect contains social change.

Beyond these four central appeals, colonialist speakers also appealed to *Independence/Representation* and *Colonialism not Negative* in their discussions on NSGTs. Similar to the anti-colonialist deployment of *Legalism* and *Proceduralism/Practicalism*, however, *Independence/Representation* was not a key appeal in the explanation and justification of voting behavior for colonialist speakers and perhaps was only deployed to signify adherence to emerging global norms of democracy. While the *Colonialism not Negative* appeal *was* an important appeal in the explanation of voting behavior, its relative dearth can perhaps be explained by the shifting global climate as well, as it directly contradicted these emergent norms of democracy.

Debate on Trusts

In comparison to the debate on NSGTs, many more debates, spanning many more meetings, were held regarding Trusts. Since theoretically, Trusts were already to be brought to independence under the institutional purview of the United Nations, the issues of concern were not as exclusively about the legality of UN competence but rather, about procedure—how to implement Trust agreements and how to develop machinery to implement Trust agreements; how to induce the Union of South Africa to take up its "obligations" as an administering authority and place South West Africa into Trust status; how to address the particular issue of administrative unions, an institutional tactic configured by administering authorities to administer their Trusts in union with other territories they were responsible for; and finally, such concerns with regard to specific Trust territories.[12]

On the distinct context of Trust territories, institutionally, anti-colonialists made several moves. First, they expanded the membership of the Trusteeship Council to include explicitly anti-colonial countries such as China, Iraq, Mexico, and the Soviet Union. Second, over protests of violations of sovereignty, they passed two important resolutions as well. The first of these sought to take the information and reports about conditions within Trust territories as instituted in the Charter out of the exclusive control of the Trusteeship Council and place it in the hands of the GA as a whole through the secretary-general and through a special

(Re)negotiating the "Colonial" Problematic 61

ad hoc committee composed of anti-colonial countries like China, Cuba, Egypt, India, Philippines, Soviet Union, and Uruguay. The second of these resolutions called on those members who administered Trust territories to convene a special conference of the representatives of the peoples living in these lands in order that they might articulate their wishes and aspirations for self-government (Lauren 1998: 215).

Despite these distinct maneuvers regarding Trusts as opposed to NSGTs, however, the patterns of appeal regarding Trusts for each group remained the same. For anti-colonialist countries, key appeals continued to be *Independence/Representation* and *International Cooperation (United Nations)*. Regarding the issue of administrative unions and independence, for example, one anti-colonialist speaker argued:

> [We have previously adopted resolutions that] an administrative union must remain strictly administrative in its nature and its scope, and that its operation must not have the effect of creating any conditions which will obstruct the separate development of the Trust Territory, in the fields of political, economic, social and educational advancement as a distinct entity . . . however, these General Assembly resolutions are being violated by the Administering Authorities . . . [because their] policy . . . is designed to rob them of their special status and annex them by amalgamating them with the neighboring colonies under the cloak of so-called administrative unions. The application of this policy by the Administering Authorities will clearly preclude any independent development of the Trust Territories as distinct entities, as required under the terms of the General Assembly resolution . . . It will thus prevent the development of the Trust Territories toward self-government or independence (Mr. Demchenko, Ukrainian Soviet Socialist Republic, Sess 6, 1952: 351).

Once again, anti-colonialist appeals for *Independence/Representation* were made together with appeals to *International Cooperation (United Nations)*. For example, in response to a statement by the representative from Denmark that the Union of South Africa was legally not obligated to place South West Africa into Trust status, one speaker argued that it was indeed the obligation of the General Assembly to ensure this was the case, as the General Assembly "represents the conscience of the world (Mr. Chieh, China, 1947, Sess 2, p. 600)."

Similar to the discussion on NSGTs, anti-colonialists again appealed secondarily to *Proceduralism/Practicalism* and *Legalism* in the discussion on Trusts, though once again, these functioned more as rebuttals than key arguments justifying voting behavior.

For colonialist speakers, the most common appeals were again to *Legalism* and *Proceduralism/Practicalism*. For example, regarding the anti-colonialist argument that South Africa was obligated to place South West Africa into Trust status, one speaker replied:

> My delegation feels fairly certain that there is no legal obligation under the Charter to place mandated territories under the Trusteeship System . . . . There is sufficient *prima facie* proof, not only to us, but to a great number of States, of the non-existence of such an obligation. There being, in our view, no legal obligation . . . we cannot go any further than invite the Union of South Africa to do what is asked for (Italics in original, Mr. Kerncamp, Netherlands, Sess 2, 1947: 606).

The appeal to *Proceduralism/Practicalism* is demonstrated in the discussion of administrative unions below. In this example, in response to a resolution that attempted to problematize these unions as compromising the territorial and political integrity of dependent territories, one speaker claimed:

> What would happen if my Government were to attempt to implement a resolution such as this? It would be required to disrupt the unified administration, which has existed in Togoland and the Cameroons for some thirty years. The new organs thus established would be in direct competition with the organs already in being, and would make it impossible for my Government to fulfill the injunctions of the Trusteeship Agreements (Lord Tweedsmuir, UK, Sess 6, 1952: 354).

Beyond these key appeals, colonialist speakers also again made secondary appeals to *Independence/Representation* and *International Cooperation (United Nations)*. Finally, they also appealed once again to *Sovereignty/State's Rights* and *Colonialism not Negative*.

Understanding the Patterns: The Renegotiation of Kinship

For both anti-colonialists and colonialists, then, there were central patterns of appeal that shaped discussions on both NSGTs and Trusts. For the first, these appeals centered on *Independence/Representation* and *International Cooperation (United Nations)*, while for the second, they centered on *Legalism* and *Proceduralism/Practicalism*. While each side also made some use of the

(Re)negotiating the "Colonial" Problematic 63

central appeals identified with the other, these secondary appeals appeared more in the form of rebuttal to the other side than genuine explanations and justifications for voting behavior. Additionally, *Colonialism not Negative* and *Sovereignty/State's Rights* were much more likely to be used by colonialist speakers than anti-colonialist speakers.

How do we understand the distinction between the sorts of appeals made by anti-colonialist speakers and those made by colonialist speakers? On the simplest level, one may argue that while the (anti-colonialist) appeals for *Independence/Representation* and *International Cooperation (United Nations)* advance the scope of globally expanding norms of democracy, representation and cooperation, the (colonialist) appeals to *Legalism, Proceduralism/Practicalism, Colonialism not negative* and *Sovereignty/State's Rights* serve the interests of imperial and colonial powers. Alternatively, one may argue that both sides advance arguments that suit their interests. Beyond both of these explanations, however, is the conversation that is occurring here between two crystallizations of *transnational collective identity*. That is, the distinction between patterns of appeal in this conversation seems to go to the heart of the tension between the identity of European imperial/colonial rule and the identity that anti-colonialist Asia-Africa crafts in response. Hence, if the kinship politics of European colonialism historically prioritizes the disembodied over the embodied, or the rational over the irrational, the colonialist appeals in these debates to *Legalism, Proceduralism/Practicalism, Sovereignty/State's Rights*, and even *Colonialism not negative*, all perpetuate this argument for the rational and indeed, can be seen as constituting a meta-appeal to the rational.[13]

Meanwhile, for its part, the anti-colonialist contingent's appeals to *Independence/Representation* and *International Cooperation (United Nations)* can thus be understood as an attempt to *reorder* the logic of this kinship politics—of the meta-appeal to the *rational*—with a meta-appeal to the *moral*. Such an interpretation particularly makes sense in the light of the way Asia-Africa distinguished itself from "the west" at Bandung, Cairo and Accra: as the unique voice of the moral, spiritual and cultural, with its crucial part to play in contemporary politics of decolonization, war, and so forth. For example, recall the statement of the Delegation of Thailand at Bandung (1955): "the sense of moral and spiritual values in life is ingrained in our nature: it is part of ourselves, it is our essential way of life."

Ultimately, these tensions manifest in each side's approach to the Charter (and indeed, as was discussed above, to international community itself).[14] While for colonialists, they manifest in a "literal" interpretation of the Charter—in an appeal to remain in the limits of the "letter" of the Charter, for anti-colonialists, the goal is to move beyond legalized and institutionalized impediments and focus on the "spirit" of the Charter—for a liberal, interpretive approach rather than a "narrow, hairsplitting, legalistic attitude (Mr. Menon, India, Sess 1, 1946: 1341)." Hence, colonialists insisted, "the Charter was a contract. By definition, that contract could not express anything other than the common will of all the contracting parties (Mr. Garreau, France, Sess 4, 1949: 457)." Indeed, the transgression of the letter of the Charter and the infringement upon the sovereignty of states was often posited as detrimental to the very foundation and purpose of the United Nations. Colonialist meta-argument thus especially appealed to the images of order and controlled change inherent in the appeals of *Legalism, Proceduralism/Practicalism,* and *Colonialism not negative.* Speakers argued against what they saw as "revolutionary movements rather than a balanced evolution towards self-government (Mr. Riemens, Netherlands, Sess 7, 1952: 348)." Others argued that the "liberal" attitude of anti-colonialist groups towards the Charter was "dangerous" and "extremist" rather than "undertaken in the spirit of realism and compromise," that the actions and arguments of anti-colonialist groups in general were "too fast," "hasty," proceeding at "an unduly rapid pace," suffering from "lack of wisdom," "unwise," "irresponsible," "not practical," "improper," "inappropriate," "inopportune," "ill-considered . . . in the light of practical, commonsense considerations," "insane," "premature," "immature," and "in the emotion of the moment."

In contrast, anti-colonialists attempted to disrupt the disembodiment-embodiment distinction by insisting on the moral over the rational. In the following, for example, in response to the argument by the Union of South Africa that it has no legal or moral obligation to place South West Africa into Trust status, one speaker replied:

> The Government of the Union of South Africa has argued that it is under neither a legal nor a moral obligation to place South West Africa under the Trusteeship System. I do not claim to be a lawyer, but speaking purely from the common sense point of view, and in view of the history of the last quarter of a century, it seems to me an astounding statement to make in this General Assembly before the nations of the world, that no *moral obligation* exists in this matter. *What would the Charter be but a medley of words, were it not sustained by the spirit* which lies behind and which has inspired the peoples of the world to join together to solve their common problems? . . . We must not forget the fate of hundreds of thousands of Africans in South West

(Re)negotiating the "Colonial" Problematic　　　　　　　　　　　　　65

> Africa who will look to this Assembly for the safeguarding of their interests (Italics added, Mrs. Pandit, India, Sess 2, 1947: 598).

Regarding the reluctance of administering authorities to provide information on NSGTs, another speaker argued:

> We do not see why a *legalistic, narrow and limited interpretation of paragraph e of Article 73* should be relied upon in order to frustrate or misinterpret the legitimate interests of this General Assembly—a representative body of the free peoples of the world, fully conscious of its duties and responsibilities towards mankind—in being fully informed of the progress of other peoples in the achievement [of] their ultimate independence and freedom (Italics added, Mr. Mendez, Panama, Sess 2, 1947: 708–709).

Hence, embedded in these patterns of appeal and evident particularly when we examine patterns of meta-appeal is that these debates are not merely negotiating the status of Trusts and NSGTs, or even simply legal decolonization. *They are fundamentally re-negotiating the logic of kinship politics*. That is, they are negotiating the legitimacy of the distinction between the disembodied and the embodied and the prioritizing of the disembodied over the embodied. Whereas for colonialists, legal decolonization must be a process of controlled change organized by the logic and privileges of kinship politics, for the anti-colonialist contingent centered around Asia-Africa, legal decolonization involves fundamentally disrupting this logic as it applies to administering authorities, remaining dependent territories, and themselves.

CONCLUSION: NEGOTIATING THE COLONIAL PROBLEMATIC BY RE-NEGOTIATING KINSHIP

Historically, kinship politics provided a range of imagery, especially the binaries of parent/child, masculine/feminine, and rational/irrational, to naturalize association and hierarchy between distinct lands and peoples. Those *embodied* by this logic—infantilized, feminized and/or made "irrational"—required the mastery, tutelage or guidance of those *disembodied*, or positioned as the parental, masculine and/or rational. In the Charter, this hierarchy of the disembodied over the embodied was institutionalized on one level through the relationship set up between colonialist powers (now administering authorities) and some of their dependent territories (now Trusts) through the trusteeship system, where the latter were to be given political tutelage and guidance by the former in order to be "prepared" for political independence. Additionally, this hierarchy was also institutionalized through the relationship set up between administering authorities and the rest (bulk) of their dependent territories (now NSGTs), where these dependent territories were to remain in such dependency indefinitely, since the rights of the former unconditionally trumped the rights of the latter.

Over the decade of the fifties, the emergence of the entity of Asia-Africa was the central locus of anti-colonial resistance to this bounding of the colonial problematic in the Charter. This entity firstly constructed itself through the concept of *similarity*, or the notion that "we are similar in our experiences of oppression." A second important concept in this identity was the notion of masculine or brotherly *unity*, or that "we are one, we are brothers, we are the sons of Asia and Africa." The final component was a unique sense of *moral and spiritual heritage*: "we are distinct from the 'west' in our spiritual, cultural and moral heritage." In the debates in the GA, this identity was especially important in contesting the parent/child hierarchy, as former and contemporary dependent territories were constructed as "orphans without a home" and the rational/irrational hierarchy, as the focus on the moral and spiritual disturbed the prioritizing of the rational over all else. The consistent focus on brothers and sons, however, would do little to disturb the masculine/feminine hierarchy, and as will be examined later, would have important implications for the anti-colonialist renegotiation of space, identity and international community.

We can understand patterns of appeal in the debates in the GA, then, in the context of this larger negotiation of kinship politics. The colonialist contingent especially appealed to images of order and controlled change, or *the rational*, with its repeated arguments for *Legalism, Proceduralism/Practicalism, Sovereignty/State's Rights* and *Colonialism not negative*. Anti-colonialists centered on Asia-Africa, on the other hand, countering with arguments for *Independence/Representation* and *International Cooperation (United Nations)*, sought to disturb this image of kinship and this prioritizing of *the rational* with an emphasis on *the moral*.

While easily overmatched at the moment of the writing of the Charter, over the years examined here, this anti-colonialist contingent would continue to grow as more and more formerly dependent territories gained political independence and became members of the UN (see Table 1 for date of membership for every member; see Table 2 for information on Trusts and NSGTs in the UN since 1945). In the latter half of the 20th century, the United Nations would emerge as a major institution of knowledge production with global reach. With the incorporation of anti-colonialist voices centered on a specific construction of Asia-Africa into its machinery, the

(Re)negotiating the "Colonial" Problematic

United Nations would help to shape and distribute new meanings of the "colonial" crafted from the perspective of this location. What would be the impact of this new constellation of social, political and institutional forces in negotiating the colonial problematic? What difference would it make that growing post-war anti-colonial sentiment was primarily assimilated into the institutional logic of the UN via the entry of newly independent nation-states—that a central condition of possibility for the articulation of anti-colonial resistance in the UNGA was the politico-cultural form of the nation-state? And if this newly independent, "postcolonial," anti-colonialist nation-state made possible new negotiations of oppression, freedom and justice, would it close off others?

Chapter Three
The Limits of the Anti-Colonial Critique: Anti-Colonialists' Visions and Divisions

If in the UNGA, anti-colonialists' anti-kinship critique was fashioned by elite representatives of "postcolonial" nation-states, representing peoples indelibly marked by colonial-era administrative categories of space, time and the social (Anderson 1991), how did these conditions of possibility impact the formation and deployment of the anti-colonialist exegesis? Even more, how was the anti-colonialist critique shaped by Asia-Africa's formation within the context of declining European power, various new and informal methods of colonial rule, and numerous struggles between the two rising superpowers? Was the anti-kinship, anti-colonialist argument that eventually emerged in the UNGA consistent for every "perpetrator?" For every dependent territory? What was its scope? How did it orient to dependent territories not under the purview of the UN, as in the case of the satellites of the USSR? Beyond the Communist bloc, how did it orient to territories for whom, though formally independent, autonomy, independence and self-representation were still compromised? In this chapter, I combine a close examination of GA debates on specific territories with secondary sources on these territories to offer some thoughts on these questions. I argue that though launching an important intervention into colonialist kinship politics, the anti-kinship critique was uneven, partial, and at times thoroughly plastic, shaped by the particular priorities and limitations of newly independent, "postcolonial" nation-states located within a broader constellation of identities and interests.

In what follows, I delineate the variegated contours of this critique in several steps. I begin by mapping the UN system's bounding of the colonial problematic, or the scope of what it institutionally included within the problem of colonialism via its NSGT and Trust statuses. As discussed in the last chapter, in its debates on NSGTs and Trusts, the states of Asia-Africa especially sought to expand this bounding. Next, I move on to complicate this analysis by exploring the limits of Asia-Africa's anti-kinship, anti-colonial argument in three distinct scenarios. In the first, I examine several cases in which administering authorities sought to remove a dependent territory they were "responsible" for—all NSGTs—from the purview of the UN and hence from its colonial problematic. Specifically, I look at the cases of the Netherlands and its NSGTS, the Dutch West Indies and Dutch Guiana, the United States and its NSGT, Puerto Rico, and Denmark and its NSGT, Greenland.[1] Theoretically, from the perspective of Asia-Africa, the unsanctioned removal of an NSGT from its NSGT status and hence from UN supervision represents a thwarting of its goal of decolonization and thus is subject to its anti-colonial critique. However, I argue that the three cases were politicized differentially, with the Netherlands and Dutch West Indies/Dutch Guiana case politicized the most thoroughly and the other two politicized relatively little. Why is this the case? I argue that within the immediate post-war, world-historical moment, there existed a complex set of transnational relationships in which the states of Asia-Africa stood in differing relation to declining European powers versus the superpower United States. Specifically, in contrast to the historical experience of colonial denial, the United States offered a model of economic and political possibility to newly independent states, leading to an uneven targeting that chose to "excuse" the actions of the United States but not those of the Netherlands. Regarding Denmark, the United States' interests in Denmark also helped to deflect criticism of that colonialist power.

Beyond such uneven targeting of problematic practices within the purview of the UN, how did Asia-Africa approach such cases outside of the UN? In other words, how broad was Asia-Africa's anti-colonial critique? What was its scope? To explore this question, I move on to examining the scenario of the republics and satellites of the USSR, which, while also theoretically representing a thwarting of the pro-democratic impetus of Asia-Africa, were not included in the colonial problematic as defined by the UN. Nevertheless, their case was brought to the attention of Asia-Africa quite forcefully at the Bandung Conference. Similar to their approach to the United States, however, anti-colonial states also neglected to politicize the practices of the USSR. Why might this be the case? I argue that similar to the US, the USSR also offered a model of economic and political possibilities after the historical experience of colonial dependence. Thus, a set of forces parallel to those that served to insulate the United States from the anti-colonialist critique were also in operation here.

The anti-colonial critique of colonialist practice, then, was shifting and contingent. Beyond these approaches to dependency, how did anti-colonialist states orient to the complexities of "postcolonial" independence—and

The Limits of the Anti-Colonial Critique

particularly to the UN's role regarding this independence? To explore a small piece of this question, I turn to the third scenario, the conjoining of the dependent territories of the Gold Coast and British Togoland into the first state that would gain independence from within the UN system, the new state of Ghana. A colony of the UK with a strong independence movement, the Gold Coast had already negotiated its independence with the UK, with both agreeing that the territories of Gold Coast and British Togoland should be amalgamated into the new state. Popular opinion in British Togoland, on the other hand, did not support this arrangement, and Togolander movements for independence lobbied for a separate state. How did anti-colonialists in the UN negotiate these conflicting demands for democracy and self-representation? I argue that these states adopted a statist politics that prioritized political independence via the nation-state form above all else—above their own anti-kinship critique and their own pro-democracy/self-representation politics. Indeed, in this first case of a territory emerging out of the UN system into "postcolonial" independence, the states of Asia-Africa abandoned their anti-kinship, anti-colonial critique, using the hierarchical discourse of kinship to simultaneously support the Gold Coast and deny British Togoland. Thus, the anti-colonial critique in the UNGA for the period examined was not merely uneven or contingent—it was thoroughly plastic. Over the years, then, though "Ghana" would come to be a symbol of the success of decolonization and the triumph of the anti-colonial movement, from the first two scenarios examined here, it differed little. For quite like Greenland, Puerto Rico and the other aforementioned dependent territories, though officially outside of the colonial problematic as defined by the UN, British Togoland would continue in a non-democratic state thereafter. As a distinct space and identity, however, unlike most of these territories, British Togoland would disappear from the global map.

THE SYSTEM OF NSGTS AND TRUSTS: DEFINING THE COLONIAL PROBLEMATIC

In the last chapter, I described the institutional-discursive bounding of the colonial problematic within the UN Charter. I discussed how the UN distinguished between two statuses of dependent territories (i.e., NSGTs and Trusts) and constructed a hierarchy between them, with the former designated to continue in its dependent status while the latter was to be prepared for eventual independence. In this institutionalization, then, the UN bound the colonial problematic in a particular way (see Figure 1). Only those dependent territories that were voluntarily submitted to UN supervision by colonialist powers, or taken from those vanquished in the recent war, were visible as part of the colonial problematic from the perspective of the UN (in either NSGT or Trust status). Beyond these, territories whose sovereignty was in some way compromised by another state were institutionally and discursively defined out of the colonial problematic—and hence were invisible to the UN. For example, the dependent republics of the USSR, as well as Puerto Rico in its contemporary relationship with the United States and the Dutch West Indies in its contemporary relationship with the Netherlands would fall into the first column in Figure 1 and hence would be defined out of the colonial problematic. Similarly, nominally independent states such as the satellites of the USSR would fall into the third column in Figure 1 and hence would also be defined out of the colonial problematic. Likewise, territories incorporated on an "equal" basis but against local wishes, such as the Hawaiian Islands into the United States, would fall into the third column and also be defined out of the colonial problem.

The UN bounding of the colonial problematic, then, was partial and contingent at best. Moreover, for those not fully ready to cooperate with the impending "wave of democracy"[2] or for those who wished to avoid it altogether, the bureaucratization of the colonial problematic offered another option. As long as their dependent territories were kept out of the middle column identified in Figure 1, they were not colonialist powers and their territories were not dependent territories. In the debates examined below, the Netherlands, US, Denmark, USSR, UK and Gold Coast would all take up this strategy. How would the newly independent states of Asia-Africa respond? It is to this question that I now turn.

THE (IN)CONSISTENCY OF THE ANTI-COLONIAL CRITIQUE: COMPARING THE CASES OF THE NETHERLANDS, UNITED STATES, AND DENMARK

That the Asia-Africa critique was uneven is clear when we examine how it dealt with the cases of the hierarchical relationships between the Netherlands and Dutch Guiana/Dutch West Indies, the United States and Puerto Rico, and Denmark and Greenland. Each of these relationships could potentially come under the colonial problematic as envisioned by Asia-Africa, as each involved issues of compromised independence and representation. For example, regarding the Netherlands-Dutch Guiana/Dutch West Indies relationship, although there were slave revolts and resistance movements throughout the centuries, the Hague insisted that these populations had no desire for democracy and were "not yet ready" for it (Goslinga 1990). Regarding the US-Puerto Rico relationship, democratic reforms over the 20th century did not, in the final analysis, alter the U.S. Congress's authority

The Limits of the Anti-Colonial Critique

over Puerto Rico nor the less-than-independent political status of the island (Montalvo-Barbot 1997). Similarly, though an Inuit-led politicization of dependency status after World War II resulted in some democratic reforms in 1953, Greenland nevertheless also continued in its unequal relationship with Denmark (Arter 1999; Janussen 1999).

The dependent territories of the Netherlands, the United States and Denmark came under NSGT status in the UN, requiring each power to regularly supply information on these territories to the GA under Article 73 e of the Charter. However, in the early fifties, each informed the GA that it would stop sending information on these territories and incorporate them "on an equal constitutional basis." Their justification for these incorporations was based on the *Legalism* and *Sovereignty/State's Rights* appeals identified in the last chapter (i.e., that the UN had no legal competence in considering the matter to any extent as this was a domestic matter) and the *Independence/Representation* (especially representation) appeal (i.e., such incorporation was justified because these territories had themselves *chosen* to become incorporated with them). With this third appeal, colonialist speakers especially attempted to make the argument that democracy, freedom, and representation—some of the core values espoused within the Charter—could be achieved in multiple forms and even without full political independence.

Examining the response of the states of Asia-Africa to these requests is particularly instructive, as they unambiguously and forcefully problematized the case of the Netherlands, problematized but ultimately excused the case of the United States, and more or less ignored the case of Denmark. For example, regarding the case of the Netherlands and the Dutch West Indies/Dutch Guiana, the anti-colonialist contingent insisted that independence could take only one form, and that incorporation did not offer the territories another form of self-government but rather that it violated *Independence/Representation* because these territories were to be unequally incorporated: "we have studied the Charter for the Kingdom of the Netherlands, and this instrument does not guarantee full equality to the three parts of the Kingdom (Miss Brooks, Liberia, 1955, Sess 10, 460)." It also contested the *Legalism* and *Sovereignty/State's Rights* argument that the General Assembly had no competence over NSGTs and only the administering authorities did, arguing that not only did the General Assembly have competence here, but that these questions required cooperation and compromise with the UN (i.e., the *International Cooperation (United Nations)* appeal).[3]

In contrast to Asia-Africa's fairly united discourse against the incorporation attempts of the Netherlands, their stance in the comparable case of the United States and Puerto Rico was much more conflicted. For example, colonialist speakers added the new argument in this case that the US could be trusted in its dealings with Puerto Rico because it was a "good" colonial power—and a number of anti-colonialist speakers agreed:

> When we speak of Puerto Rico today in my country, we think of it as an island where progress is in full swing, where freedom is fully enjoyed by all, and where a painstaking group of honest and very conscientious young men work ceaselessly to give their country an efficient government with far-reaching powers, an island to which students from my country already go to seek knowledge and from which they return with what they sought. . . . Puerto Rico today has the status of a free associated State, which its inhabitants accepted by a free plebiscite, and is not the colonial territory it was before, but one which possesses not only an independent but a good government. . . . Puerto Rico is a beautiful and true example of a stable and democratic government (Mr. Canas, Costa Rica, Sess 8, 1953: 310–311).

> As a result of its constitutional status and its recent transformation into a free State associated with the United States, Puerto Rico has attained self-government, and therefore the submission of information under Article 73 e of the Charter is no longer required of the late administering Power, the United States. Moreover, the decisive factor for us has been the principle of the self-determination of peoples, in which, as expressed through various electoral processes, we found an overriding argument in confirmation of Puerto Rico's status in international law within the meaning of Chapter XI of the Charter (Mr. De Marchena, Dominican Republic, Sess 8, 1953: 320).

Interestingly, then, for some in this group, while *Independence/Representation* could only be obtained by complete political independence for Dutch territories, such was not the case for this U.S. territory. However, others did counter that this change in Puerto Rico's status *did not constitute independence* in the spirit of the Charter or of Article 73e:

> We are not called upon to decide whether the status which has been granted to the Puerto Rican people is good or bad, or whether or not it helps that people to realize fully its national aspirations. It is not for us to grant or to deny liberty to the Puerto Rican people. Our task is a different one: it is simply to determine whether or not the degree of self-government which the Puerto Rican people have

The Limits of the Anti-Colonial Critique

75

> reached corresponds to what the United Nations Charter calls "a full measure of self-government." . . . the present government of Puerto Rico is, in practice, subject to such limitations and depends so much on the United States that the country cannot be regarded as having reached the full measure of self-government which the United Nations requires (Mr. Mendoza, Guatemala, Sess 8, 1953: 312).

Still others added that this unequal status between Puerto Rico and the United States rendered problematic any "choices" that the territory of Puerto Rico might make:

> The degree of self-government enjoyed by the Puerto Ricans under the new constitutional arrangement does not keep it outside the scope of Article 73 e. . . . while we do not deny Puerto Ricans the right to enter into any kind of arrangement with the United States or any other country, we hold that this can be done validly only after two conditions have been met: when Puerto Rico is fully independent of external pressures at the time of executing such a compact; and when the democratic processes claimed, such as a referendum or plebiscite, are conducted in an atmosphere of complete democratic freedom. . . . My delegation is not convinced that Puerto Rico, under its present association with the United States, has become a self-governing territory. . . . we believe that independence should precede any voluntary association (Mrs. Menon, India, Sess 8, 1953: 321).

But even detractors, those that thought the incorporation was problematic, agreed with the colonialist argument that the US was a trust-worthy, "good" colonial power. For example, one speaker argued, "My delegation has always accorded its full measure of appreciation to the United States Government for the loyalty, sincerity and devotion with which it has always fulfilled its obligations under the Charter (Mrs. Menon, India, Sess 8, 1953: 321)." Another added, "My delegation, which represents a country allied by ties of kinship to Puerto Rico, has for centuries followed the Puerto Rican people's struggle for freedom and enthusiastically applauds its progress towards self-government. In doing so, we heartily congratulate both this sister nation and the US government, which has made such progress possible (Mr. Mendoza, Guatemala, Sess 8, 1953: 312)." One of the most interesting elements in the discussion on the United States and Puerto Rico, then, is the degree to which colonialist and anti-colonialist discourse actually overlapped.

One speaker resolved such contradictions within the anti-colonialist camp with a statement in which, noting a United States' claim that its actions were supported by 80% of the people of Puerto Rico in a referendum, and then noting that various parties in Puerto Rico who contested this result were denied their requests for oral hearings before the UN, summed up the situation in this way:

> I do not believe any representative will maintain that Puerto Rico is independent or that it has attained a full measure of self-government. . . . but the traditional generosity and freedom-loving spirit of the people of the United States, which impelled them to spontaneously grant freedom and independence to the peoples of the Philippines and Cuba, and which today has made Puerto Rico among the most advanced of the Non Self-Governing Territories, will, we believe, in due course bring to the people of Puerto Rico a full measure of self-government (Mr. Lawrence, Liberia, Sess 8, 1953: 309).

Ultimately, then, the matter was one of *willingness to trust*: these anti-colonialist speakers were *willing to trust* the United States in a way they would not trust the Netherlands. While the GA had considered the Netherlands' case for a total of three sessions, the debate on the US lasted for only one. Ultimately, speakers accepted the United States' request to cease sending information on Puerto Rico, and the draft resolution on this matter also passed.

In contrast to both of these debates is the case of Denmark, whose request to incorporate Greenland and stop sending information on Greenland was debated for less than one session and passed with almost unanimous support. Again, the most common colonialist appeals in support here were *Legalism* and *Sovereignty/State's Rights* (i.e., the notion that the United Nations had no legal competence in interfering in the internal affairs of sovereign states and their NSGTs), *Independence/Representation* (i.e., that the people of Greenland chose this course of action), as well as *Colonialism not negative* (i.e., "Congratulations to Denmark for its success in civilizing the people of Greenland"). To the representative from Australia (Sir Spender, Sess 9, 1954: 300–01) who commended Denmark's "wise guidance," for example, Denmark responded, "We Danes have felt it a responsibility and a privilege to lead the people of Greenland to a richer life and to full equality and participation in the government of our country. United we will work for the further advancement and development of the Greenland community . . . the new order will be a blessing and a benefit to the people of Greenland (Mr. Lannung, Denmark, Sess 9, 1954: 307)."

The Limits of the Anti-Colonial Critique

In the anti-colonialist camp, speakers once again insisted that the United Nations did have the legal right to concern itself with NSGTs and several speakers also pointed out the need to confirm Denmark's claim that Greenlanders indeed supported the move for incorporation. Interspersed, however, were numerous "congratulations" to Denmark and Greenland on their happy news and the discourse of kinship (i.e., "the important work done by Denmark"). Interestingly, speakers cautioned that this was a unique case:

> We support the draft resolution because we consider that in view of the geographical situation and the economic resources of Greenland, as well as the high education level attained there and the work done by Denmark, the United Nations could not find a more satisfactory procedure than that Greenland should so freely express its will to become a permanent part of what for so many years has, morally speaking, been its mother country. I must state, however, that this. . . . is in no way a precedent for the future. On the contrary, in keeping with our position in this matter, we shall become increasingly cautious with regard to the rights of peoples still living under a colonial system (Mr. Vergara, Chile, Sess 9, 1954: 306).

> Although my delegation does not entirely approve of the procedure followed for the integration of Greenland within Denmark, it believes its attitude [of support for Denmark] to be justified by the special situation of Greenland, by the age-old ethnic bonds which tie that country to Denmark, by the fact that no objections have been raised against integration, which in many respects appears to be the only possible solution in the present case, by the Danish Government's close cooperation with the United Nations in the transmission of information—even political information—on Greenland, by the equality between Greenlanders and Danes resulting from the change in the political status of Greenland, and by a number of other factors (Mr. Itani, Lebanon, Sess 9, 1954: 304).

These statements suggest that Greenland's geographical location, economic resources, and "special situation" made this incorporation an acceptable option. Both of these speakers also emphasized the idea that Denmark was a "good" colonial power. Additionally, Lebanon posited that there were "old ethnic bonds" between the two territories that justified this incorporation, thus implying that the hierarchical territorial relationship between the two was not associated with a racial-ethnic dimension—despite the fact that over 80% of the population of Greenland is estimated to be Inuit (Arter 1999; Caulfield 1997).

Thus in these debates, while the Netherlands, the United States and Denmark all sought to remove their dependent territories from the colonial problematic as defined by the United Nations, the states of Asia-Africa did not deploy their anti-kinship critique against all three consistently. How do we understand this selective politicization of these cases? Some have discussed Asia-Africa as a strategic coalition of states pursuing their "interests" on the world stage. For example, one author argues that because the General Assembly is based on a majority voting structure, individual states formed voting groups or "blocs" with other states to aid passage of draft resolutions they cared about. He argues that especially after the Bandung Conference, such a bloc was formed by a group of Asian and African countries (Hovet Jr 1960). From this perspective, this grouping of Asian and African countries was merely strategic; in this vein, perhaps Asia-Africa's differential politicization of the colonialist practices of the Netherlands versus the United States and Denmark largely reflected shifting global power relationships, in which the Netherlands as representative of European colonial powers in general was on the decline and the United States was on the rise (more on Denmark below).

While I do not deny the "strategic" element of the politics of Asia-Africa, I argue that this perspective neglects one important dimension of Asia-Africa as a collectivity, particularly as demonstrated at the Bandung, Cairo and Accra conferences reviewed in the last chapter. That is, beyond such "strategic interests," this grouping represents a racialized, anti-imperialist, anti-colonialist *collective identity* forged by formerly dependent territories from Asia and Africa. To deny this element of the emergence of Asia-Africa is to deny the collective experiences—however socially constructed—of racialized groups across Asia and Africa who had their territorial and cultural autonomy compromised by numerous colonialist projects since the 16th century. From this perspective, then, the differential politicization of the problematic practices of the Netherlands versus the United States and Denmark, while certainly shaped by transforming global power relationships, was also affected by the particular angle of vision afforded to Asia-Africa by its collective history. Specifically, this "angle of vision" was shaped by Asia-Africa's own experiences of (western European) colonialism, how western European powers versus the US defined their political identities historically (and Asia-Africa's acceptance of these identities, in a sense), and how Asia-Africa ultimately situated itself in relation to these identities.

The Limits of the Anti-Colonial Critique

From the perspective of Asia-Africa, for instance, the colonial experience was shaped within the structure of an overseas empire, where the rule between peoples/lands separated by vast amounts of territorial space was naturalized. The traditional theatres of conflict regarding these empires were the territories of Asia and Africa, and the racialized objects of these empires were the peoples of Asia and Africa. From the beginning, then, a traditional colonial power such as the Netherlands fit the colonialist profile from the perspective of Asia-Africa in a way that the U.S. did not. Furthermore, western European colonialist powers produced a powerful narrative of self as colonial and imperial. Indeed, their colonial and imperial identity was an integral part of their European-ness. Delanty (1995) argues that it was just such a conception of self-as-Europe—a geopolitical name for civilization and indeed, a metaphor for "complex" civilization—that served as a legitimation for the politics of the secular and territorial (colonialist) state.[4] From this perspective, then, in its thorough politicization of the colonialist practices of the Netherlands as a part of "Europe," Asia-Africa simply accepted the colonialist/imperialist identity and narrative that Europe itself produced.

One could argue that the United States had a similar history of colonialist practice, given its history of overseas dependent territories in the Western hemisphere, the legacy of contiguous empire via Manifest Destiny[5], its ongoing informal intervention in countries in Latin America, Asia and Europe, its continuous siding with the western European colonial powers on issues of decolonization in the GA, and contrary to its claims, its ongoing domestic problems with race, of which Asia-Africa was acutely aware. Regarding this last element, a letter from the American white supremacist group, the Ku Klux Klan, was distributed to the delegations of the Asian and African states within the UN with the title "White America rejects a bastardized United Nations." The delegation of Nigeria actually introduced the document into the GA discussions during Session 15 in order to "put it on record (Mr. Wachuku, Nigeria, Sess 15, 1960: 1236)." The letter read, "A foul stench spreads out from the East River and hangs over New York like a pall. It is the smell of sweat, the greasiest sweat of the black races of Africa and the yellow races of Asia which have invaded the United Nations. It is enough to make every white Protestant American vomit (Letter by KKK introduced by Mr. Wachuku, Nigeria, Sess 15, 1960: 126)." The letter went on to compare the "races" of Asia and Africa to animals that whites were intended to rule over.

However, in contrast to its politicization of the Netherlands, Asia-Africa seemed to "excuse" the United States' colonial practices. Why is this the case? One important factor is that unlike the European narrative of self as colonial and imperial, in contradiction to its actual colonialist practices, the United States historically produced a strong anti-colonial narrative of self, beginning with the original revolt against British colonial rule. Moreover, the ideology of American exceptionalism, as espoused for example in the Gettysburg Address, associated the United States' political identity intimately with democracy: Four score and seven years ago our fathers brought forth, upon this continent, a new nation, conceived in liberty, and dedicated to the proposition that "all men are created equal (Gettysburg Address, 1863)." Moreover, regarding the case of Puerto Rico, the United States maintained this image by co-opting local demand, molding public opinion, and manipulating outward symbols of popular representation. Grosfoguel (2003), for example, argues that the US response to local demands in Puerto Rico were always conditioned by its perceived needs within the international context. For example, until the 40s and through WWII, this interest was primarily military, and wanting to avoid a local population hostile to its military use of the island during WWII, the US extended basic democratic rights in exchange for military exploitation. Regarding resistance to the elected governor, Congress had a referendum on the bill for the elected governor so that it could demonstrate its commitment to the values of political representation and yet, despite local calls from separatists, statehood supporters and nationalists, the referendum—support for which was also built through widespread public relations campaigns—gave voters only one choice: that of an elected governor. Later, in 1953, when the Eisenhower administration would inform the UN that it would no longer provide information on Puerto Rico, it added that this referendum demonstrated that Puerto Rico had "freely chosen" this relationship with the United States (Montalvo-Barbot 1997: 127–135).

But the value of Puerto Rico to the United States went far beyond its military use. In the context of the international "independence boom" but especially of the Cold War, the US wanted to make Puerto Rico a symbol of democracy and capitalism in the eyes of the international community. Hence, it initiated during this time not only massive programs for industrialization but also Truman's Point Four Program, where Third World elites were brought in to be trained in the techniques of "development" but even more, in the American model of development as opposed to the Soviet model (Grosfoguel 2003). This symbolic role especially explains the massive US federal assistance in housing, health, and education that Puerto Rico received during this time (ibid).

Perhaps this manipulation of symbols of popular representation was efficacious, as anti-colonialist speakers in general, with the important exception of the USSR, seemed to largely accept the anti-colonial, democratic narrative of self advanced by the US. This acceptance is evident in the repeated referral of these speakers in their *Independence/Representation* appeals to American texts and symbols. Iceland began, for example, with the statement, "Perhaps the greatest blow it [colonialism] ever suffered was delivered here during the America Revolution (Mr. Thors, Iceland, Sess 15, 1960: 1147)." To this, others added, "Although a man's body might be conquered for a while, he had also been endowed with a soul which could not be crushed. The cry of Patrick Henry, 'Give me liberty or give me death' had been a cry from the soul, which still echoed from all parts of the earth (Mr. Cooper, Liberia, Sess 4, 1949: 532);" "To paraphrase George Washington's words, 'it is folly in a colonial country to look for disinterested favors from the colonizers (Mr. Winiewicz, Poland, Sess 15, 1960: 1024);'" "In the words of Abraham Lincoln, 'It is true that you may fool all the people some of the time; you can even fool some of the people all the time; but you can't fool all of the people all the time (Mr. Aw, Mali, Sess 15, 1960: 1066).'" And finally,

> One of the great ironies of the present age is the curious inability of the colonial Powers to comprehend the fundamental urges of freedom and independence. . . . Have they forgotten that a great American said: "that all men are created equal. That they are endowed by their Creator with certain inalienable rights. That among these are life, liberty and the pursuit of happiness (Mr. Asha, United Arab Republic, Sess 15, 1960: 1047)."

Beyond the "strategic reasons" provided by Hovet Jr (1960) and the constructivist reasons outlined above, there is a third and final dimension to the uneven treatment of the Netherlands versus the United States by Asia-Africa. That is, enabled fundamentally by the transformation in global power relationships between the declining European powers and the new superpowers, dependent territories on the cusp of independence and newly independent territories were finally to be "included" in the world community. Scholars of world culture argue that in the modern period, the only agent with legitimacy to act on the world stage is the bounded, purposive, responsible, rational nation-state (Meyer 1997; Meyer 1999; Boli and Thomas 1999; Finnemore 1996; Finnemore 1998). It is precisely this agency that dependent territories had been historically denied and of which they were now on the threshold. Scholars of world culture also argue that while various "rationalized others" in the world polity have always provided a set of prescriptions to the nation-state on how to conduct itself appropriately (i.e., provide security, individual citizenship, etc), after World War II, prescriptions for appropriate agency and behavior on the part of the nation-state have especially intensified (Meyer 1999; Meyer 1997). For example, the "good," "rational," "modern" nation-state in the post-war period is especially expected to pursue economic development (Meyer 1997; Finnemore 1996; Chabbott 1999), among other goals. States that enjoy the most legitimation within the world polity and so are "successful states" offer models for other states to follow (Finnemore 1998; Meyer 1999). In the post-war period, the two superpowers each offered two alternative models of legitimate or "successful" statehood and also of economic development. I will discuss the Soviet Union more extensively in the next section. Regarding the United States, in addition to offering such a model for development and successful statehood for newly independent countries, it also, critically and in full cognizance of the alternatives offered by the USSR, offered development *aid*. For example, as mentioned above, Puerto Rico was the international training ground for Truman's Four Point Program, intended to demonstrate to Third World elites the efficacy of this American model of development as opposed to the Soviet model (Grosfoguel 2003: 57–58). Hence, the states of Asia-Africa were located in a complex constellation of identities and interests in which they had every incentive to distinguish the United States from western European powers and turn a blind eye on the former's colonialist practices.

Beyond the U.S., while Denmark could certainly have been grouped with western European powers in its colonialist practices, it was also similarly "excused" for a number of reasons. First of all, it was a relatively small colonialist power, and neither the indigenous peoples of Greenland, nor peoples with a sense of ethnic connection to them, were anywhere visible within the collective identity of Asia-Africa or in the General Assembly. The racialized, anti-colonialist identity represented by Asia-Africa, thus, perhaps did not easily incorporate Danish rule over the indigenous peoples of Greenland as racialized rule—perhaps did not include these indigenes as part of European colonialism's racialized others. This may be why one anti-colonialist speaker argued that Denmark's incorporation of Greenland is acceptable partly because of the ethnic bonds between the two, indicating an assumption of ethnic overlap between the two territories that was in direct contradiction to their actual demographic makeup. Beyond such de-racialization of Danish-Greenlandic relations, another possibility is that a number of the states of Asia-Africa, many of which were inheritors of the arbitrary territorial borders and identity categories of colonial administrators (Anderson 1991:165–69; Deng 1993; Nugent 2002; Mengara 2001a), did not orient to the one-to-one relationship between ethnicity or nation and state borders in the same way as did liberal theorists of the nation-state. Particularly in Africa, colonial borders played havoc with long-standing affinities, deconstructing and reconstructing them according to extra-local priorities (Nugent 2002; Mengara 2001a; Deng 1993). As representatives of elites within these Asian and African states, then, perhaps these speakers viewed the state form not as problematic in its inability to align neatly with ethnic cleavages, but instead as offering a solution to these cleavages by transcending them.

Moreover, in a strategic sense, Denmark was a relatively weak colonial power, and its relationship with Greenland was conditioned by the geographical position of Greenland close to the North American continent and thus the United State's sphere of interest (i.e., the Monroe Doctrine). One example of the influence of this third party is that in 1941, Denmark entered into an agreement with the United States which allowed the latter to build military bases on the territory (Janussen 1999). This influence especially made itself felt in the wake of an emerging post-war Inuit-led politicization of dependency status (Arter 1999). For example, a 1951 agreement gave the US permission to supplement its wartime bases with a larger military base at Thule. In connection with the building of the Thule base, the local population was compulsorily and traumatically moved off the land (Janussen 1999). In my examination of the debates in the General Assembly, in contrast to extensive politicization and discussion of the forced movement of a local population in one of the territories of the British Empire,[6] this particular movement was not even mentioned. Furthermore, the United States stored nuclear rockets on the Thule base despite official Danish promises to the locals to the contrary. Janussen (1999) suggests that these favors to the United States were assets in connection with its membership in the North Atlantic Treaty Organization. Ultimately, there was an amendment to the Constitution in 1953, giving the territory limited representative institutions. Even decades later, however, as indigenous movements within Greenland demand complete independence and a revision of the 1951 agreement between the United States and Greenland, and even in the wake of the development of a private association called Hingitaq 53 (Thrown out in 53) which has formed to take Denmark to court for the forced 1953 movement of the indigenous population connected to the Thule base, the fate of Greenland seems somewhat ambiguous. For all of these issues "involve an allied great power with which Denmark under no circumstances wishes to seriously fall out (ibid 1999)."

THE SCOPE OF THE ANTI-COLONIAL CRITIQUE: THE CASE OF THE USSR

This uneven politicization of colonialist practices by different states on the part of Asia-Africa is underscored by its treatment of the case of the

USSR. The USSR's hierarchical relationships with its numerous republics "within" and satellites "without" were not officially recognized within the colonial problematic as defined by the UN (and hence can be placed in columns 1 and 3 of Figure 1 respectively). Asia-Africa, however, was decidedly aware of their situation. Lloyd writes, thus, that Soviet imperialism was hotly debated behind closed doors at Bandung, but never openly acknowledged (Lloyd 1959). Regarding the case of the republics, for example, before the Bandung Conference got underway, Said Schamyl, the Former Chief of National Defense of North-Caucasus and Isa Yusuf Alptekin, General Secretary of Eastern Turkestan State, submitted a memorandum entitled "Appeal to the Chairman of the Conference of Afro-Asiatic States in Bandung" to the organizers of the conference. Calling themselves the "Moslem Nations under the URSS Imperialism," and representing the National Centers of Azerbaijan, North-Caucasia, Idil-Ural, Crimea and Turkestan, they asked their "African and Asian brother states" for help against "oppression, torture, massacres and mass-deportations (Memorandum, 1955)." The Memorandum included two annexes, which listed the various violations, including routine violence, the suppression of movements for self-determination and nationalism, and Russification policies which sought to stamp out local languages, histories, cultures, and so on. The issue, however, was not placed on the conference agenda. In response to this lack of response, Said Schamyl wrote a second memorandum during the conference: THE HESITATION OF YOUR HONOURABLE CONGRESS TO TAKE A DIRECT STEP OF INTERVENTION TO BETTER THE DESTINIES OF THESE FIFTY MILLIONS OF UNFORTUNATE MUSLIM BROTHERS INSPITE OF THEIR SAD SITUATION WILL BE A CAUSE OF TOLERANCE FOR THE CONTINUATION OF SUCH TRAGEDIES (Memorandum, Capitalized in original, 1955). At the end of the conference, when the resolutions passed were widely distributed and it became apparent that they did not directly deal with these territories, this final letter from Said Schamyl stated: The Bandung conference dealt with the problems concerning East from one angle unfortunately, and they passed silently on the rightful question of the dependent peoples of the East in the Red Russian Imperialism. . . . their brothers Behind the Iron Curtain (Memorandum, 1955).

On the case of Soviet satellites, too, as discussed in the last chapter, the decision was made to make a categorical distinction between UN membership and dependency status at the Bandung Conference. That is, if a state was a member of the United Nations, by definition it could not be a dependent territory. Ultimately then, whether regarding republics or

The Limits of the Anti-Colonial Critique

satellites, the hierarchical territorial practices of the Soviet Union were not politicized and thus "went unremarked (Bell 2001)."

And yet, the principles of the Bandung Conference continued to be an important referent for some of the independence and nationalist movements within the areas of Soviet influence. Hungarian Prime Minister Imre Nagy, for example, saw the principles of independence, sovereignty, equality and non-interference espoused by the Bandung Conference as ones that should be applied to the Soviet camp, where they were being opposed by the "remnants of Stalinist autocratic rule." His "uprising" was of course crushed (Brzezinksi 1967).

So, why were the colonialist practices of the USSR regarding its satellites and republics—practices of which Asia-Africa was decidedly aware—not politicized? I argue that this is primarily because the same complex of identities and interests that served to mitigate the practices of the United States were also in operation here. First, like the United States, the Soviet Union was also a superpower and so strategically not as convenient a target as European colonial powers on the decline. Second, like the United States and in contrast to Western Europe, the USSR also produced a powerful anti-colonial narrative within its political identity. For example, the USSR was officially anti-imperialist and anti-colonialist, as it associated these terms with capitalism and hence the capitalistic "west." Interestingly, however, if the ideological construction of "Europe" was so intimately tied to colonialist practices (Delanty 1995), while there was an ambiguous relationship between Russian identity and this idea of Europe before the 1700s (Bassin 1991),[7] this

> changed dramatically in the first quarter of the eighteenth century as Peter the Great undertook the far-reaching reform of the Russian state and Society [and so emerged a]. . . . fundamentally new understanding of the distinction between Europe and Asia. . . . [where now, there was an acknowledgement of] the singular importance of the European continent and the unconditional preeminence of European civilization. . . . [and hence] the country was to be given a European appearance and to be thoroughly reorganized along European patterns. . . . apparent at all levels, from the infamous ban on beards at court to the construction of the new and quintessentially European capital city (Bassin 1991).

Hence, as the colonial and imperial idea of Europe grew in the 18th century, it affected Russia as well and even after 1917, remained the dominant sense of self in the Soviet Union (Bassin 1991).[8] The Soviet state even deployed hierarchical kinship language here, as it constructed itself as the "senior brother" with the power to rule over and guide "junior brothers" in its domain (Szporluk 1997; Shlapentokh 2001).

Of course, an important way in which the Soviet empire distinguished itself from western European empires, however, was that it saw itself as providing an alternative model of modernity, superior to that represented by the "west"—a Soviet Utopia. Based on the idea that the nation-state was the political form of capitalism, socialism was to be international and after World War II, was "extended" to the formally independent states of Eastern and Central Europe (Szporluk 1997). Significantly, thus, whatever the complexities in terms of its relationship with "Europe" and whatever its territorial practices in contrast to western European colonialist powers, the Soviet Union did not publicly construct itself as a colonial/imperial power. Moreover, its conquest of contiguous territories, like the ideology and practice of Manifest Destiny on the part of the United States, materialized in a contiguous empire and hence looked very different from traditional European overseas empires. Ultimately, then, like its acceptance of the anti-colonial, democratic narrative of self crafted by the United States, Asia-Africa also seemed to accept the anti-colonial, anti-imperial narrative of self produced by the Soviet Union.

Beyond such strategic and constructivist reasons, the Soviet Union was similar to the United States in one final way: it offered a model of development and of successful statehood after independence. This model had the added appeal for some newly independent states of not being associated with western capitalism—a point the Soviet Union sought to underscore with its active support, in important contrast to the United States, of Asia-Africa in both voting agenda and patterns of appeal in the General Assembly.

THE PLASTICITY OF THE ANTI-COLONIAL CRITIQUE: THE CASE OF GHANA

Against the hierarchical territorialist practices of the Netherlands, the United States and Denmark discussed above, I argued that Asia-Africa deployed its anti-colonialist critique selectively. Against parallel practices on the part of the USSR, I examined how Asia-Africa withheld its critique. In this section, I argue that this critique was completely plastic, borrowing from colonialist kinship politics as required. Specifically, I turn to the interesting case of the amalgamation of the dependent territories of the Gold Coast colony and the trust Territory of British Togoland into the new independent state of Ghana. Here, while the Gold Coast enthusiastically supported such a merger, British Togoland did not. The plasticity of its anti-kinship critique is especially evident here, as Asia-Africa launched this critique in support of the Gold Coast, but fell back on crude kinship imagery to deny the wishes of British Togoland. In what follows, I first examine the case of Ghana to introduce the complexity of the West African nationalist project of translating political identity into territorial borders. I give a brief overview of the multiple contingencies with differing agendas in this regard, and I end with how this all fared in the debates in the GA.

Stories about Ghana and West African independence movements typically begin with the Gold Coast, and the review offered here is no different. Hence, I start with Grimal, who argues that the territory of the Gold Coast was "confined within purely artificial borders (Grimal 1978: 295)," and was rife with ethnic, religious and economic class divisions, as well as divisions between nationalists and those who had a stake in the imperial order. Korang (2004) writes that the nationalist effort to create the oneness of the territory began with the creation of a historical past for the Gold Coast. A central piece of this project was the thesis of a genealogical connection between the Akan majority of the Gold Coast and the imperial kingdom of Ghana of the medieval western Sudan. This thesis was especially taken up in the 1920s by the nationalist Danquah, who founded the United Gold Coast Convention in 1947 (Grimal 1978; Korang 2004). In 1948, Danquah publicly proposed that the name of the colony be changed from Gold Coast to Ghana, as the former was a colonial trademark to which "Ghana" would be resistance. Hence, Korang (2004) argues, Danquah invented, academized, and popularized this essential "Ghana," and "Ghana" became a successful symbol for the anticolonial struggle. Additionally, his quest for national character and essence was also assisted by various imperialists, who aimed to create a "future filled with grateful ex-savages chanting to the Astraea Redux, metropolitan culture—at the service of imperial political economy (Korang 2004:164)."

But the peoples of the territories that would be affected were still divided in various ways. Multiple parties emerged, each of which claimed to represent different identities and sought a different materialization of these identities via different territorial borders. For example, the All-Ewe Conference claimed to represent the Ewe tribe, which was split between the Gold Coast, French Togoland and British Togoland, and sought to unify these groups under British trusteeship (they perceived the British as somewhat more responsive to local demand for reform than the French). This movement faded after 1947 and was replaced in prominence by the Togoland Union, which wanted to reunite the British and French Togolands into a unified Togoland and ultimately exclude the Gold Coast. (The two

Togolands had previously been one territory, which became the German Protectorate of Togoland, and which was then split into British and French mandates after World War I). This movement for Togoland unification began to gain mass support, formed the new unificationist party termed the Togoland Congress (TC) in 1950, and also gained increasing support for its case at the UN (Nugent 2002:147–98).

For their part, however, the British had long administered the Gold Coast colony with the Trust territory of British Togoland, and preferred to grant independence to the two integrated together. Hence, Nugent (2002b:147–98) argues that the "official strategy" of the British became to stall the impetus to Togoland unification at the UN, while nurturing a local constituency that would favor the integration of British Togoland with the Gold Coast.

Scholars disagree about the precise role of Kwame Nkrumah and his Convention People's Party (CPP) in this scenario. In Grimal's (1978) victorious account, Nkrumah chafed under the moderate politics of Danquah and founded the CPP in 1949 as a base for more radical independence politics. His ongoing contentions with the British government eventually resulted in more democratic reforms, then full internal autonomy, and eventually, independence within the Commonwealth in 1957. Korang (2004) differs slightly in arguing that the significant contribution of Nkrumah was to advance the cause of independence by moving beyond Danquah's pure ethnos, which actually failed to unite Gold Coast's divided groups, and build a different kind of collectivity—a virtual nativity where if people were not united by descent, they could still be one by consent. Specifically, the argument was the *similarity* argument of Bandung: if we are not all essentially alike, we are alike in our burdens at the hands of the colonial power. We are the same in our common oppression, and in our common dream of freedom. Perhaps then, as in the case of Denmark and Greenland, in this approach the state form was to be the solution to multiple cleavages within the Gold Coast.

As Nugent (2002:147–98) tells it, however, in contrast to such an image of the CPP "as a black nationalist knight that slew the imperialist dragon," behind closed doors, the CPP actually worked closely with the British. While the British sought to "buy time" at the UN and not look too supportive of the CPP, the CPP assumed the task of building the constituency for integration of the Gold Coast with British Togoland. The British even coached the CPP on how to present its case at the UN. Why such collaboration? According to Nugent (2002), Nkrumah thought hydroelectric power was the key to modernization, but the viability of this depended on the new government having complete rights over the Volta River. If British

The Limits of the Anti-Colonial Critique

Togoland was allowed to secede, however, the left bank would be touching foreign soil and thus, the status of British Togoland was of fundamental importance to the whole nationalist project of the Gold Coast. Ultimately, in the battle between the TC and the CPP for British Togoland, the "annexationist agenda (Nugent 2002:147–98)" of the CPP won. In 1956, the people of British Togoland were asked by the UN to vote in a plebiscite for either union with an independent Gold Coast or separation from the latter pending ultimate determination of the future of the territory. Most (58%) voted for unification. At the UN, the plebiscite results were decisive, and on March 1957, British Togoland was integrated with Gold Coast, emerging as the newly independent Ghana. Across the border, French Togoland would gain separate independence as the Republic of Togo (ibid).

In this third version, the story of the role of Nkrumah, the CPP, and the process of gaining independence is very different from the first two version. Interestingly, a central difference between the first two and the third versions is which part of Ghana the focus is on—the Gold Coast or British Togoland. For the first two, stories of Ghana begin with the Gold Coast and are more positive stories of the attainment of independence from colonial rule. In the third, Nugent describes the independence of Ghana from the perspective of British Togoland, using the term "annexation." In what follows, I examine how the GA came to support this independence-annexation in its debates on British Togoland and in doing so, negotiated the graduation of the first Trust territory from UN supervision to "political independence."

In the early fifties, the Togoland Congress appeared before the Fourth Committee and the General Assembly several times in order to plead the cause of Togoland unification, creating support within the anti-colonialist contingent in the UN for the unificationist case as early as 1953. Anti-colonialists articulated this support in the GA debates with the usual appeal to *Independence/Representation*, and the GA passed a resolution instructing the British and French governments to convene a Joint Council for Togoland Affairs, which was to represent the populations of both French and British Togolands, to deliberate on the future of this "divided nation (Documents 1954)." The two administering authorities, however, never convened the Joint Council for Togoland Affairs. In July 1953, the Acting Secretary of the All-Ewe Conference wrote a letter to the Secretary-General of the United Nations, enclosing a copy of a document entitled "Most Secret: The Future of Togoland Under United Kingdom Trusteeship" to share with all members of the GA. In the letter, he wrote that it was important to forward this document to the UN, as its contents were "diametrically opposed to the aspiration of the Ewes and Togolanders to-day (Atiogbe, I.K., Ag. General

Secretary, Petition to UN Secretary-General, 1953, Documents, 1954)." According to Mr. Atiogbe, the document itself laid out a joint strategy on the part of the British government and the CPP on how to outwardly satisfy the democratic prerequisites of anti-colonialists in the UN but still integrate the Gold Coast with British Togoland. The document acknowledged that both the Togoland Congress and the Ewe-unificationists enjoyed support in different areas of the territories in question. Hence, it proposed a two-step plan in which, first, the CPP was to go about building support for the integration of Gold Coast and British Togoland among locals on the ground through whatever means necessary, including bribery of specific leaders and second, the UN was to be bombarded by petitions from locals demanding this integration. Such locals were to be coached by the UK government and the CPP on how to do this. Moreover, in order for the first step to succeed, this matter could not come before the UN until 1954—until the necessary local support could be obtained.

Following the delivery of this document and Mr. Atiogbe's letter to the UN in July 1953, Mr. Antor, the representative of the Joint Togoland Congress, addressed the Fourth Committee in November of 1953, arguing that its resolution that the British and French governments set up a Joint Council for Togoland Affairs to determine the future of the two Togolands still remained unheeded and that instead, the UK was going ahead with its plans as laid out in the "Most Secret" document. In early December, the UK circulated a cablegram allegedly from locals supporting the case of integration of British Togoland with the Gold Coast in the GA. Two days later, representatives of the All-Ewe Conference and the Togoland Congress wrote the Fourth Committee a letter in which they disputed this cablegram, arguing that its signatories were all members of the CPP and did not represent the Ewes or the Togolanders. In this letter, they further asked the UN to itself take action to ascertain the wishes of the people.

How did GA members react to this barrage of contradictory messages from the Gold Coast and Togoland territories? In 1954, consistent with its alleged plan as laid out in the "Most Secret" document, the UK itself was ready for a plebiscite to "determine what the people of British Togoland wanted." Some anti-colonialists seemed sympathetic to the notion that the results might be manipulated, and they offered objections to the plebiscite. Interestingly, these objections were a confused medley of the *Colonialism not negative* appeal and the *Independence/Representation* appeal. For example, the Philippines argued that this was an attempt on the part of the UK to "annex" British Togoland and that the UK was violating the sacred trust which had been entrusted to it. It was supposed to develop the people of the territory; however, from the beginning, it had integrated British

The Limits of the Anti-Colonial Critique 91

Togoland and Gold Coast and administered them together: "We are now faced here with a situation where we are being asked to give the blessing of the United Nations to the annexation of a Trust Territory (Mr. Carpio, Philippines, 1954, Sess 9, p. 500)." It argued further that the people had never been allowed to develop: "Before we take a plebiscite . . . [we need to] determine first whether the people of the Trust Territory are or have been developed enough or are in such a condition that they can now *be trusted to determine their own future* (italics added, ibid)."

Despite the above complications and the resultant misgivings on the part of some, however, most anti-colonialists ended up supporting the plebiscite. India, for example, offered the curious argument that, "some apprehensions have been voiced. . . . because the [British Togoland] Territory has been administered as part of the Gold Coast and because its future has sometimes been spoken of in terms of that situation. The main element, however, is the independence of the people of the Trust Territory. [This is a] march forward to independence (Mr. Menon, India, Sess 10, 1955: 456)." This argument, in essence, encouraged detractors to focus less on the uncomfortable issue of "annexation" and more on the positive element of progression toward formal independence. Indeed, other anti-colonialists that supported the plebiscite also supported their stances based on appeals to *Independence/Representation*, and in December 1955, the GA voted for the plebiscite to take place.

The difficulties of the situation, however, did not end there. When the plebiscite was administered in May 1956, it offered the people of British Togoland only one of two options: union with an independent Gold Coast or continuation of existing Trust status. Alternative options, as preferred by the Ewes or the Togolanders, were not made available. As mentioned earlier, the result was that 58% of the people chose the former, and so the GA voted for the integration of Gold Coast with British Togoland.

In what follows, I examine the debates on this last draft resolution on the integration of Gold Coast and British Togoland. I focus especially on the positions of different speakers—were they supportive of this integration of the Gold Coast with British Togoland? What appeals did they use to make their cases? I found that beyond the colonialist group, which supported integration, anti-colonialists for the most part also supported integration, and they used their usual appeal (i.e., *Independence/Representation*) to do so:

> The Togoland people were offered free union with an independent Ghana, where all were to enjoy full freedom . . . the people . . . decided in favour of union with Ghana . . . [this supports] the will of

> the people. . . . we in Ethiopia have followed with great interest the struggle of the people of the Gold Coast in their march towards independence. . . . . The emergence of Ghana and its subsequent admission to the United Nations will add one more voice to the voice of Africa (Mr. Yifru, Ethiopia, Sess 11, 1956: 691).

Only a few anti-colonialists, most of which were not part of Asia-Africa proper, (specifically Uruguay, Venezuela, Guatemala, the Philippines, Afghanistan and the USSR) problematized this integration as violating *Independence/Representation*.

Beyond these typically anti-colonialist appeals, however, these speakers also made use of typical colonialist appeals such as *Colonialism not negative* (i.e., "British Togoland has now been prepared for independence"). For example, one speaker argued "British Togoland was placed under trusteeship some time ago and now, as it reaches a level enabling it to exercise its right of self-determination freely, it has been given that chance (Mr. Mahgoub, Sudan, Sess 11, 1956: 681)." Once again, these speakers from Asia-Africa who were in support of integration were opposed in this argument by anti-colonialist speakers who were *not* a part of Asia-Africa proper. The oppositions of this second group to Asia-Africa's kinship logic were incidentally also made with different kinship logic:

> the international trusteeship system, as set up, safeguards the advance of a group of underdeveloped territories to a stage at which their peoples are capable of self-determination, of deciding their own internal system of government and of acting independently in international affairs. . . . It is the duty of countries which administer Trust Territories to promote the political, economic, social and educational advancement of the inhabitants. . . . peoples' . . . inadequate development has caused them to be placed under trusteeship. . . . We cannot believe that the mere incorporation of Togoland under British administration in Ghana is the appropriate step to take (Mr. Balay, Uruguay, Sess 11, 1956: 679).

There was a small intervention into this kinship-ridden discussion by one speaker, who argued, "I believe all peoples are ready. . . . it is not as though we today were conferring civilization upon them: they are re-emerging into their new youth (Mr. Menon, India, Sess 11, 1956: 682)."

Ultimately, the central anti-colonialist arguments for unification made a case for the typically colonialist appeal of *Proceduralism/Practicalism* and to the historicity of "Ghana." Anti-colonialists actually made the appeal to *Procedurlism/Practalism* in this case more often than colonialist speakers did.

The Limits of the Anti-Colonial Critique

They argued that British Togoland was too small to be on its own, and that integration with the Gold Coast was efficacious since it had already been integrated with the Gold Coast by the administering authority for administration purposes for so long. Additionally, they argued that the Ewe tribe, parts of which were in Gold Coast, French Togoland and British Togoland, could not be practically united.

But why the integration of British Togoland with Gold Coast instead of with French Togoland? Here, the focus shifted to the historicity of "Ghana" (i.e., Gold Coast) as opposed to the constructed nature of any connection between the two Togolands:

> "Togoland" was a name given by the Germans, and the Territory [of the two Togolands] has no national historical background. . . . any feeling that any delegation may have that we are preventing the unity of a people is . . . erroneous. [Moreover] this part of West Africa has an ancient history going as far back as the empires of the pre-Roman days, but even in more modern times, what is now to be called Ghana, which is the new name that the Gold Coast proposes to adopt, has a very glorious and a very honourable history [this history of the ancient kingdom of Ghana]. . . . It is this history that the new nation will inherit (Mr. Menon, India, Sess 11, 1956: 685).

Repeatedly, then, in the argument for integration, the focus shifted from British Togoland to Gold Coast, from the wishes of the Togoland Congress, which did manage to build a mass following, to a plebiscite that only offered Togolanders freedom via uniting with Gold Coast, and again from the wishes of this Congress, to the mythical history of Gold Coast.

In this manner, British Togoland was the first Trust territory to "graduate" from the UN Trusteeship System—to move from the colonial problematic as defined by the UN (i.e., column 2 in Figure 1) to official statehood. Hence, the emergence of "Ghana" can be seen as a metaphor for the complexities of postcolonial independence, accompanied by negotiations, compromises, and silences. It was enabled by Asia-Africa, who not only bound the colonial problematic unevenly with its differential politicization of different NSGT cases and the case of the USSR, but also with its willingness to "take what it could get" when it came to freedom.

CONCLUSION

Ultimately, then, anti-colonial states centered on Asia-Africa in the UNGA launched a multi-layered, anti-colonialist critique that targeted particular colonialist practices based on their own positioning as newly independent states within shifting global power relationships. Regarding the historic kinship politics of the colonial era, thus, Asia-Africa's interventions were selective, limited and at times, non-existent.

Was this fragmentary nature of its challenge to the kinship politics of the Charter merely a strategic sacrifice of principle? Alternatively, considering especially the problem of Ghana, did the power of the kinship narrative affect the way anti-colonialists defined the colonial problematic as well? In the next chapter, I explore such questions further by turning to the narratives invoked by different groups in understanding the nature of the colonial problematic, the role of colonialist powers, and the role of dependent territories.

Chapter Four
Contending Perspectives?: The Overlap between Colonialist and Anti-Colonialist Narratives on Dependency and Sovereignty

Given the great overlap between the discursive appeals used by colonialist and anti-colonialist speakers examined in the previous chapter, and given the inconsistency of especially the latter, in this chapter I seek to explore these discussions in greater depth. In what follows, I examine the central narratives shaping the politics of different groups in their discussions of colonialism and decolonization; specifically, I examine these discursive exchanges as attempts to renegotiate space through the renegotiation of identity. As mentioned in a previous chapter, I see these exchanges as both *persuasive* and *constitutive*. They are persuasive in the sense that they are based on a set of appeals that aim to justify a speaker's stance on a draft resolution under discussion and also to convince others to take on a similar stance (and so ultimately, vote similarly). Additionally, following Tischer, Meyer, Wodak and Vetter, they are also constitutive. They are "simultaneously constitutive of social identities, social relations, and systems of knowledge and beliefs (Titscher, Meyer, Wodak, and Vetter 2000)." From this perspective, we may understand the historic, kinship politics previously identified to posit two overarching, distinct categories of social identity: the *disembodied* or rational/paternal/masculine on the one hand versus the *embodied* or irrational/childlike/feminine on the other; a hierarchical set of social relationships between the two, whereby the first category can and indeed must "rule over" or "guide" the second; and the system of knowledge inherent in these constructions, namely the notion that dependent territories require rule/tutelage from sovereign states. From the eighteenth to especially the twentieth century, I argued in Chapter One that this politics moved away from "harsher" notions of colonial rule to "softer," paternalistic notions of guidance and tutelage. In this chapter, I am interested in to what extent this politics—in either form—is evident in the GA debates in the fifteen years examined. Moreover, given the great overlap in colonialist and anti-colonialist argument identified thus far, how do anti-colonialists respond?

In what follows, I begin by performing a cluster-agon analysis of different speakers' talk about dependency and sovereignty in order to tap into potentially varying meaning systems. I note patterns by former and contemporary status in the European colonial system, position and allegiance in the Cold War, and other elements, in order to explore the competing meaning systems inherent in the language deployed. Next, I examine how in the use of this language, different discourses bring together different imagery in order to weave contending narratives of the colonial experience and the meaning of political independence.

In this way, I identify four different narratives advanced by colonialist and anti-colonialist speakers within the United Nations General Assembly for the fifteen years leading up to the onset of legal decolonization. Focusing on how these different narratives constitute identities, relationships between these identities, and knowledge about them, I argue that in this setting, colonialist speakers continued in their articulation of a softer kinship politics of colonial rule for the beneficence of dependent peoples, producing a colonialist narrative that worked to advance their own subjectivity while denying the subjectivity of dependent peoples. Specifically, this narrative made categorical distinctions between mature, wise, and rational administering authorities versus their young, immature charges, posited a set of paternalistic relationships between them, and so produced concomitant paternalistic and controlling knowledge about them.

Interestingly, while countries situated within the anti-colonialist perspective also prioritized the subjectivity of "their group"—former and contemporary dependent territories—the anti-colonialist response here was quite different. For in contrast to the relatively distinct and consistent character of the colonialist narrative, anti-colonialists produced three overlapping but conflicting narratives, distinguished primarily by the different stances each took on the colonialist narrative. One narrative wholly accepted the central narrative produced by the colonialist perspective, including its paternalistic construction of identities, relationships between identities and knowledge about them. Against this, a second rejected a number of the major premises of the colonialist narrative, while accepting others. The consequence for the resultant discursive production of identities, relationships and knowledge was ambiguous. A wholesale rejection of the colonialist narrative and its implications for identity, power and knowledge was also evident, though this narrative was a minority perspective at best. Overall, then, when it came to softer kinship images of the nature and rationale of colonial authority and rule, the bulk of anti-colonialists largely agreed.

THE COLONIALIST NARRATIVE: A CONTINUATION OF "SOFT" KINSHIP POLITICS

Since the central interest here is the negotiation of dependency and sovereignty, I first performed a cluster analysis of the key terms/symbols political independence, freedom, autonomy, and sovereignty. As language is necessarily inexact, I examined any discussions of these terms/symbols without requiring this precise language (this is discussed in greater detail below). The terms found to cluster around these key terms were: *progress, advancement, development, evolution, higher civilization,* and *modernity* (see Figure-1). In the following statement on colonialism, for example, *development* and independence are placed in a cause-and-effect relationship where (political) *development* is seen as a precondition for independence:

> We recognize that the colonial system is useful in a great many cases; we recognize that the colonial system is the best way of slowly guiding, by gentle but ever-lengthening steps, peoples of little political education so that they can develop their political sense and become independent nations able to take their places with us here and thus constitute a truly universal assembly of nations. We know that England, for instance, may be considered a great teacher of mankind (Mr. Sourdis, Colombia, Sess 2, 1947: 689).

Likewise, in the following statement made by a colonialist speaker on the exclusive rights of administering authorities to determine the status of their territories, the terms *self-government* and *development* are positioned within a cause-and-effect relationship where *development* is seen as a precondition for obtaining *self-government*: "Only the administering Power is left in the position . . . to decide when a particular Territory under its administration has reached a stage of political development when it can be deemed to be self-governing (Sir P. Spender, Australia, Sess 9, 1954: 301)." For my purposes, I interpreted this discussion of *self-government* as a discussion of *political independence* in the sense I am interested in, and I included this discussion within my cluster analysis.

Moreover, all six of the terms that clustered around the key terms seemed to define each other, as they repeatedly appeared in close proximity to each other, appeared in conjunction with each other, appeared in cause-and-effect relationship with each other, and functioned interchangeably within statements. In the following statement on the Danish administration of the dependent territory of Greenland, for example, the terms *development* and *advancement* are joined together by the conjunction *and*: "United we will work for the further advancement and development of the Greenland community. . . . the new order will be a blessing and a benefit to the people of Greenland (Mr. Lannung, Denmark, Sess 9, 1954: 307)." Similarly, in this next statement, the terms *advancement* and *progress* seem to be defined in terms of each other: "On principle, we sympathize with the advancement of the NSGTs and consider that their political, social, and economic progress should lead them to assume full responsibility for their own destinies, in accordance with the spirit and the letter of the Charter (Mr. P. Perez, Venezuela, Sess 10, 1955: 461)."

After exploring this first cluster, I next performed a second cluster analysis concerning the key terms political dependence and lack of sovereignty. The terms that repeatedly clustered around these key terms were: *native, primitive, backward, underdeveloped, incompetent, uneducated, lack of civilization* and *simplistic civilization* (See Figure-2). The logic of this cluster seems inherent in the logic of the first cluster. That is, if development, advancement, progress, modernity, and so forth are prerequisites for political independence, it follows that the lack of these qualifying conditions is a justification for political dependence. Indeed, the most common argument made by colonialist powers and administering authorities to legitimate their rule over a dependent territory was the notion that they were in fact "preparing" and "training" their dependent territories, by virtue of imparting modernity, progress and so forth, for independence at some future date. In the following statement, for example, *lack of education* and *preparation* (which I interpret here as a synonym for *competence*) are associated with political dependence and so offered as the justification for political dependence by Brazil: "We must encourage the political education of the peoples that are not yet ready for independence, and prepare the ground for them so that they might shape their own future and direct their own affairs (Mr. De Oliveira, Brazil, Sess 12, 1957: 518)."

While this argument was usually used to legitimate continued conditions of dependency for dependent territories, there were also cases in which this logic could be turned on its head. For example, in 1946 the Union of South Africa submitted a report (and request) to the General Assembly claiming that the people of their then mandate South West Africa had expressed the desire to become "incorporated" into the Union of South Africa. As such, the Union of South Africa appealed to the now commonly pledged norm of self-representation as it claimed it only sought to give the people what they wanted. In this case, however, the alleged lack of the qualifying conditions (for independence) of development, advancement, modernity and so forth were used by opponents to argue that the international community need not recognize these expressed opinions here: "African inhabitants of South West Africa have not yet secured political autonomy or reached a stage of political development enabling them to express a considered opinion, which the Assembly could recognize, on such an important question (Mr. Lannung, Denmark, Sess 1, 1946: 1324–25)." Over the fifteen years examined, speakers who deployed these arguments more often articulated the conditions for independence (Figure 1) rather than the reasons why specific territories were in a dependent state (Figure 2). Nevertheless, both clusters relied on each other for their meaning and significance within the debates (i.e., were defined in opposition to each other, see Table 1). Considering the two in conjunction, then, colonialist discourse in these fifteen years conjoined the abstractions of progress, advancement, development, evolution, higher civilization and modernity into a singular narrative of *linear progression*. Separately and together, these abstractions were quantified and placed on a linear scale, where countries that were "higher" or "more advanced," with a quantitatively greater amount of the qualities listed therein, were associated with political independence while countries situated as "lower" on the scale, or "less advanced," and possessing quantitatively less of the qualities listed therein, were associated with political dependence.

While differential placement of territories on this scale of linear progression helped to construct central identity distinctions such as independent territories versus dependent territories, an additional set of images and symbols helped to construct appropriate kinds of *relationships* between these categories of identity. Thus, a second set of terms clustered around the key terms/symbols political independence, freedom, autonomy and sovereignty and its associated imagery of linear progression: *growth*, *maturity*, *responsibility* (including *responsibility for self*), *autonomy*, and *the ability to make decisions for self* (See Figure 3). How did this imagery facilitate certain kinds of relationships between those "higher" and those "lower" on the scale of linear progression? To start, consider how the following speakers associate level of advancement on the scale of linear progression and *responsibility*: "The struggle over backwards populations has passed from London to Washington, from Lisbon to Rio, Rome to Addis Ababa; but the situation always remains the same: a population of higher civilization, responsible for the well-being and advancement of peoples of another race (Mr. Ryckmans, Belgium, Sess 2, 1947: 672)." Similarly, "On principle, we sympathize with the advancement of the NSGTs and consider that their political, social and economic progress should lead them to assume full responsibility for their own destinies, in accordance with the spirit and the letter of the Charter (Mr. P. Perez, Venezuela, Sess 10, 1955: 461)." Hence, a higher level of advancement on the scale of linear progression meant not just the ability to be responsible for self, but also be responsible for others—for colonialist powers, anyway. Meanwhile, a lower level on the scale implied an inability to be responsible for self. Through such imagery, political independence for dependent territories was envisioned as the end product of a naturalized, evolutionary process of tutelage under a "more responsible" state until one was determined capable of "taking responsibility for self." This argument could of course also be used to justify the denial of political independence, as in the following case where the United Kingdom explained its views on political independence in a general sense:

> Democracy is a growth. . . . In the case of all the territories coming under our jurisdiction, we have been attempting, will continue to attempt, to provide all the assistance we can towards this growth—and, as I have said, it is essentially a growth. With all our cooperation and all the help we an offer, time is needed to build tradition and, to create political and public responsibility and to create the social services which are the only sound foundation for political freedom (Mr. McNeil, United Kingdom, Sess 2, 1947: 666).

This imagery was also particularly useful for both sanctioning and disciplining the behaviors of those seeking political independence. For example, the final negotiations for the territorial demarcations of Ghana occurred between the administering authority of the Gold Coast and British Togoland (Britain), the UN machinery, and a number of different and differentially interested groups (Nugent 2002), and it left numerous unificationist and nationalist groups within the affected territories unsatisfied.[1] In the following statement, consider how a great supporter of the final conditions for the independence of Ghana, the United States, associates independence with *responsibility* and *maturity* in order to legitimate one territorial and institutional arrangement and delegitimate others:

> A word about the opinion of my delegation concerning the magnificent accomplishments of the Administering Authority, the United Kingdom, with the supervision of the Trusteeship System. . . . [for the UK] has not only brought knowledge of modern medicine, education and government administration to the people under its charge, but it has also instilled in them knowledge and experience in truly democratic government, honesty in administration, impartial judicial

Contending Perspectives?

procedures . . . and many other principles and practices which form the basis for truly self-governing institutions. . . . However, we would also like to utter a word of caution. . . . there are still some West Africans who are somewhat dissatisfied with the decision of the General Assembly [regarding the boundaries of Ghana]. One of those dissident groups seeks a federal form of government in Ghana. Another seeks a form of independence for both Territories of Togoland. We would strongly urge those groups to accept the principle that political maturity seeks to achieve political change by peaceful means, and to operate on the democratic premise that minorities should yield to majorities. . . . We are confident that the soon to be independent new peoples of the new State of Ghana . . . will prove themselves to be responsible, progressive and politically mature, and thus play a major role as a strong, free and democratic State which can be an example for the entire world (Mr. Nash, United States, Sess 11, 1957: 681–82).

As in the two opposing clusters for linear progression, if this second set of terms of maturity, responsibility and so forth clustered around the key terms of political independence, autonomy, freedom and sovereignty (Figure 1), its binary opposites again seemed to cluster around the key terms political dependence and lack of sovereignty (See Figure 2 and Table 2). Particularly evident were the terms/symbols *immaturity, lack of responsibility (including responsibility for the self), dependency, wards,* and *children* (See Figure 4). In the following statement, for example, the speaker makes clear the connection between political dependence and *immaturity*: "[The terms of the Charter apply to] countries, which, by reason for their social immaturity, have not yet reached the stage of full independence (Mr. Sourdis, Columbia, Sess 2, 1947: 692)."

Even beyond the justification of political dependence, such imagery could be used to deny even "lesser" forms of self-representation. For example, when the Fourth Committee submitted a draft resolution on allowing indigenous inhabitants of NSGTs to participate in the Committee on Information from Non Self-Governing Territories (a committee formed to collect information on social, economic and educational progress in the NSGTs), the UK opposed this draft resolution with the following argument associating *lack of responsibility* with lack of sovereignty:

We do not believe that direct participation of the Non Self-Governing Territories in the work of the committee can in fact be of assistance in promoting the progress of those Territories and their peoples towards the goal set for them in Chapter XI of the Charter. . . . we wish to remain the sole judges as to the composition of our delegations to international bodies, and we consider further that membership of the committees of the General Assembly must be confined to Members of the United Nations. These committees must remain associations of sovereign and responsible governments. They cannot be converted into tribunals in which States of the United Nations can be confronted with the indigenous inhabitants of these Territories (Mr. Lloyd, United Kingdom, Sess 7, 1952: 344).

Hence, dependent territories, those on the right hand side of the binary in Table 1 and with quantitatively less "advancement," "development," "evolution," "civilization" and so on, were imaged here, above all, as *children*.[2] The easy slippage between the naturalized condition of childhood and the status of political dependence, with no "autonomy" in the existing geopolitical system, is evident in the characterization of dependent territories throughout the fifteen years examined as "minors or incomplete states," "wards of the international community," "not yet able to stand alone in the modern world," "unable to govern themselves," and "not developed enough to have an opinion that counts." Lack of sovereignty was especially figured as a state of irresponsibility. Against this, the state of independence was characterized as the ability to have "full responsibility for the self."

In contrast to this construction of dependent territories as children, administering authorities were "parents" given the "duty," "the sacred duty," and "the sacred trust" of "guiding dependent people," providing "wise guidance," "tutelage," "political education," and "teaching responsibility for the self." Administering authorities added that the colonialist system existed merely to provide an important source of tutelage for dependent territories around the world. Toward the close of the fifteenth year, when it became increasingly clear that legal decolonization was to become a reality, the notion that such tutelage should continue through the provision of United Nations programs for economic and technical assistance to newly independent states was also an important part of this discourse (this will be discussed in greater detail in the following chapter).

Hence, in the period examined, the colonialist construction of identities, relations between these identities, and knowledge about them, consisted of two primary sets of images. First, the image of *linear progression* provided an entire lexicon of quantified and linearized abstractions, including *progress, advancement, development, modernity, evolution,* and *higher civilization*—all terminology that has been identified as constituting a post-Enlightenment metanarrative (Harding 2000; Wallerstein 1996; Lyotard 1984). This metanarrative produced particular kinds of identities based on where territories

Contending Perspectives?

were located within the scale of linear progression, including "backwards," "primitive," and "less evolved" dependent territories versus "advanced," "modern," and "civilized" countries. Fundamentally, these identity distinctions posited an ontological difference[3] between different categories of humanity. For example, speaking of indigenous peoples within colonialist states as well as people in faraway dependent territories, one speaker argued:

> They are so backward that, where they do not altogether escape the administration of the State to which they belong, they are placed under a special legal or administrative constitutional system. . . . Furthermore, they are totally different, not only by reason of their primitive character, but also race, language and culture from the peoples from whom the government administering the State emanates (Mr. V. Langenhove, Belgium, Sess 8, 1953: 310).

But location on the scale of linear progression does not necessarily explain the hierarchical sets of relationships *between* these identities that colonialist discourse legitimated. To understand this, we must turn to a second set of images, that of kinship relations. That is, this hierarchical metaphor of kinship, where more "childlike" and "incompetent" dependent territories were distinguished from "wiser" and "more competent" administering authorities, produced and indeed naturalized the paternalistic relationship of tutelage and guidance between them:

> We in the United Kingdom are proud of what we are doing in the colonial field. It is with great pride that we have been able to bring various members of the British Commonwealth and Empire along the road to full self-government. We feel the same pride that a parent feels when he sees his children going out into the world and making their own way. Sometimes the children, when they are given the key to the door, may kick over the traces a little bit but we do not mind that any more than the parent does. More often we have seen growing affection between ourselves and our children and we look forward to an extension of that process. We shall feel increasing pride as we see ourselves able to bring more and more of the dependent peoples who look up to us, along this road to self-government and independence (Mr. Thomas, United Kingdom, Sess 1, 1946: 1271).

Ultimately, in constructing these identity distinctions and the relationships between them, these two sets of images simultaneously produced the knowledge that while the dependent territories were children "who were not developed enough to have an opinion that counts," that the guidance of the more responsible administering authorities could bring them into "growth" and "maturity" (See Table 3). In doing so, they continued the softer kinship politics of colonial rule, evident earlier in the eighteenth century, into the mid-twentieth.

CONFLICTING ANTI-COLONIALIST NARRATIVES: NECESSARY GUIDANCE OR IMPERIALIST DOMINATION?

While this language of paternalistic rule for the beneficence of dependent peoples was certainly not new, then, what the fifteen-year period examined here reveals is that the anti-colonialist response was ambivalent at best. It consisted of two primary responses, along with a minor third response.[4] Of these, the first accepted the colonialist narrative wholesale, including its identity distinctions of "backwards, dependent territories" versus "advanced, independent territories," the paternalistic kinship relationship between these identities, and (colonialist) knowledge about them. In contrast, the second anti-colonialist narrative also accepted the identity distinctions of "backwards, dependent territories" versus "advanced, independent territories" produced by the colonialist narrative. However, not only did it reject the purported relations of paternalistic kinship between these identities but also the (colonialist) knowledge produced about these identities. The third anti-colonialist response rejected all three elements of the discourse under consideration: the colonialist production of dependent territories as "backwards" and independent territories as "advanced," the paternalistic kinship relationship between the two, as well as any (colonialist) knowledge about them (See Table-4).

A key term within especially the first two of these anti-colonialist discourses was that of *backwardness*. For these discourses, thus, I performed a cluster analysis of backwardness (see Figures 5 and 6), which reveals that each actually constructed the *meaning* of backwardness differently. Given these different meanings, each then also proposed very different solutions to the task of eliminating this backwardness. For the first response, what I term the "colonialist" anti-colonialist narrative, backwardness was tantamount to lack of development, advancement, progress and evolution, or a lower status on the scale of linear progression. In consequence, this approach argued that dependent territories must be prepared for independence, and so must be developed, advanced, and must be helped to evolve. This colonialist, anti-colonialist narrative, thus, also appealed to both sets of images that the colonialist narrative deployed. That is, it joined images of linear progression together with images of hierarchical kinship relations.

Contending Perspectives?

Describing the duties of the Trusteeship System, one speaker in the anti-colonialist camp proclaimed:

> The trusteeship system must raise these at present backward territories to such level that they should be able to take their place in the family of nations as self-governing or independent peoples. The peoples of these territories have an equal right to enjoy the benefits of contemporary civilization and to improve their welfare. . . . our first concern for the backwards peoples of Trust territories is to ensure that these possibilities are realized. . . . at which period these territories would be sufficiently mature enough to receive self-government and independence (Mr. Novikov, USSR, Sess 2, 1947: 1278).

Of course, the USSR did not really identify as a (former) dependent territory, and perhaps its own location as a global power conditioned its view. However, even territories fully identified with the (former) dependent territory status responded similarly:

> The Charter, with the object of leading the backward peoples step by step towards the light and towards an evolution which will enable them to take their responsibility for their social and political destinies upon their shoulders [and]. . . . the Trusteeship System [are] more in keeping with our modern ideas, which require that the peoples of the world should rise from one stage of civilization to the next (Mr. Vieux, Haiti, Sess2, 1947: 611).

But if this anti-colonialist response to the colonialist narrative adopted this narrative wholesale, why is it a distinct discourse? Why is it an *anti-colonialist* discourse? As mentioned earlier, the two overarching perspectives, "colonialist" and "anti-colonialist," were determined in terms of the sorts of arguments they advanced, the sorts of appeals their arguments were based on, and who they supported in the debates. Perhaps the most decisive factor was that the first consistently prioritized the subjectivity and the rights of the colonialist countries, while the second did the same for dependent territories. Hence, for the "colonialist," anti-colonialist discourse, appeals to alleviate conditions of backwardness were always made from the perspective of the dependent territories and with an eye to advancing the cause of moving the independence process forward. One of its most important maneuvers was to take the colonialist narrative's discursive construction of "the duty of a higher civilization towards a lower civilization" and transform it into obligations that the administering authority had for increasing the material welfare of inhabitants in dependent territories and for advancing these territories towards political independence. In contrast, colonialist discourse consistently prioritized the subjectivity and rights of the colonialist countries, or administering authorities. Typically hinging on the exclusive and sovereign right of these authorities to administer their territories and affairs as they sought fit, on a concrete level these tended to hinder the process towards independence. The consequence was that while the colonialist countries advanced a conservative colonialist discourse aimed at preserving their rights and privileges, the first anti-colonialist approach advanced a colonialist discourse aimed at social change.

Furthermore, the peculiar position of an anti-colonialist subject advancing colonialist knowledge produced particular kinds of tensions within this discourse. First, there was an ambiguous relationship to the cultural and racial hierarchy inherent in the colonialist images of linear progression and kinship. The notions that "backward populations, most of whom had many centuries of their own type of civilization" after independence, may "return to [the] rich cultural heritage of these civilizations" and indeed, their civilizations "will enrich the whole world" were joined with the idea that "without imperialism, [these civilizations] would presumably have remained primitive." Second, although there was an overwhelming reliance on the argument that the "backward peoples must be lead, evolve, so that they can take responsibility for their own social and political destinies," or that they required "guidance, assistance to reach [the right] level for self-determination," this was *not* the colonialist appeal of a Belgium, a Union of South Africa or a France. Hence, this discourse added: "countries need to develop themselves economically, politically, socially, and culturally to the most advanced conception of modern civilization . . . [as] this is the only guarantee of freedom." Thus the colonialist, anti-colonialist appeal was not merely for linear progression, but for the conditions of freedom in a world of colonial realities. Third, the UN Charter made certain obligations for progress in administered territories incumbent upon administering authorities. While in the basic colonialist narrative, these requirements were read as "assistance for progress" that flowed from more advanced territories to less advanced territories, for the colonialist anti-colonial appeal, they were also read as conditions only enabled by, and hence stemming from, *the international community*: "sovereignty is lying latent in the people, and [this territory] should come under the tutelage of the world community (Mr. Menon, India, Sess 8, 1953: 324)." Similarly, in the following example, the system that matched a dependent territory with an administering authority was a global system: "The essence of the mandate system was to place certain backwards peoples under the guardianship of the League of Nations and under the supervision of the conscience of the world. . . . the responsibilities of the League of Nations in the wide field of moral authority have been assumed by the United Nations (Mrs. Pandit, India, Sess 2, 1947: 598)." Ultimately, such an interpretation of the UN trusteeship system muted (the significance of) the hierarchical relations inherent therein.

Finally, there was also an ambivalent analysis of the nature of post-independence assistance. Hence, the argument that after independence, domination would be "over" and that newly independent countries "will need help . . . aid . . . economic development" co-existed with the argument that beyond political independence, the hierarchical relations of economic dependency would continue to be problematic.

Ultimately, then, while the colonialist, anti-colonialist narrative certainly drew on the identity distinctions, hierarchical relations and knowledge inherent in the colonialist narrative, this discourse was much more cognizant of the power relations inherent therein.

While the colonialist, anti-colonialist narrative deployed the notion of backwardness—though from its unique location—in contrast, the second anti-colonialist narrative defined backwardness very differently. For this perspective, backwardness was indeed about lack of development (lower position on the scale of linear progression), which was also connected to a lack of political independence. However, the significant difference here was where this approach placed *the cause* of dependent territories' lower placement on the evolutionary scale. While the first anti-colonialist narrative accepted that dependent territories were not advanced, were in fact dependent because they were not advanced, and required tutelage, the second argued that while dependent territories certainly lacked advancement, that this lack of advancement was actually not an inherent condition but caused by the exogenous factor of European colonialism. Hence, this approach argued, "colonialism is not civilization," that "before colonialism, Africans were highly developed," that "colonialism [itself] is bad for development," is indeed "emasculating," and that there is a "new kind of backwardness [that of] those who continue colonialism."[5] From this perspective, the "civilizing mission" or "white man's burden" was seen as mere "paternalism," as a "guise" and an "excuse." One speaker argued: "you've been claiming to train us for 350 years, and haven't done so." Another claimed:

> At this moment, over 100 million of our brothers and sisters are still experiencing the horrors of a system which has inflicted indescribable sufferings on the dependent peoples. . . . [It was] brute force or force cleverly disguised in the best paternalistic traditions. . . . a

> force designed primarily to hold back the development of the colonial peoples whenever development was not seen to be essential in one form or another, to the development of the colonial interests. It was therefore basically a force opposed to the people's development . . . [and it] did not allow people to develop except in so far as their development was essential to its own existence. . . . So the colonial system, by the support it gave to the forces of social reaction in subject territories and to tribal classes and hierarchies which would otherwise have disappeared, distorted the dynamic working of the forces of change and froze political and social development at the primitive stage. This is why colonialism must be held responsible for the considerable backwardness of the dependent countries in relation to the general progress throughout the world, and for the tragic gulf between these dependent countries and the industrialized countries (Mr. Vakil, Iran, Sess 15, 1960: 994–998).

Furthermore, because this discourse dissociated colonialism from "development," this approach could deconstruct the notion of advancement or progress on a linear scale as the *precondition* for independence. This discourse thus inverted the relationship between progress on a linear scale and independence, arguing that progress did not so much lead to independence, but rather, that "independence would lead to progress" or "development." With regard to the image of kinship, it argued that "independence would lead to maturity," and that "independence is the best way to mature the people."

In this vein, this narrative was also much more critical of international relationships after legal decolonization than was the colonialist, anti-colonialist narrative. While the first made some note of the potentially problematic aspects of continuing relationships of economic development after independence, this second anti-colonialist narrative was much more prolific on these dangers. It repeatedly made reference to the "new colonialisms," "neo-colonialism," "new dangers," "new forms of colonialism beyond political domination," "the new type of colonialism under the guise of liberation," and the "conquest of the mind." Specifically, it referred here to new kinds of economic relationships formed between older colonialist powers and newly independent territories, the ideological and other power relationships inherent in economic assistance to newly independent territories, the military alliances of various powers, the military bases that began to dot the world as a result of the Cold War, and the emerging "spheres of influence" of various older and newer powers.

Once the practices of colonialist countries, or administering authorities, were incorporated into the narrative in this way and once the image of

Contending Perspectives?

linear progression was dismantled, colonialism could no longer be about "paternalistic guidance" or "tutelage." Hence the image of hierarchical kinship was also deconstructed. One speaker argued, "We are of age from the moment when we have the full use of our freedom. There are no countries which are under age when it comes to the exercise of freedom (Mr. Kaka, Niger, Sess15, 1960: 1125)." Youth could even be a positive quality from within this perspective, about a closer association with a more authentic self, where political independence would lead to nations being "reborn." Now, this approach argued that "none of us are too immature for independence," and that "notions of immaturity are about racism." Following the colonialist link between kinship status and political status, it argued that hence, "dependent territories do not need guidance, " that "every territory is capable of governing itself" and "can develop itself," that immaturity "should not be the pretext for delaying independence" and that "guidance is just a justification of colonialism."

In sum, while this narrative accepted the identity distinctions of backwards versus advanced of the colonialist narrative, it rejected the purported relationship between these identities as well as the colonialist knowledge about them. In the process, it redefined the significance of those identity distinctions themselves.

Against both of these perspectives, the third anti-colonialist narrative rejected the idea that the dependent territories were somehow backwards. For example,

> The former colonial peoples and those who are still not independent have their own cultures, their own civilizations, their own traditions, their own languages and their own customs. They are not only proud of their heritage but they want to maintain it. They are determined to preserve it and to develop it in their own way. . . . If some colonial Power would venture to say it . . . that some colonial territories are not prepared to assume independence, then we must treat with the greatest suspicion the assertion advance by that Power (Mr. Asha, United Arab Republic, Sess 15, 1960: 1049).

Hence, this narrative also rejected the notion that the territories required any sort of tutelage or that there was any relationship between "development" and political independence: "Complete, unconditional and immediate liquidation of colonialism in all its manifestations must be our irreducible decision. . . . Let the parties concerned begin immediate negotiations to transfer full sovereignty and authority to the rightful people without delay and let us welcome them in this world Organization (Mr.

Asha, United Arab Republic, Sess 15, 1960: 1050)." It necessarily, then, also rejected colonialist knowledge about these entities, and thus ultimately, this discourse rejected *each element* of the colonialist discourse. Relative to the other two, however, this argument was quite rare in the fifteen-year period under discussion.

PATTERNS OF ARGUMENT

Attempting to "quantify" or "compare" discourse is a tricky business—particularly when contending images develop in relation to each, have no definite boundaries, and notoriously defy quantification. With these strong qualifications in mind, I attempted to gauge the relative strength of particular imagery by comparing the frequency of different associational clusters over time and by institutional-discursive context. Speakers engaged in discussions about colonialism and decolonization in three institutional-discursive contexts: through their discussions on Non Self-Governing Territories (NSGTs), through their discussions on Trust Territories (Trusts), and through their discussions on the Declaration on the Granting of Independence to Colonial Countries and Peoples (Declaration). The first two sets of discussions involved the two statuses allowed dependent territories within the machinery of the UN, with the Trust status incorporating territories into the Trusteeship System and explicitly seeking to "prepare" dependent territories for political independence, and the NSGT status merely maintaining a status quo. The third discussion regarded a draft resolution on the general problem of dependent territories, which sought to initiate the process of legal decolonization across both statuses of dependent territories. While the first two sets of discussions took place largely during the first fourteen years of debate examined, the third took place in the final year.

Before comparing associational clusters over the fifteen years of debate, it must be reiterated that throughout the period, the colonialist discussions occurred from the perspective of the administering authorities, while the anti-colonialist discussions occurred from the perspective of dependent territories. In terms of colonialist discourse, despite attacks from a growing anti-colonialist contingency, it remained remarkably consistent in its espousal of the colonialist narrative identified above, including its images of linear progression and hierarchical kinship relations. This included a discursive construction of dependent territories as having a lower status on the scale of linear progression and thus lacking in a number of linearized abstractions such as advancement and development, where such abstractions were general concepts incorporating political, social-cultural, and economic elements. Through this imagery, speakers engaged in a discursive construction of self as further along this scale of linear progression, and possessing the "sacred duty" or the "peculiar duty" of helping dependent territories along as well.

Anti-colonialist discourse largely accepted this notion of lack of progression or backwardness—or at least failed to challenge it. This discourse alternated over the fifteen-year period between the arguments that dependent territories required help to progress from territories further along the scale of linear progression and that dependent territories were only lower on the scale of linear progression because of the experience of colonialism. While the first was evident particularly in the case of NSGTs, in the case of Trusts, it was challenged largely by the argument that the administering authority, given its "sacred trust," was not doing a proper job, or that it was violating its sacred trust. In these discussions on Trusts, then, speakers introduced the crucial question of *who* should really have the task of generating progress for dependent territories: administering authorities or the UN?

These discussions became more complex in the last year of debate, which was also the year of the discussions on and passage of the Declaration on the Granting of Independence to Colonial Countries and Peoples, the document which would initiate legal decolonization. During this final year, the anti-colonialist challenge to the colonialist narrative developed some new dimensions. While it still articulated colonialist notions of backwardness, these articulations were overwhelmed by the argument that the backwards conditions of the dependent territories were due to colonialism, imperialism and exploitation and by the argument that the dependent territories actually were not backwards at all. Instead, against the colonialist narrative of hierarchical kinship relations, anti-colonialist argument demanded non-hierarchical kinship relations between territories—relations between more or less equal *brothers*[6] rather than between *parents and children*. They demanded cultural autonomy and a return of masculine dignity. And, they insisted there was only one dimension in which they required assistance: the economic dimension. Hence, they argued for economic development.

CONCLUSION

The narrative contentions explored in this chapter demonstrate that while colonialists generally continued to articulate the "soft" kinship politics that emerged first in the eighteenth century, anti-colonialists, for the most part, failed to challenge this logic. Regarding the colonialist perspective, a fairly consistent and distinct colonialist narrative brought together the images of linear progression and kinship to construct the ontologically distinct identity categories of "backwards" versus "advanced" territories, paternalistic relationships between these identities, and colonialist knowledge about them. In contrast, a much more conflicted anti-colonialist discourse produced three narratives, two of which accepted major premises of the colonialist narrative. While a third completely dismantled this narrative, it was rare.

Given this great overlap in the understanding of the nature of dependent territories, as well as what advancement looked like, how did different speakers ultimately seek to resolve the colonial problematic? How did they address issues of the colonialist construction of space, differential personhood and embodiment? Of race, gender, culture, progress, freedom? What would the new international community that resulted from these conversations look like? It is to these questions that I now turn.

Chapter Five
Masculinity, Time and Brotherhood: Resolving the Colonial Problematic

> *Nationalist texts were addressed both to "the people" who were said to constitute the nation and to the colonial masters whose claim to rule nationalism questioned. To both, nationalism sought to demonstrate the falsity of the colonial claim that the backward peoples were culturally incapable of ruling themselves in the conditions of the modern world. Nationalism denied the alleged inferiority of the colonized people; it also asserted that a backward nation could "modernize" itself while retaining its cultural identity. It thus produced a discourse in which, even as it challenged the colonial claim to political domination, it also accepted the very intellectual premises of "modernity" on which colonial domination was based.*
> —Partha Chatterjee, 1986

In the fall of 1960, anti-colonialists moved beyond the particulars of Trusts and NSGTs and introduced a debate on the general problematic of colonialism, initiating a set of conversations that would end with the passage of the 1960 Declaration on the Granting of Independence to Colonial Countries and Peoples and thus, the onset of legal decolonization. In conventional understanding, this shift signaled a transition from the exclusions of the colonial era to a progressively more democratic era (Cassese 1995; Theodoropoulos 1988). If international law until now had been based on the systematic denial of the subjectivity of various "others" (see Chapter 1), as one scholar put it, now, both individuals as well as liberation movements could claim subjectivity in some limited sense. This transformation was especially signified by the decision of the international community, after 1960, to attribute a heightened status to a select group of principles considered more fundamental than other general principles of international law: those of *jus cogens*. Theoretically, these meant that now, no state was to deviate from the right of self-determination, or of the values of peace and human rights—even if this was at the expense of competing national interests (Cassese 1995).[1]

But did the 1960 Declaration really signal democratic progress in the sense indicated above? How did it relate to colonialist constructions of space, identity and international community—particularly the racial, cultural and sexual dimensions of these constructions? If, as I argued in Chapter 3, anti-colonialists disrupted the hierarchies of colonialist kinship politics especially with an appeal to the moral and to brotherhood, how did this discourse relate to the final "resolution" of the colonial problematic? Furthermore, what difference did it make that this resistance politics was conditioned on entering the nation-state system—that it could only be articulated by (representatives of) states (see Chapter 4)? And perhaps most important of all, how did the fact that most anti-colonialists actually accepted some of the central premises of the colonialist narrative—specifically, colonialist understandings of progress, modernity and development (see Chapter 5)—figure into all of this? In other words, what sort of a shift did the 1960 document really signify? And for whom?

In this final analysis chapter, I argue that the ambiguities and complexities of the anti-colonialist critique elaborated in the previous three chapters critically shaped the way the colonial problematic was finally resolved. As the emerging identity of Asia-Africa continued to develop as a masculinist, anti-colonialist, transnational entity united in its unique moral culture and its brotherhood (see Chapter 3), this identity made itself felt in the UNGA by 1960 in particular ways. Specifically, anti-colonialists offered a three-tiered argument that can be directly linked to the Asia-Africa conferences examined in Chapter 3. First, they argued that colonialism emasculates grown men and that decolonization is required to restore lost manhood. Second, they incorporated a critical temporal dimension: if colonialism was ever justified because the colonized were once "children," this is no longer the case. Time has passed and the children have grown into adult men. Third, they argued that thus, the appropriate relationship between territories must no longer be as between "parents and children," but rather, as between "brothers." To the colonialist construction of hierarchical space, identity and international community based on paternalistic kinship relations, then, anti-colonialists advanced the notion of a "more equitable," masculinist set of international relations based on fraternal kinship relations, or brotherhood.

At the same time that they launched this challenge to legal colonialism, however, anti-colonialists' acceptance of colonialist definitions of progress, modernity and development meant that they also accepted the designation of their peoples/states as somehow "behind" on economic, scientific and technical, social, and other fronts. Thus, while they fought to end formal political tutelage, they nevertheless would actively pursue such tutelage in the so-called, "non-political" scientific and technical, economic, social, and even cultural arenas. Indeed, as representatives of newly independent states, it seems they only asked for a shift in the source of this tutelage (or in the era of the UN, of development assistance) from paternalistic colonialist powers to a "more equitable" international community of brothers.

In what follows, I discuss this contradictory resolution of the colonial problematic in three steps. First, I relate patterns of appeal in this last year of argument, making the case that while colonialist speakers resorted still to the colonialist logic of kinship politics, anti-colonialists responded with an insistence on masculinity, time and brotherhood. However, given their contradictions regarding "political" versus "non-political" forms of tutelage, next, I more fully explore this ambiguous positioning. Starting not in 1960 but from 1946, I examine anti-colonialists' efforts in this regard in different branches of the UN system, arguing that while seeking an end to political tutelage, they actually provided a key impetus for the elaboration of the UN's machinery for "development assistance" in economic, educational, social, cultural and other "dimensions of development." Indeed, such development assistance from the UN was a key ingredient in their nation- and state-building efforts. But how could anti-colonialists define freedom as the condition of sovereign statehood and then seek assistance on how to be proper states? Finally, I explore this contradictory orientation to the politics of dependency and tutelage further from the perspective of the culture of the state-system. Specifically, I argue that once freedom was defined in the GA as the attainment of statehood—as inclusion via the nation-state form into the system of nation-states—newly independent states were compelled to act "like states." Thus, they were obliged to perform and practice their statehood within certain culturally acceptable parameters, including the pursuit of progress, modernity and development. While there is certainly some room for negotiating precisely what constitutes the conditions of progress, modernity and development, anti-colonialist activity in the UN for the period examined demonstrates that they largely accepted the definitions provided by the colonialist narrative.

Thus, the fifteen-year period examined here was not generally a transition to a "more democratic" era. Rather, it signified a particular renegotiation of the racial, cultural and gender hierarchies of the colonialist narrative. Specifically, to especially the racial and cultural hierarchies of this narrative, anti-colonialists responded with masculinity—with a retreat to gender. This resort to masculinity illustrates that rather than launching a wholesale challenge to the multifaceted, paternalistic logic of kinship, anti-colonialists were willing to merely reconfigure this hierarchy so that "postcolonial" men—as brothers—could be included. Ultimately, this masculinist politics of inclusion certainly provided access to the nation-state system. However, it left the hierarchies of the colonialist narrative largely intact.

"RESOLVING THE COLONIAL PROBLEMATIC": DEBATE IN THE FINAL YEAR

On September 23 1960, Nikita S. Khrushchev, then Chairman of the Council of the Ministers of the USSR, asked for the inclusion on the GA agenda of "the complete and final liquidation of peoples languishing in colonial bondage," submitting to the GA for consideration the Draft Declaration on the Granting of Independence to Colonial Countries and Peoples (Kruschev, United Nations, 1960). As discussed in Chapter 4, of course, this only meant European and United States' colonialism. Fearing a misappropriation of the decolonization issue in the Cold War climate, on November 28th Asia-Africa advanced an alternative to the Soviet draft with the explicit aim of finding "formulae and solutions which would be acceptable to the greatest possible number of delegations (United Nations 1960)." Initially sponsored by a group of 26 Asian and African countries, eventually the group of sponsors grew to 48 (United Nations 1960). In addition, several amendments to the two drafts on decolonization also emerged. The discussion on this series of items lasted for over two weeks, comprising debate on the general issue of decolonization within a field of possibilities. During these conversations, over 70 delegations expounded on matters of colonialism and decolonization, oppression, gender, and the nature of racial and cultural difference. Ultimately, these conversations ended with the adoption of the Asia-Africa version of the declaration on December 14 1960, thus formally "resolving" the colonial problematic and initiating the process of legal decolonization.

In these conversations, some speakers attempted to expand the definition of the colonial problematic, pointing to the narrative of the "white man's burden," the role of capitalism, and the contemporary military and ideological struggle that was carving up the globe into "spheres of influence." There was also some discussion of the scope of this problematic, with speakers from different ideological locations pointing to not just "land-grabbing colonialism" but also to "ideological colonialism" and "neo-colonialism," as well as to the practices of particular states such as the United States, the USSR, China and Israel. Despite such attempts to extend the parameters of the discussion, argument nevertheless tended to revert

Masculinity, Time and Brotherhood

to the colonial problematic as constructed by Asia-Africa (see Chapter 4), with the targeted European colonial powers reacting in defense. In this last year, anti-colonialists especially made appeals to *International Cooperation (United Nations)*, *Independence/Representation*, and *Peace* (see Chart 1 for a comparison of appeals for NSGTs, Trusts and the Declaration). For their part, European colonialists and their allies appealed to the colonialist narrative (i.e., the appeal of *Colonialism not negative*) as never before:

> When the Portuguese nation was set up and extended over other continents, usually on unoccupied or unused land, some very striking features became apparent: to those peoples which had not yet conceived the idea of a homeland, it offered one; it also offered a common language, the guarantee of peace and an organized economic and community life (Mr. Garin, Portugal, Sess 15, 1960: 1115).

> The colonization process was the outcome of Europe's tremendous impulse for expansion at the end of the Middle Ages. There is no doubt that the "little peninsula backing on Asia" as it was once described, comprised within its narrow confines a collection of peoples gifted with the most extraordinary qualities of intelligence, inventiveness, and enterprise that mankind has ever known . . . [who] soon found the territory assigned to them too small and went off to the four corners of the earth in search of new theatres for the expansion of their creative genius. That was the beginning of the great colonial adventure. . . . [Today, we hear critiques of this but in English and French. To these critiques, then, we say that] when a people has received from another country such a valuable treasure as language, it cannot assert that it owes that country nothing. . . . [moreover, there have been other benefits:] the victorious campaign against disease, the educational work of the missionaries and the constructive efforts of technicians (Mr. Amadeo, Argentina, Sess 15, 1960: 1006).

This colonialist narrative, as discussed in Chapter 5, combined notions of linear progression and hierarchical kinship relations, where entities more advanced on the scale of linear progression were to teach, guide and "bring to maturation" entities less advanced. Michael Adas (2004) argues that the horrors of war during World War I especially catalyzed the critique of this discourse among many thinkers in Asia and Africa, undermining its moral authority and its ideals of racial superiority. In its challenge to this narrative in the GA, then, Asia-Africa reframed this tutelage as "paternalism," a "pretext," a "guise," a "myth," and even "neo-slavery." Speakers pointed to the problematic racial and cultural distinctions on which colonialist practices were based:

> It was in the nineteenth century that a very famous international lawyer, Professor Lorimer, Professor of International Law at Edinburgh, divided the world into three kinds of humanity. There was civilized humanity, as represented by Europe; there was barbarous humanity, as represented by a few Powers like Turkey and Iraq . . . and there was savage humanity, which covered the rest of Africa and Asia (Mr. Perera, Ceylon, Sess 15, 1960: 1001).

Mr. Perera argued that these distinctions led to the different types of mandates within the League of Nations Mandates System as well as the different kinds of territories in the UN Trusteeship System. Other speakers added that such practices, far from teaching or imparting civilization, violated the norms of civilization, imposing foreign practices on cultures that already had their own traditions[2]:

> The colonial powers have all contended that the purpose of their remaining in other peoples' lands is to spread their language and culture to the peoples of these colonies . . . to carry out a "civilizing mission." . . . The former colonial peoples and those who are still not independent have their own cultures, their own civilizations, their own traditions, their own languages (Mr. Asha, United Arab Republic, Sess 15, 1960: 1048).

Added others, "There is an infinite distance between colonization and civilization (Mr. Aw, Mali, Sess 15, 1960: 1965)" and "Civilization is not a peculiar monopoly of any part of the world. All we mean by making this distinction is that those of us who speak about it probably do not understand other peoples' civilizations (Mr. Menon, India, Sess 15, 1960: 1242)."

As discussed in previous chapters, the colonialist narrative naturalized unequal relations between "more and less advanced" entities with the hierarchical nature metaphors of the body and family. In its challenge to this narrative, Asia-Africa introduced three new elements into the discussion. First, it invoked *masculinity* with the argument that hierarchical kinship relations were unjust because the recipients of this tutelage were not children but rather, fully growth men. Hence, colonial rule did not derive from nature but rather, constituted a violation of nature. In the GA, then, anticolonialists used the same nature metaphors of the body and family as the colonialist narrative, but depicted their "violation" through the language of

Masculinity, Time and Brotherhood

"unnatural" family or bodily disease. One argued that colonialism was so extensive that "contrary to the rules of creation, the child was manifoldly bigger than its parents, indeed all the parents put together (Mr. Shukairy, Saudi Arabia, Sess 15, 1960: 1013)." Others added, "the remnants of this system in present-day society stand out like suspicious and unhealthy cancerous growths (Mr. Djordja, Yugoslavia, Sess 15, 1960: 1026)," a "cancer on the body politic of the world (Mr. Menon, India, Sess 15, 1960: 1244)." As a violation, this unnatural rule was a "moral prostitution. . . . a rape (Mr. Perera, Ceylon, Sess 15, 1960: 1001)" that took "the manhood out of those exposed to it (Mr. Dosumu-Johnson, Liberia, Sess 15, 1960:1069)" and that deprived "the man living under colonialism of his identity and human dignity (Mr. Vakil, Iran, Sess 15, 1960: 990)." Decolonization, from this perspective, would help to redress this emasculation. One speaker described having freedom returned after being colonized, for instance, as once again being "master in [one'] . . . own house (Mr. Thors, Iceland, Sess 15, 1960: 1147)." Speaking of the decolonization process already underway, another argued that "nearly a thousand million men have recovered their outraged dignity and freedom (Mr. Champassak, Laos, Sess 15, 1960: 1108)."

On perhaps an even more fundamental level, the notion of differential position on a scale of linear progression, imparting greater and lesser quantities of advancement, as well as development, modernity and so forth, relied on a certain temporality, as discussed in Chapter 5. Advanced, modern and developed peoples were the peoples of the present and future, while "backwards," "under-developed" and "traditional" people belonged to the past (McClintock 1995). This temporality is clearly demonstrated in the following statement by Australia on a territory it is "responsible" for, Eastern New Guinea:

> Eastern New Guinea has long been isolated from the rest of the world. Its people had no contacts with other peoples for hundreds of years. . . . they have lived primitive lives. . . . they were dominated by sorcery and witchcraft. In many cases they practiced cannibalism. These are not people who, until recent times, formed a nation with a highly sophisticated political or social structure. I am not one of those who confuses civilization with Western ways of living, but [imagine] peoples living with primitive lives, with limited traditions, and with, up to the present, limited opportunities . . . this shows the immensity of the task. It is a question of bringing men in a few years from the stone-age up to the modern complicated civilization. . . . they have quite a way to go before they can take their place among us. This view is

> not based on any feeling of racial superiority. . . . Australia has had the task . . . of bringing these people into the twentieth century (Mr. Plimsoll, Australia, Sess 15, 1960: 1091).

Dependent territories like Eastern New Guinea, thus, were "behind" and needed to be sufficiently advanced along the scale of linear progression to be able to have political independence and be "responsible for themselves." Moreover, this progression was to be guided by colonialist powers or administering authorities in a gradual, controlled manner. A second key element in the anti-colonialist challenge, then, was a critique of this temporality. Again and again, in this last year, anti-colonialists insisted that the time for decolonization could no longer be delayed with such gradualism—that the *time for decolonization was now:* "Here we are, the peoples of the United Nations, giving historic expression to this universal moment of truth. It is a moment between a past of inequality and a glorious future. . . . an irresistible and irreversible movement of peoples towards full emancipation (Mr. Vakil, Iran, Sess 15, 1960: 990)." Speakers argued that this was a "historic moment," "a great landmark in the history of the world," "the opening of a new and decisive era in universal evolution," "a new page in the history of mankind," and "a new era in the history of human society."

Finally, building on both *masculinity* and *time*, anti-colonialists argued that if the hierarchical international community of the colonial era relied on unnatural, paternal kinship relations between grown men, then the time had come for a transition to a more "natural and equitable international community"—made up of more equal, fraternal kinship relations between men—in effect, *brotherhood*. In this regard, some speakers also mentioned the comparable image of sisterhood. Nevertheless, there was an overwhelming focus on brotherhood as opposed to sisterhood, which should perhaps not be surprising considering the simultaneous attempt to recover "lost masculinity." Indeed, both the elements of the recovery of lost *masculinity* and of *brotherhood* relied on each other. For example, one speaker argued, "men are born free, and no man should be allowed to enslave man. This is not only right and just, but it is the dictate of human brotherhood under the fatherhood of God (Mr. Shukairy, Saudi Arabia, Sess 15, 1960: 1014)." Another added, "our age is one of co-operation among free and equal peoples and men. More still, it is an age of human brotherhood, association and mutual assistance (Mr. Ammoun, Lebanon, Sess 15, 1960: 1162)." These statements on masculinity and brotherhood point to an important dimension of this renegotiation of the colonial problematic: in these conversations, both the colonial experience and the freedom and

Masculinity, Time and Brotherhood

equality being fought for were masculinized. Even the mention of women did not negate this masculinization:

> Where the soldier stands in defense of the honor of his nation, from the exile where the patriot is deported from his fatherland, from the shabby place where the refugee is expelled from his home, from the prison where the hero languishes, and this cry for freedom comes from every man and every woman. . . . fraternity. . . . how pleasant life will be when nations live in real brotherhood (Mr. Rifa'I, Jordan, Sess 15, 1960: 1057).

In the GA, anti-colonialist and newly independent countries also used the notion of brotherhood to connote association with ongoing movements for independence. With this language, then, speakers transformed the struggles of still dependent peoples into the masculine battles of "our brethren in Africa," "our Algerian brothers," and "our brothers in courage."

Hence, to the paternalism of the colonialist narrative, the anti-colonialist challenge consisted of masculinity, time, and brotherhood. Interestingly, however, this challenge was somewhat ambiguous. For while on the one hand, speakers critiqued the notion of political tutelage with the argument that "there was no country in the world that had not always been capable of governing itself," on the other, they also argued that territories required "preparation" and "political maturity" before they could be granted political independence. Likewise, while for some anti-colonialists every territory was "always already of age," for others, the once young territories had only now come "of age" and so only now deserved freedom. Describing his own country of India, one speaker transformed one of the oldest civilizations in existence into a "young country," and the representative from Ghana described his country as at once "ancient" and "reborn." This ambiguous relationship of many anti-colonialists to the imagery of birth, youth, growth, tutelage and preparation, and adulthood, clearly emergent from the hierarchical kinship image, is especially evident in the following speech:

> Every child, in his youth, inexperience and lack of initiative, lives under the wing of his parents. When he grows up, he leaves his parents' home, goes out into the world and makes a home for himself far from those who reared him, because he feels free in his person and personality. Then should the colonized, ever submissive, have his freedom rationed by his colonizer?. . . . Not long ago we were being poisoned with the sugared venom of colonialism. . . . but we have outgrown the stage

of servitude, we are no longer credulous children who can be made to believe in Santa Claus forever. Those days are over, and colonialism has been outstripped at every point (Mr. Lheyet-Gaboka, Congo (Brazzaville), Sess 15, 1960: 1178).

Here, the speaker moves between the image of a (male) child that grows up and obtains his freedom to the notion of a fleeting credulity or gullibility which is now decidedly gone.

What are the implications of this ambiguity? Did anti-colonialists fully challenge the paternalism of the colonialist narrative? Or perhaps better stated, what really was the nature of their challenge? Examining the debates on the draft declaration on independence, it appears that while the anti-colonialist critique of paternalism was especially aimed at the notion of "political" tutelage, this critique was not meant for other arenas deemed separate from the political arena. Hence, some newly independent countries insisted that though the time had come for an end to political tutelage, that they nevertheless continued to require economic or technical assistance:

> Assistance and co-operation are indispensable for the progress of underdeveloped countries, [as] the gap separating them from the technically advanced countries can only be bridged if loyal cooperation is established within the framework of national independence for all countries, for the task of transforming and industrializing the economic structures of backward countries (Mr. Ismaël, Guinea, Sess 15, 1960: 1083).

Moreover, this assistance had nothing to do with colonial domination, as the Soviets, for instance, insisted:

> We badly need international technical assistance. . . . as we listened to some representatives, however, we received the impression that these needs were sometimes overlooked, and that the provision of assistance to under-developed countries like ours was sometimes regarded as a manifestation of neo-colonialism in that it crystallized the inequality between the country assisting and the country assisted. I therefore wish to state, on my country's behalf, that economic aid or technical assistance of any kind, rendered with no thought of domination, that is to say on an equitable basis and in respect for our freedom and independence, cannot be dubbed neo-colonialism (Mr. N'Goua, Gabon, Sess 15, 1960: 1181).

The challenging of hierarchical kinship relations whilst taking up the language of linear progression—notions of development and under-development and

Masculinity, Time and Brotherhood 123

backwardness, for example—was dangerous in that the two were intimately related. Ultimately, a failure to deconstruct the latter would only buoy the former—even after decolonization. This problem is evident in the following statement from a colonialist sympathizer:

> The most important problem which the end of colonialism brings in its wake is the imbalance between the desire for independence of formerly subject peoples and their economic and technical possibilities for self-development. . . . this problem has already arisen and been solved in various ways. In some cases the independent countries have retained close links with the former metropolitan country, which provides them with equipment, technicians and financial assistance. It is precisely this type of co-operation which has been vilified as "neo-colonialism." We should find it impossible to agree with this attitude because the cooperation and assistance of the former dominating Power to its newly emancipated colony do not seem to us to be intrinsically evil but appear rather to be in keeping with the natural order of things. Who, after all, is more aware of the country's problems, who has greater experience of its needs. . . . [how else can] a country structurally in its infancy . . . alone, and without external aid, achieve the status of a mature nation (Mr. Amadeo, Argentina, Sess 15, 1960: 1007)?

In this statement, the colonialist speaker legitimates continuing relations of tutelage and guidance between newly independent countries and their former "dominating Power" after decolonization as "the natural order of things" in order to help a country in its "infancy" to "achieve the status of a mature nation." From this perspective, despite legal decolonization, hierarchical kinship imagery is left intact. Nevertheless, for their part, newly independent countries distinguished between the paternalism of the colonialist narrative and this sort of "economic and technical" assistance between "brothers." For example, according to one speaker, "real brotherhood [means that] the strong supports the weak; the wealthy helps the needy; the developed assists the under-developed; and when all such aids are made without conditions or strings attached (Mr. Rifa'I, Jordan, Sess 15, 1960: 1057)." Such assistance from their "already developed brothers" suited them just fine. Given their troubled history with the colonialist powers, what accounts for such an inconsistency in their critique? Perhaps one explanation is that they sought such development assistance not necessarily from their former "dominating Power," but from their brothers in the United Nations:

> The inadequate level of political, economic, social and educational advancement has in the past always been used by the administering powers as a reason for delaying the independence of the colonial countries. . . . in fact, . . . they have delayed giving the peoples the necessary training for various aspects of their national life, while on the other hand they have argued that, since independence requires a certain minimum degree of training, it cannot be granted to them without this. . . . Today, the difficulties which always spring from an inadequate level of development . . . do not frighten the colonial peoples unduly. . . . if their economic, social and political backwardness necessarily imposes a state of relative dependence . . . there is no reason to think that such dependence should be imposed on them by the former Administering Power. The international community and the United Nations, among others, can easily give them the necessary aid and assistance (Mr. Vakil, Iran, Sess 15, 1960: 994).

In this last year, then, colonialist speakers reverted to the colonialist narrative to legitimate their practices. Drawing on the growing identity of Asia-Africa (see Chapter 3), anti-colonialist speakers challenged this narrative by introducing three new elements into the discussion: *masculinity, time, and brotherhood*. While calling for immediate political independence, this critique was partial and problematic in that it masculinized not only the colonial experience of domination but also the imagination of "postcolonial" independence and freedom. Moreover, the challenge was quite ambiguous in that while it focused on hierarchical kinship relations between colonialist powers and dependent territories, it continued to reinforce images of linear progression. Hence, while anti-colonialists contested the notion that they were children, they nevertheless sought assistance for "development" and "progress" from the international community. Perhaps the argument for *masculinity, time, and brotherhood*, then, was not really an attempt to dismantle hierarchical kinship, as much as to reconfigure it so that excluded territories could be "included" into the existing nation-state system. What were the implications of these conversations? How would these particular negotiations manifest institutionally? It is to these questions that I now turn.

INTERNATIONALIZING LINEAR PROGRESS AND KINSHIP: THE INSTITUTIONALIZATION OF DEVELOPMENT IN THE UN SYSTEM

The United Nations system consists of 6 main organs (see Table-1) and is also in relationship with a number of specialized agencies such as the

International Trade Organization (ITO), the Food and Agriculture Organization (FAO), the United Nations Educational, Scientific and Cultural Organization (UNESCO), the International Bank for Reconstruction and Development (World Bank), and the World Health Organization (WHO), to name a few. In 1946, the colonialist narrative and its associated cluster of linearized abstractions (i.e., development-progress-modernity-advancement-education), as well as its hierarchical kinship relations between territories, were institutionalized throughout this system on a number of levels.[3] Most visible in this regard was the Trusteeship System, which oversaw the "development" of "peoples who are not yet ready to stand in the modern world" by specific administering authorities as discussed in Chapter 3. Beyond such explicit development of dependent territories, moreover, this sort of "assistance" was also available for formally independent territories. The ITO, for example, was to provide such guidance to member states who sought it for the purpose of carrying out "economic development" while the FAO was also concerned with the "agricultural and industrial development" of "less developed countries (United Nations 1946: 687–822)." Ultimately, through these organs, such assistance was institutionalized within discrete but overlapping fields of practice that the UN termed "economic," "political," "cultural," "social," and "educational" dimensions of development.

How did anti-colonialists situate themselves in relation to these multiple instantiations of the colonialist narrative? The response to this question may tell us something about how they envisioned freedom. Through their initial participation in the Trusteeship System, they sought to take part in the oversight by the UN of the "development" practices of particular administering authorities; their part in this political tutelage ending only in 1960 with the demand for an immediate end to political dependency and equal access to the nation-state system. But beyond this "development" of dependent territories, how did they understand the needs of newly independent territories? An examination of anti-colonialists' discourses and practices within the UN system regarding these territories—not just in 1960 but from 1946—demonstrates that though they sought to bring political tutelage to an end, they pursued tutelage in every other arena. Hence, they asked for "development assistance" in the economic, technical, and educational fields. Despite Asia-Africa's aim of reclaiming oppressed "cultural personalities" due to the colonial experience (see Chapter 3), after decolonization, interestingly, they also sought such development assistance in the cultural and social fields. In what follows, I first briefly describe anti-colonial participation in the Trusteeship System for the development of dependent territories. Next, I move on to their pursuit of development for newly independent states.

For the Trusteeship System, "peoples who are not yet ready to stand in the modern world" were to be developed in "economic," "social," "cultural," "political" and "educational" dimensions for Trusts, while with the exception of the "political" field, the same was also true for NSGTs (United Nations 1951: 571). Hence, administering authorities were to carry out a series of development projects within the aforementioned dimensions of development, with the Trusteeship Council overseeing these projects on a regular basis. Specifically in regard to the "political development" of Trusts, for example, the Council asked for increasing the numbers of indigenous people in local political institutions so that they could gain experience and "develop" political skills. On "educational development," the Council oversaw education facilities and expenditures, and on "economic development," training facilities for locals in areas such as "agricultural and industrial development" were of interest. The "social" arena was particularly interesting, as it was comprised of a broad array of activities including "demographic and sociological" matters, medical and water facilities, women's sexual autonomy, polygamy and women's status, human rights, public welfare, and so on. Finally, regarding the "cultural" arena, there were some interesting contradictions in the UN institutionalization of progress and oversight. For example in the case of NSGTs, the Council asked administering authorities to engage in the "protection" but also the "development" of indigenous arts, literature and folklore. Exacerbating this contradiction, progress on this matter was measured by the extent to which the administering authority contributed to the formation of various cultural institutions such as the press, cinema, radio and museum within a territory (United Nations 1947: 722–723)—entities that were not always part of "indigenous arts, literature and folklore." Such complications notwithstanding, in each of these arenas the Trusteeship Council sought to guide the "development" of indigenous populations within educational, political, cultural, economic, and social institutions that it associated with progress (see for example United Nations 1950; 1951; 1952).

Given the construction of dependent territories as requiring assistance in the colonialist narrative, this institutionalization of the narrative within the Trusteeship System should not be surprising. Beyond such guidance for dependent territories, however, such assistance was also available for formally independent member states if requested by these states.[4] Initially, such assistance to member states did not necessarily fit the logic of the colonialist narrative, as it was primarily intended for the reconstruction of areas occupied during or devastated by the recent war. Indeed, the GA adopted a resolution to encourage the speedy opening of the World Bank for just this purpose, which also then became one of the Bank's main goals (United

Nations 1946: 479–747). Newly independent and anti-colonialist countries, however, sought to change the direction and tenor of this assistance for member states. In contrast to the assumption that often seems to be made in critiques of the development project that development was somehow imposed upon the Third World,[5] my examination of the UN records demonstrates that newly independent countries, often amidst some resistance from "more developed countries," more often than not pursued this goal themselves. Indeed, though images of development may have originated in the space and time of an industrializing Europe, and some time before Truman flattened two thirds of the world into the undifferentiated condition of "under-development," development became a universal goal (Escobar 1995). Hence in 1946, Lebanon proposed a resolution for placement on the GA agenda that would provide member states "expert advice in connection with their own internal development (United Nations 1946: 182)," and after considering the resolution, with some amendments, the GA unanimously passed the following:

THE GENERAL ASSEMBLY,

CONSIDERING that the Members of the United Nations are not yet all equally developed:

CONSIDERING that some Member Nations may need expert advice in the various fields of economic, social and cultural development;

RECOGNIZING the responsibility of the United Nations under the Charter for assisting in such development;

RECOGNIZING the importance of such development for the peace and prosperity of the world;

RECOGNIZING the responsibility of the specialized agencies in their respective fields;

DECIDES to refer to the Economic and Social Council for study the question of providing effective ways and means for furnishing, in cooperation with the specialized agencies, expert advice in the economic, social and cultural fields to Member nations who desire this assistance.

Source: United Nations, 1946: 183.

Similar to the assistance provided to dependent territories in multiple arenas, this "expert advice" to "not yet all equally developed" member states was also to transpire in "economic," "social," "educational" and "cultural" fields—though, of course, not in the "political" field since presumably, these territories were already sufficiently politically developed to be politically independent. (Though it should not surprise anyone that some thought such development assistance would also advance progress in the theoretically already-achieved "political" field). In the "economic" arena, while some countries like the United States argued outside of the European colonialist narrative that underdeveloped countries were primarily responsible for their own economic welfare[6], anti-colonialists such as China, Egypt, Haiti, India, Iraq, Mexico and the Philippines argued that the UN needed to do more to assist in the economic and technical development of "economically under-developed areas" and that the World Bank should shift its focus from reconstruction of war devastated areas to such development in under-developed areas. In 1948, then, the GA adopted several resolutions to do just that (United Nations 1948: 432–438), and in the following year, the GA also unanimously voted for an expanded program of technical assistance, the "Expanded Programme of Technical Assistance for Economic Development of Under-Developed Countries." The program was launched in 1950 (United Nations 1949: 440; United Nations 1950: 3–12).

Beyond this technical assistance, newly independent and anti-colonialist countries also sought to increase financial assistance for economic development. As the UN's own documents note:

> The geographical distribution of the total disbursements made by the Bank up to 31 December 1950, in round numbers by areas of expenditures, was as follows: $471,000,000 in the United States; $56,500,000 in Latin America; $38,600,000 in Canada; $71,000,000 in Europe; $2,200,000 In Africa; $2,500,000 in the Near East; and $100,000 in the Far East (United Nations 1950: 949).

Hence, newly independent countries argued that this distribution of Bank loans needed to change (United Nations 1951: 377). In 1953, to this end, the GA considered the recommendation for the Special United Nations Fund for Economic Development, or SUNFED, which would take voluntary contributions from "more developed countries" and make these available specifically for the purpose of the economic development of "under-developed areas." These "more developed countries," such as the United States and United Kingdom, however, argued that the monies for such assistance were unavailable (United Nations 1953: 292).

These disagreements, in which anti-colonialists positioned themselves as lacking in development and requiring development assistance, occurred year after year, and by the end of the fifties, their efforts started to bear fruit. For example, in 1957, a compromise was reached on the matter of SUNFED, where SUNFED would especially provide technical assistance but also some financial assistance based on voluntary contributions (United Nations 1957: 142), and by January 1959, SUNFED launched 44 projects in "under-developed areas" from Asia to Africa to Latin America. Geographically now, in contrast to the distribution of World Bank loans in 1950, 80% of SUNFED's assistance went to Africa, with the rest going to the Americas, Asia and the Far East, the Middle East, and then to Europe, in that order (United Nations 1959: 110). Moreover in 1957, the World Bank itself expanded its lending in Asia (United Nations 1957: 422). This success of anti-colonialists in bringing development assistance to their territories was underscored in 1960, when the GA decided to place special emphasis on the provision of development aid to newly independent countries during their "critical formative period (United Nations 1960: 269)."

Development is typically conceptualized as an economic project. Beyond the "economic" arena, however, the UN system also offered such development assistance in "social," "cultural" and "educational" arenas. For example, the purpose of the GA's Third Committee, or Social, Humanitarian, and Cultural Committee, was to focus on "social, humanitarian, cultural, educational and health matters [for the sake of] social progress and development (United Nations 1946: 54)." ECOSOC also focused on the issue of "social development" for particular "socially under-developed populations" such as the Aboriginal populations of the Americas (United Nations 1950: 610). In the area of "cultural development," the central institution was UNESCO. In 1946, UNESCO came into being with the explicit purpose of contributing to the cause of peace through the fostering of collaboration in culture, education and science (United Nations 1946: 704). In this same year, at the behest of the GA, ECOSOC considered the matter of "cultural development" and decided to assign to UNESCO the task of translating the world's classics—which were to be drawn from multiple cultures—into member country languages (United Nations 1946: 541). For this, ECOSOC adopted the following resolution:

THE ECONOMIC AND SOCIAL COUNCIL

TAKING NOTE of the resolution No. 60 (1) of the General Assembly of 14 December 1946 whereby the question of the translation of the world's classics into the languages of the Members of the United Nations was referred to the Economic and Social Council for reference to the United Nations Educational, Cultural, and Scientific Organization, and of the principles CONSIDERING

(a) That the translation of the classics is a project of international concern and of great significance for the promotion of international cultural cooperation;

(b) That the successful implementation of this project is linked closely with all the activities of UNESCO which tend to raise the general level of culture among the people of the world;

(c) That certain nations do not have sufficient facilities and resources for the authentic translation of numerous classics into their languages;

(d) That such translation is greatly conducive to their cultural development; and

DECIDE TO REQUEST UNESCO to submit by 1 June 1948, to the Economic and Social Council a report giving recommendations for needed action, and including particularly data on objective methods of selection of great books, the needs of various cultural regions, and suggestions for general assistance in translation, publication and distribution.

Source: United Nations, 1946: 541.

Hence, UNESCO was assigned the task of raising "the general level of culture among the people of the world," of providing aid to nations with insufficient resources in this regard, and of generally promoting "cultural development," with the primary goal of such a task being "international cultural cooperation." While conversations on such projects within the UN system were replete with commentary on the need to protect state sovereignty and respect cultural rights, similar to their stance on "economic development," newly independent and anti-colonialist countries did not exactly resist such efforts. For example in 1949, the representative of Lebanon made the following statement to the GA:

> While a series of general studies on the world economic situation had been initiated by the [Economic and Social] Council, no comparable action was contemplated in the social, humanitarian and cultural fields. However. . . . in order to fulfill its double function, the Economic and Social Council would need a world survey of the social and cultural as well as of the economic situation (United Nations 1949: 619).

Although initially floundering in the definition of its functions, by 1950, UNESCO's purpose was fairly stabilized (United Nations 1950). In 1950, it established the International Committee on Monuments, Artistic and Historical Sites, and Archeological Excavations (Sewell 1975: 180), and at the request of member states, it engaged in a series of activities in which development in the cultural arena was to be pursued through the attainment for example of skills in how to "restore," "preserve," and "educate" about "national culture." In this vein, UNESCO sent experts to advise member states on art education and restoration and on how to preserve and restore monuments and archaological and historic sites and "national treasures." In 1952, UNESCO held a seminar on how to use museums for the purpose of "education (United Nations 1952: 845)," and from 1953, it advanced the notion of "cultural property" with its International Study Centre for the Presentation and Restoration of Cultural Property (United Nations 1953: 746). With its program "Direct Aid to Member States" in 1955, it provided direct aid in the development of museums, libraries and communications services (United Nations 1955: 393)." In the mid-fifties, at a meeting in New Delhi with ten Asian states and Egypt, then UNESCO Director-General Evans was told that their peoples were not being given adequate UNESCO assistance. Specifically, representatives from these countries argued that "western advances in natural sciences and education would help them; in turn, the abiding values of Eastern culture or cultures might help others (Sewell 1975: 167)." In the same year, UNESCO began to engage in a significant way in a program for the "mutual appreciation of Eastern and Western cultural values." UNESCO had already begun in this arena with activities such as determining "the characteristic features of each country's culture and ideals" and offering "help developing in each country sympathy and respect for other countries (Valderama 1995: 31)." Now, this program included activities such as examining different teaching syllabi in the humanities for inclusion of the different civilizations of "East" and "West," traveling exhibitions representing the art of different cultures, translating the representative literature of different cultures and so on. Finally, beyond such efforts in the cultural arena, in the areas of "modern science and education," too, there was consistent demand for UNESCO training and expertise (United Nations 1952). Pierre Auger, then UNESCO Secretariat, once said:

> Some people think you can attain peace by just crying "Peace! Peace!" but this leads to nothing. . . . You must start obliquely—creating proper conditions, using civilizing influences. A good starter is weaving scientists into the international pattern, since they already have a fund of ideas in common, speak the same language, and like being with each other (ibid: 174).

Thus, UNESCO also offered assistance in "modern science and education" with numerous projects in the natural sciences and in childhood and adult education.

The above is necessarily a brief and selective introduction to the emerging UN system in its first fifteen years. For their part, while anti-colonialists sought to terminate political development, they nevertheless actively and persistently sought development in the economic, technical, social, cultural, educational and other arenas. Indeed, the UN machinery for development policies and programs was elaborated partly under pressure from anti-colonialist and newly independent countries (see also Rajagopal 2003: 27). Yet, if development was an extension in a number of ways of the colonialist narrative into the "postcolonial" era, why did anti-colonialists only challenge this narrative in the so-called political arena? Why did they orient so differently to the economic and technical and even the cultural?

NATION-STATES IN WORLD SOCIETY

To understand the contradictory approach of anti-colonialists to decolonization and "postcolonial" independence, as briefly touched on in Chapter 4, we have to examine the nation-state system they sought to be included in, not just as a geopolitical system or a politico-economic system but critically, as a *cultural system*—an arena of particular forms of subjectivity and practice. From the perspective of the nation-state system as a cultural system, the nation-state is the one agent or agency that enjoys legitimacy on the world stage in the modern era (Meyer 1997). Moreover, it is decidedly an agency that dependent territories have historically been denied (Strang 1991; Theodoropoulos 1988). The argument against political tutelage, thus, is not merely an argument for decolonization, but a bid for access to a particular form of subjectivity hitherto unavailable.

But with this argument for an end to political tutelage, why did anti-colonialists actually pursue other kinds of tutelage? Beyond mere inclusion into the system, this access to the mantle of the nation-state also brings with it particular kinds of performative requirements. That is, in the modern era and particularly after World War II with the advent of the UN and other international bodies, the nation-state is accompanied by certain world cultural or world society models, constructs regarding their "true and responsible natures, purposes, technologies (Meyer 1997)," which impart normative symbols states must don and practices states must engage in, in order to maintain their status as legitimate states (Meyer 1997; Meyer 1999; Finnemore 1998; Meyer 1976; Thomas and Meyer 1984; Finnemore 1996; Boli and Thomas 1999; Korzeniewicz, Stach, Patil, and Moran 2004: 537–547). Once "included" into the nation-state system, thus—and moreover, in a context in which independence has been denied on the basis of incompetence—newly independent states are compelled to demonstrate their legitimacy. In this vein, especially after World War II, the legitimated goals of states became centered on what can broadly be called "modernization" and consequently in the post-war period, world society scholars highlight the astonishing "diffusion of" or "isomorphism in" the modernization goals and practices of states across the globe (Boli and Thomas 1999; Finnemore 1996; Finnemore 1998; Meyer 1999; Korzeniewicz, et al 2004: 537–547). Of course, the colonialist narrative, particularly the hierarchical relations of power, knowledge and identity embedded within this narrative, as well as anti-colonialists' partial adoption of this narrative (see Chapter 5), actually predict the "diffusion" of particular models of modernization. Beyond anti-colonialists' goal of political independence for still dependent territories, hence, this adoption is evident for newly independent territories in their pursuit of one of the quintessential "modern" state goals and practices in the post-war period: economic development (Meyer 1997). Thus, though they resist political tutelage, newly independent and anti-colonialist countries actively seek economic tutelage—as well as tutelage in any arena deemed connected to the economic (which over the years would decidedly breach the "economic"/"non-economic" divide, however defined, as it moved from the technical and the scientific to the educational, the social, "women's status," the cultural, the demographic, health and so on). The possibilities and the fallacies of economic development and its associated scientific, technical and other arenas have, of course, been thoroughly expounded upon (for example, see Cooper and Packard 1997; Escobar 1995; McMichael 2000; Rist 2002), and so I will not remark on them further here.

Finally, beyond the rejection of political tutelage and the embrace of economic tutelage, access to the nation-state system also has a third significant implication: the uptake of the legitimacy myth of the nation-state that a particular state somehow represents a particular "nation." Contrary to this myth, of course, states must actively engage in the power-laden process of the nationalization of particular local identities and their articulation with a given bounding of territorial space (Balibar 1991; Anderson 1991; Hobsbawn and Ranger 1983; Hobsbawn 1990). In this regard, within the UN system, the specialized agency of UNESCO "trained" newly independent states in such activities at their request. Specifically through UNESCO, they learned the concept of "cultural property" and how to "restore" and "preserve" "national treasures, tradition, and history." They learned about how to use museums to "educate" about the nation and its history. They even learned how to educate the "west" or the "Occident" about their unique "eastern" or "Oriental" values and vice versa. With this sort of assistance, then, beyond the pursuit of economic tutelage, anti-colonialist and newly independent countries also accepted, or rather pursued, cultural tutelage.

But how could newly independent countries simultaneously seek to "develop economically" but "preserve authentic national cultures?" Conforming with my findings on the construction of the collective identity of Asia-Africa that the cultures of Asia and Africa were distinguished from the "material west" by their "unique spiritual and moral qualities (see Chapter 3)," according to Partha Chatterjee (1993), a key feature of Asian and African "postcolonial" nationalisms is that they also made a distinction between the "cultural" and the "economic." He argues that this distinction was mapped onto a second distinction between an "inner" spiritual dimension versus an "outer" material dimension. Hence, newly independent states could preserve their "authentic inner selves" while simultaneously pursuing "outward" economic development.

The pursuit of cultural preservation and nationalization via UNESCO was problematic for other reasons as well. For example, according to Wells (1987: 43), there was a division of labor between the UN system proper and UNESCO in which while the work of the former was to delve into the "political," the work of the latter was to remain "non-political" and "technical." Of course, state- and nation-building through UNESCO is fundamentally political activity. In the first instance, the borders of many of these new territories were the result of complicated histories of colonialism and decolonization (Anderson 1991). With the sovereign state posited as the resolution to histories of colonial domination and suppression, however, this complexity was elided. For example, the African freedom fighter and founder of the Party for the Independence of Guinea Bissau and Cape Verde (PAIGC), Amílcar Cabral, made the argument that "if imperialist domination has the vital need to practice cultural oppression, national liberation is necessarily an act of *culture* (italics in original, Cabral 1994)." Hence, the argument went, if colonialism suppressed distinct cultures, the political form of the nation-state would return not just political but also cultural freedom. Never mind that this expression of "distinct cultural personalities," as one speaker in the GA put it, was to be enabled by remarkably similar museums, libraries, historical sites, and so forth.

Moreover, with the uptake of the myth that states represent "nations," and in interesting contradiction to the notion that national liberation meant reclaiming "oppressed" pre-colonial cultures, newly independent countries could use the resources of UNESCO to construct and indeed invent traditions, histories, and various objects of so-called cultural property (Bennett 1995; Hobsbawm and Ranger 1983; Korang 2004; Lowenthal 1998; Hevia

2001). According to Korang (2004: 272–73), speaking of "postcolonial" states in Africa, thus, "appearing from above, it is the *force* of the State, it would seem, that "legitimates" the nation, and not the force of the nation, from a popular below, that confers on the state its true legitimacy."

Despite these complications, nevertheless, newly independent countries engaged in "restoring" and "preserving" their national cultures. In the process, they helped to universalize and naturalize the nation-state as a particular organization of territorial space and identity across the globe. According to Lentin (2005), this push for "culture" was made on the part of a strong anti-racist current in UNESCO. However, this discourse of discrete cultures merely replaced the discourse of discrete races to explain human variation. Emanating from UNESCO, "discrete culture," too, was internationalized across the globe.

CONCLUSION

Ultimately, I argue that legal decolonization signified not merely a shift from the colonial to a new more generally democratic era—but to something much more particular. For legal decolonization was less about dismantling the power-laden constructions of power, identity and knowledge of the colonialist narrative and more about inclusion—about having "access" to the prevailing system of power. In other words, this decolonization was less about doing away with the racialized, sexualized construction of transnational hierarchy and more about reconfiguring this hierarchy so that "postcolonial men" could be included. Thus, while the anti-colonialist argument of masculinity, time and brotherhood certainly challenged some of the exclusions of the colonialist narrative, it also universalized and naturalized the construction of space, identity, power, knowledge and agency inherent in the nation-state system. At the very minimum, then, while it intervened to a limited extent in the racial and cultural hierarchies of the colonial era, it also invented and solidified a new gender hierarchy— masculinizing "postcolonial" nations-states as well as "postcolonial" international community in the new democratic era.

Chapter Six
Conclusion: Twentieth Century Transformations of Space, Identity and International Community

> *Every modern nation is a product of colonization: it has always been to some degree colonized or colonizing, and sometimes both at the same time.*
>
> -Etienne Balibar, 1996

> *Decolonizing nationalism did not envision a mere return to traditional patriarchy. . . . the new patriarchy . . . was not a traditional patriarchy, but a nationalist patriarchy.*
>
> -Prasenjit Duara, 2004

In the Introduction to this study, I began with a discussion of the largely United States-based literature on intersections of racial, gender and other inequalities, and I posed a question regarding the utility of globalizing this perspective—of attempting to observe such intersectional dynamics of hierarchy on a transnational level. The findings of this research, I argue, move beyond mere utility and demonstrate the great significance of this perspective, which enables an understanding of the contradictory, gendered process of the "global advance of democracy" known as legal decolonization. Even more, it illuminates the significance of work on gender, sexuality, bodies, and the family—often ghettoized as somehow particular or local, separate and distinct from more "macro" and generalizable work on states, democracy, development, modernization, and globalization. Thus, as explored in Chapter One, there are important historical connections between notions of authority within the family and ways of imagining, thinking about and speaking about authority within imperial rule. In the first period of empire, notions of absolute authority within the patriarchal family are connected to "harsher" ideologies of imperial rule. From the 17th century and on, a series of transformations in the nature of authority and relationships within the "western" family are connected to new ways of imagining, thinking

137

about and speaking about authority within "softer" ideologies of rule. It seems quite fitting, then, that the anti-colonial argument for ending imperial rule engages this familial metaphor as well: "We have grown and are now adults (or alternatively, we have always been adults). We should no longer be treated as children, then, but as brothers."[1]

In the rest of these remarks, there are three dimensions of this renegotiation that I would like to comment on further: its temporality, its gendering, and what it tells us about resistance.

THE TIMES AND SPACES OF THE COLONIAL: THE LIMITS AND POSSIBILITIES OF THE ARGUMENT FOR INCLUSION

To the hierarchical politics of kinship and its construction of the identity distinctions of adult versus child in the GA, anti-colonialists respond either that they have now grown into, or that they always have been, adults. Rather than being treated as children, then, they seek to be treated as brothers. In this (masculine) politics of growth and adulthood, the anti-colonialist argument, hence, incorporates a certain temporality: "We are adults. The time for decolonization is now." Thus, *the renegotiation of the hierarchical, colonialist construction of space comes to revolve in the examination here around a renegotiation of time.* Why is this the case? Why does time emerge as such an important dimension of these debates on decolonization in the GA? In one sense, that the politics of time emerges in this way in this setting perhaps should not be so surprising, for as discussed in Chapter One, the colonialist denial of space relies on a certain *temporality*:

> Imperial progress across the space of empire is figured as a journey backwards in time to an anachronistic moment of prehistory. By extension, the return journey to Europe is seen as rehearsing the evolutionary logic of historical progress, forward and upward to the apogee of the Enlightenment in the European metropolis. Geographical difference across *space* [consequently] is figured as a historical difference across *time* (italics in original, McClintock 1995: 40).

From this perspective, the colonialist narrative imbues (as it constitutes) particular spaces with cultural and political meanings. Europe, America and Africa, as well as East and West, and North and South are not just spatial and geographical, but also economic, political, moral and philosophical metaphors (King 1997; Lewis and Wigen 1997; Delanty 1995),[2] all of which emerge in part through a powerful identity discourse[3] that constructs its others as perennially or transiently "behind" (i.e., traditional, pre-modern, under-developed, without history) (Wolf 1982; Fabian 1983; Wallerstein 1996; Pratt 2002).

It is precisely such a temporal identity discourse that is embodied in the image of linear progression that is so central in the GA debates, as discussed in Chapter Five. Thus, the sorts of identity distinctions made by this image—distinctions having to do with possessing lesser or greater amounts of linearized, quantified abstractions such as "progress," "modernity," "development" and so forth—are all temporal distinctions; and given the way these abstractions are deployed in the transnational politics of inequality, power, and privilege in the GA, moreover, "progress," "modernity," and "development" in this case act as *time concepts*. Thus, it is to this temporally based denial of the spatial and identity claims of various "others," that the anti-colonialist argument for growth and adulthood responds: "We are adults. The time for decolonization is now."

But is this argument sufficient? Does it adequately contend with the space-time of the colonialist narrative? Can the children simply grow up and join the adults in brotherhood and equality? Can the non-modern simply develop to the level of modernity and join the rest of the modern world? As time concepts, "progress," "modernity," and "development" "foreground the temporal dimension of existence, moving the spatial to the background (Wallerstein 1996)." In other words, as time concepts, they narrativize time from a particular location, the space of a colonizing Europe, in the meantime making other spaces with simultaneous but different experiences of "progress," "modernity," and "development" invisible. The work of sociologist Anthony Giddens offers a particularly illustrative example of such a Eurocentric theorization. In *The Consequences of Modernity*, Anthony Giddens defines modernity as "modes of social life or organization which emerged in Europe from about the seventeenth century onwards and which subsequently became more or less worldwide in their influence (Giddens 1990: 1)." For him, the modern is distinguished from the pre-modern by a particular temporality and spatiality. That is, modernity can be understood as the gradual emergence of a "separation of time from space. . . . uniformity in the social organization of time. . . . the 'emptying of time' [which is then] the precondition for the 'emptying of space.' . . . the separation of place from space." He adds that the "discovery" of "remote" regions of the world by Western travelers and explorers was the necessary basis for this emptying of time and space. "The progressive charting of the globe that led to the creation of universal maps, in which perspective played little part in the representation of geographical position and form, established space as 'independent' of any particular place or region (Giddens 1990: 17–19)."

This work exemplifies a central problem is such Eurocentric but unmarked, universalized treatments of concepts such as modernity. For such an "emptying out" of time and space in which "perspective played little part"—from the problematic location of seventeenth century Europe no less—silences the history of the space-time of the colonialist narrative, including its definitions of self (Europe, civilization, and so forth) and other (Non-Europe, barbarism, savagery, etc). Perhaps it is only from the perspective of the unmarked "center" that such an "emptying out" is even possible.

The particularity of this theorization of modernity is especially evident when we contrast it to theorizations situated in other locations. For example, in his essay "'Race,' Time and the Revision of Modernity," Homi Bhabha interrogates the Eurocentric understanding of modernity from the perspective of space and speaks of something called "contra-modernity." Specifically, he asks: what is modernity in those colonial conditions where its imposition is itself the denial of historical freedom, civic autonomy (1994b)—of conditions the "center" always associates with modernity? In a somewhat similar fashion, in *The Black Atlantic*, Paul Gilroy (1993) seeks to demonstrate the "variations and discontinuities in modern experience and . . . the decentered and inescapably plural nature of modern subjectivity and identity (Gilroy 1993: 46)." Here, akin to Bhabha's "contra-modernity," Gilroy writes of the Black Atlantic as a "counterculture of modernity." From still another vantage point, Tani Barlow uses the term "colonial modernity" as a way to think through the fundamentally transnational space-time of modernity:

> Because it is a way of posing a historical question about how our *mutual present* came to take its apparent shape, colonial modernity can also suggest that historical context is not a matter of positively defined, elemental or discrete units—nation-states, stages of development, or civilizations, for instance—but rather a complex field of relationships or threads of material that connect multiply in space-time and can be surveyed from specific sites (italics added, Barlow 1997: 6).

In this vein, scholars have also examined how modernities take shape in multiple, complex ways "outside" of the metropolitan core. Barlow (1997), for example, argues that there have been multiple modernities in

East Asia that have been missed because the Eurocentric modernity narrative was not prepared to recognize them outside of the "West." Similarly, other scholars have discussed a "selective" modernity within Indian nationalism (Chatterjee 1993: 121), "peripheral modernities" in Latin America (Pratt 2002), a "militarized modernity" in South Korea (Moon 2005), and particular "negotiations of modernity" in Africa (Korang 2004). Hence, in opposition to the exclusivist notion of modernity provided by Europe, Mary Louise Pratt argues for a concept of modernity that is global and relational, focusing on relations of contradiction, complementarity and differentiation in the "periphery" with respect to the "center" (Pratt 2002).

Thus, the temporal identity discourse embedded within the colonialist narrative constructs differential and hierarchical distinctions between peoples and territories from a particular, unmarked, but universalized space. Such a Eurocentric temporal discourse serves to deny the alternative spatial and identity claims of various "others," constructing them as lacking in progress, development, modernity and so on. As Roland Robertson argues, then, it is only with the fading of the temporal unidirectionality of the "modernity narrative," as he puts it, that the representational space within which other narratives may be added can be expanded (Robertson 1997). Thus, with "We are adults. The time for decolonization is now," anti-colonialists do address this temporal dimension—to an extent.

But does this politics of adulthood and brotherhood sufficiently disrupt the space-time of the colonialist narrative so that other spatialities and temporalities—other experiences of progress, modernity and development—may be recognized? My argument is that while this politics disrupts the conservative gradualism of colonialist kinship politics in the mid-twentieth century, nevertheless, it does not go far enough. In the first instance, the argument for adulthood and brotherhood only asks that kinship politics be reconfigured so that grown men may be "included." It does nothing to challenge this politics or the space-time of the colonialist narrative more fundamentally. These speakers do not want to challenge the family or even leave the family, but only be equal members in brotherhood within the family. In contrast to actually dismantling the space-time of colonial modernity by bringing other spatialities and temporalities into the conversation, thus, they ask for the "homogeneous empty time (Anderson 1991: 24)" and "space (Alonso 1994)" of the nation. In doing so, they leave the discourse and hierarchies of kinship intact, making them available to be used again, on still dependent territories, on newly independent countries, and on others.

THE CONTRADICTIONS OF INCLUSION: THE PRODUCTIVE POWER OF THE NATION, GENDER, AND (HETERO)SEXUALITY

A number of scholars have written about the problematic nature of the post-war moment of "inclusion." In the era of American globalization, for example, there is a particular form of power that is not about completeness and does not work for completeness but rather: A form of capital which recognizes that it can only . . . rule through other local capitals, rule alongside and in partnership with other economic and political elites. [Thus] it does not attempt to obliterate them; [rather] it operates through them (Hall 1997a: 28). Hall is interested here in the power relations inherent in post-war "global mass culture." Beyond mass culture, Howard Winant problematizes inclusion in a similar fashion, but from the perspective of race. He argues that the racial reforms achieved in the second half of the twentieth century were contradictory in that "they expanded democracy and lessened racial hierarchy, but they also allowed white supremacy to survive, to modernize, to adapt to post-colonial and post-apartheid conditions (Winant 2001: 146)." Hence, he argues, "the world racial system underwent a transition from *domination to hegemony*. Segregation and colonialism . . . were abandoned. . . . but. . . . the new world racial system could maintain much of the stratification and inequality, much of the differential access to political power and voice, much of the preexisting cultural logic of collective representation and racial hierarchy (italics added, Winant 2001: 307)."

Continuing in this vein, some authors argue that particularly from the vantage point of the United States, the nation-state form was never intended to extend freedom but rather, to contain it:

> The US in the first instance was at least as interested in reducing the economic and political powers of the European empires as it was in advancing the cause of the downtrodden, colonized nations. . . . [Moreover,] the US leadership planned for the replacement of all bilateral economic negotiation with a large and complex apparatus of new global institutions—a World Bank, an International Monetary Fund, Global Agreements on Tariffs and Trade, and an International Trade Organization (later WTO)—institutions that in reality, even while they invented themselves restricted dramatically the possibilities of self-determination that the nation-state was said to embody (Kelly and Kaplan, 2004: 131–150).

Thus, the "UN world" became an "engine for limiting political will":

Conclusion 143

> This is the predicament of post-coloniality—not so much, as so many theorists of the postcolonial have sought to define it, the incompleteness of decolonization or the continuing importance of inherited colonial relationships, but this, the fact that decolonization as actually experienced was entry into a new world order already tooled for purposes at best differing from aims of anticolonial movements, and at times clearly obstructive of them (ibid 2004: 141).

Hence, Kelly and Kaplan argue that the very meaning of the state shifted from the colonial to the "post-colonial" era. While in the former, what was called the "national state" was about competition, conflict and conquest, a "vehicle for expressing and extending" national will, what became the "nation-state" in the latter was a form of containment (ibid 2004: 137).[4]

Consequently, rather than framing legal decolonization in the UNGA through the terminology of the global advance of democracy, or as a transition from oppression to liberation, perhaps it is more accurate to deploy Foucault's notion of power as a positive or productive force (Foucault 1977; Foucault 1988b). Because now, formerly dependent territories take up the notion of freedom as the practice of state- and nation-building without really disturbing the ideology of "catch up" embedded in the image of linear progression. This is the case most clearly with the pursuit of economic, technological and other forms of development, which some argue have simply replaced earlier colonial discourses (Rajagopal 2003: 27–34), and still continue to be about colonial hierarchies such as race (Winant 2001: 16).

Thus, there is a real contradiction between the anti-colonial bid for freedom via inclusion into the nation-state form and the performative demands of this form of agency in the post-war world. The notion that oppressed selves must be reclaimed or protected sits uneasily with the notion that postcolonial nations must somehow develop or change. As mentioned in the previous chapter, Partha Chatterjee suggests that these states manage this contradictory position by recourse to a dichotomy of *external versus internal*, which translates into the idea that any change that postcolonial nations must undergo will only be an external or superficial form of change, while inner, more authentic traditions/cultures will be protected (Chatterjee 1993). But of course, postcolonial practice in this arena is fundamentally about creating new symbolic and material entities—of feeling, of practice, of being (Alonso 1994).

Moreover, by pursuing freedom as state- and nation-building, postcolonial states further reinforce the problematic modern co-articulation and reification of the territorial machinery and space of the state with the ideological spaces of nation-race-ethnicity-culture.[5] Etienne Balibar suggests, for example, that the nation invents and relies on a "fictive ethnicity:"

> [For every nation] the fundamental problem is . . . to produce the people. More exactly, it is to make the people produce itself continually as national community. . . . [In this sense,] fictive ethnicity is. . . . indispensable to. . . . the ideal nation. . . . for it makes possible for the expression of a preexisting unity to be seen in the state and continually to measure the state against its "historic mission" in the service of the nation and as a consequence, to idealize politics. By constituting the people as a fictively ethnic unity against the background of a universalistic representation which attributes to each individual one—and only one—ethnic identity and which thus divides up the whole of humanity between different ethnic groups corresponding to potentially so many nations, national ideology. . . . inscribes . . . a sense of belonging. . . . and the naturalization of belonging (Balibar, 1996: 138–141).

Moreover, Balibar argues that a central way in which this fictive ethnicity is built is through "a principle of closure, of exclusion"—the modern idea of race (Balibar 1996). Indeed, according to a number of authors, race and nation have been thoroughly interlinked in modernity (Nicholson 1999), and modern states actually rely on the notion of race (Goldberg 2002; Lentin 2004; Marx 1998). Thus, racism is a part of "the historical traditions of civic and liberal humanism that create ideological matrices of national aspiration, together with their concepts of 'a people' and its imagined community (Bhabha 1994b)," perhaps helping to explain, then, the "discursive slippage" or connotative resonance between "race, ethnicity, and nation (Gilroy 1993: 15)." In the post-war period, perhaps there has been a slight shift in these discourses of the nation-state as the term "culture" has increasingly come to replace the term "race." Nevertheless, either intentionally in the language of colonialist reactionaries (Cooper 1996: 17) or unintentionally in the language of progressives and anti-racists (Lentin 2005), "culture" continues to do the same work as "race"—ultimately serving to "justify exclusionary politics and policy . . . far better than traditional white supremacist arguments can (Winant 2001: 35)."

Beyond such naturalization of difference, this notion of freedom as state- and nation-building is further problematic from the perspective of gender and sexuality as the concept of community that is articulated to the state—or is even sub-state or trans-state—whether "national," "cultural," "racial" or "ethnic," has historically relied and continues to rely on gender

Conclusion 145

and (hetero)sexuality (Alonso 1992; Alonso 1994; Enloe 1989; Yuval-Davis 1997; Yuval-Davis 1994; Papanek 1994; Moghadam 1994; McClintock 1995; Kaplan, Alarcon, and Moallem 1999; Kandiyoti 1994; Hall 2000; Mosse 1985; Pierson and Chaudhuri 1998; Hoad 1999; Blackwood 2005; Puri 2004; Kim-Puri 2005; Moon 2005; Mayer 2000). As the nation is a time concept, it consists of a duality in that while on the one hand, the nation is supposed to represent a primordial essence that reaches "back" into time, on the other, it is also supposed to represent an entity moving "forward" into the future. Anne McClintock argues that nations manage this temporal duality, thus, with *heteronormative gender*. Specifically, heteronormative, gendered dichotomies manage the dual temporality of the nation by associating normative masculinity with progress and moving forward and normative femininity with maintaining the traditional and the essential (1995: 358–60). Thus, nations do not merely "invent traditions (Hobsbawn and Ranger 1983)," they typically invent heteronormative, gendered traditions. The invention of Mother's Day is one good example (Teitelbaum and Winter 1985).

"Postcolonial" nations, especially those without large settler societies, may have the additional task of bringing together local—however invented—traditions with sometimes quite foreign images of modernity. In these nationalisms, the politics of gender and (hetero)sexuality are not simply about maintaining national tradition but also about guarding the authenticity of "non-western" tradition from "the west," "the colonial," and "the modern." Hence, if freedom is defined as the reclaiming of lost/oppressed "national," "ethnic," "racial" or "cultural" tradition—particularly tradition that is "superior" to the "materialistic West" (See Chapter Three; See also Chatterjee 1993: 121; Duara 2004: 12)—the production of this tradition may have especially powerful implications for so-called traditional ideas about gender and (hetero)sexuality as well (Heng 1997; Chatterjee 1993).

Focusing on the gender dimension of Indian nationalist discourse, for example, Chatterjee (1993) argues that the *external versus internal* dichotomy identified above is a spatialized and gendered dichotomy, as this dichotomy is applied to the spaces of the home and the world:

> The world is the external, the domain of the material; the home represents one's inner spiritual self; one's true identity. The world is the treacherous terrain of the pursuit of material interests . . . practical. . . . male. The home in its essence must remain unaffected by the profane activities of the material world—and woman is its representation. . . . [Moreover, as a specifically anti-colonialist discourse, this perspective

posits that] the world was where the European power had challenged the non-European peoples. . . . [but in the spiritual realm where East was superior] the East was undominated, sovereign, master of its own fate. . . . [so] the subjugated must learn the modern sciences and arts of the material world from the West. . . . [but simultaneously] protect, preserve, and strengthen the inner core of the national culture, its spiritual essence (Chatterjee, 1993: 120–1).

Interestingly, such gender dynamics are also evident in "postcolonial" immigrant communities in various countries: surrounded by "others" and so threatened, it is up to the women of the immigrant community to maintain/uphold the community's so-called traditions (Ganguly-Scrase and Julian 1997; Appadurai 1994). Thus, Prasenjit Duara argues that "postcolonial" patriarchy is *not* a traditional patriarchy but an emergent, "nationalist patriarchy." For now with decolonization, women are "to be mothers of the nation, protecting and cherishing its inner values (Duara 2004: 10; See also Chatterjee 1993)."[6]

Furthermore, as this dichotomous gender is premised on heteronormativity (Boellstorff 2006; Puri 2004; Blackwood 2005; Alexander 1994), sexual others, those who can be positioned as outside of the authentic tradition of the nation or even merely as not sexually productive for the state, such as single women, are now made deviant (Alexander 1994; Bacchetta 1999; Blackwood 2005; Hoad 1999). For example, Neville Hoad (1999) argues that in southern Africa, gay and lesbian rights are constructed as part of a decadent western modernity and outside of the space of an authentic African tradition; thus, in regional politics, the recent advances for gay and lesbian rights within South Africa are used by its neighbors to define it as *un-African*. Similarly Bacchetta (1999), focusing on postcolonial Indian nationalism and especially on recent Hindu nationalism, argues that this nationalism constructs both "internal others" such as Muslim men and "external others" such as "the west" as hypersexual. Bacchetta offers two terms for thinking about such othering, *xenophobic queerphobia* and *queerphobic xenophobia*. While the first figures the queer as external to the nation, the second makes queer a trope for all otherness, assigning a metaphoric queerness to all outsiders regardless of sexual identity.

Of course, the politics of nation, culture, race and ethnicity, tradition and modernity, progress and stagnation, development and underdevelopment, implicate gender and sexuality in myriad and complex ways that exceed the purposes of this study. For example, the symbol "woman," as well as particular women's bodies, are vehicles for not only guarding national tradition but also for projects of modernization and can further be deployed creatively by women themselves (Greenhalgh 1994; Lopez 1998; Cano 1998; de Groot 1998; Alexander 1994). Similarly, "sexual others," too, may be incorporated into state projects and even into the nation at particular moments (Larvie 1999). Moreover in the GA, little can be said about specific national constructions of community. What can be seen from the rare angle of vision provided by the GA debates, however, is a (particular local instantiation) of a *global conversation*. That is, to the hierarchies of the colonial narrative, the anti-colonial argument for freedom and for the nation is an argument for adulthood and masculinity. The agency of the nation is envisioned in these conversations, thus, as a heteronormative, masculine agency. And the new metaphor for international community, little surprise, is brotherhood.

THEORIZING RESISTANCE: WHAT DID WE LEARN?

This is a study on conversations occurring, broadly, between transnational "colonialist" and "anti-colonialist" collectivities. The study's purpose is to understand a particular set of exchanges between different racialized, sexualized subjectivities in historical and transnational perspective. Patterns of appeal and narrative, in the manner in which they are amassed and compared here, offer a window onto such conversations. However, these findings are silent on a number of accounts. First, they say nothing about what might be occurring at other levels of analysis. For example, at the state level, we do not know what particular states might want, whether a state would follow the general pattern identified for its group in another context, what additional issues distinguish the situation of a given state, and so forth. Second, though these conversations are "global," they are happening in a particular "local" situation—in the United Nations General Assembly immediately after World War II. In that sense, like any particular "global," they are a local instantiation of the "global (Robertson 1997)"—hence they are *local-global* conversations. Other spaces and times of investigation regarding some of these same issues might reveal different elements within these exchanges. Third, these negotiations are occurring among elites—among groups in power within particular states via their elite diplomatic proxies. Overwhelmingly, the bulk of these individuals are educated, and they are male. This is true of the elite groups of both powerful and colonialist states on the one hand as well as of newly independent and anti-colonialist states on the other. As such, the conversations examined do not necessarily represent the perspectives of various "others"—women, the unlettered, and contingencies not in power within particular states. The partiality of these negotiations, however, should not detract from their significance. For this partiality is in stark contrast to the alleged universalism of the UN negotiations, underscoring the central point of this study that the negotiation of international community is a problematic, power-laden undertaking that represents itself as a moment in the global advance of democracy.

Beyond this partiality, it must be noted that the way resistance and social change are institutionalized within the complex, bureaucratic apparatus of the United Nations, only certain social locations are able to participate in the language games this apparatus presupposes. Thus, nationalist and anti-colonialist movements must learn the language games of time, space, subjectivity, agency, and representation embedded within the state-system and the global economy, at the very minimum, to negotiate their entry. The system's spatial and temporal others, who speak from within different language-games, are at a distinct disadvantage. This consideration inevitably brings us to one question: what would the renegotiation of the hierarchies of the colonial look like from these othered social locations? From the perspective of the indigenous, women, the "subaltern?" And, where would we go to get a glimpse?

Appendix
Tables and Figures

CHAPTER 2

Table 1. Distribution of Mandates by the League of Nations

Class of Mandate	Territory (Administering Power)
A	Syria-Lebanon (France)
	Palestine, Transjordan, Iraq (Great Britain)
B	The Cameroons, Togo (France)
	North West Cameroons, Togo (West), Tanganyika (Great Britain)
	Ruanda-Urundi (Belgium)
C	South West Africa (Union of South Africa)
	Caroline Islands, Mariana Islands, Marshall Islands (Japan)
	Nauru, British Empire, Eastern New Guinea (Australia)
	Western Samoa (New Zealand)

Source: Grimal, 1978: 14.

CHAPTER 3

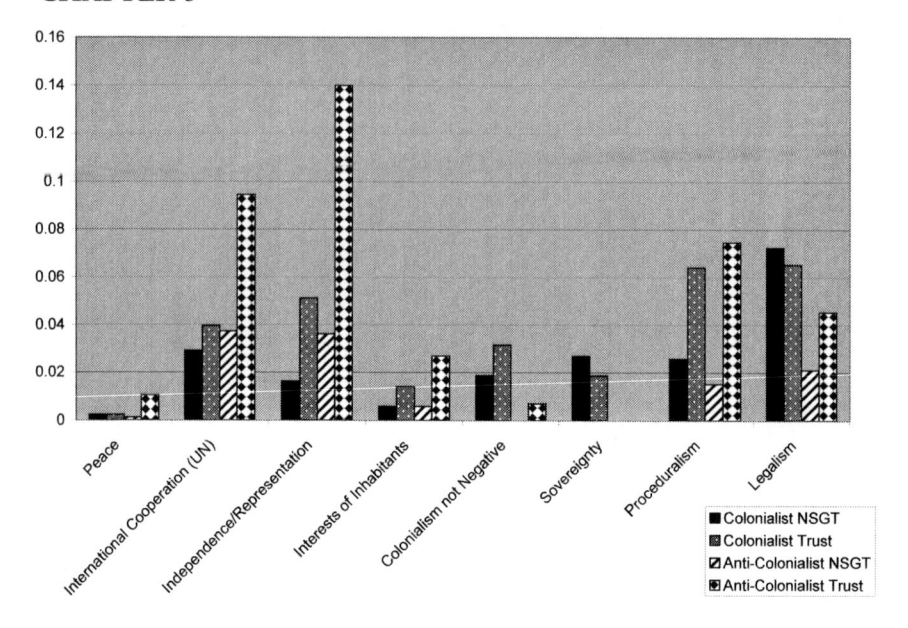

Chart 1. Prevalence of Appeals in Debates on NSGTs and Trusts, by Political Position (%)

Notes:

1. This is based on a total of 54 meetings examined, with 20 of those being on NSGTs and 34 being on Trusts.

2. Percentages are calculated for the total number of appeals across all years of debate in order to control for the different length of time spent on Trusts versus NSGTs.

Appendix

Extra-Colonial	Colonial Problematic		Extra-Colonial
(Dependent Territories)	NSGT Territories	Trust Territories	(Independent States)
			X X
X	X	X	X X
X	X X X X		X
X X	X X	X	X
X	X		
X	X X		
X			

Figure 1. The UN Bounding of the Colonial Problematic

Table 1. Growth in UN Membership, 1945 to Present

Year	Number	Member States
1945	Original 51	Argentina, Australia, Belgium, Bolivia, Brazil, Belarus, Canada, Chile, China, Colombia, Costa Rica, Cuba, Czechoslovakia, Denmark, Dominican Republic, Ecuador, Egypt, El Salvador, Ethiopia, France, Greece, Guatemala, Haiti, Honduras, India, Iran, Iraq, Lebanon, Liberia, Luxembourg, Mexico, Netherlands, New Zealand, Nicaragua, Norway, Panama, Paraguay, Peru, Philippines, Poland, Russian Federation, Saudi Arabia, South Africa, Syrian Arab Republic, Turkey, Ukraine, United Kingdom of Great Britain and Northern Ireland, United States of America, Uruguay, Bolivarian Republic of Venezuela, Yugoslavia[1]
1946	55	Afghanistan, Iceland, Sweden, Thailand
1947	57	Pakistan, Yemen
1948	58	Myanmar
1949	59	Israel
1950	60	Indonesia
1955	76	Albania, Austria, Bulgaria, Cambodia, Finland, Hungary, Ireland, Italy, Jordan, Lao People's Democratic Republic, Libyan Arab Jamahiriya, Nepal, Portugal, Romania, Spain, Sri Lanka
1956	80	Japan, Morocco, Sudan, Tunisia
1957	82	Ghana, Malaysia

Table 1. Growth in UN Membership, 1945 to Present (continued)

Year	Number	Member States
1958	82²	Guinea
1960	99	Benin, Burkina Faso, Cameroon, Central African Republic, Chad, Congo, Côte d'Ivoire, Cyprus, Democratic Republic of the Congo, Gabon, Madagascar, Mali, Niger, Nigeria, Senegal, Somalia, Togo
1961	104	Mauritania, Mongolia, Sierra Leone, United Republic of Tanzania
1962	110	Algeria, Burundi, Jamaica, Rwanda, Trinidad and Tobago, Uganda
1963	112	Kenya, Kuwait
1964	115	Malawi, Malta, Zambia
1965	117	Gambia, Maldives, Singapore
1966	122	Barbados, Botswana, Guyana, Lesotho
1967	123	Democratic Yemen
1968	126	Equatorial Guinea, Mauritius, Swaziland
1970	127	Fiji
1971	132	Bahrain, Bhutan, Oman, Qatar, United Arab Emirates
1973	135	Bahamas, Federal Republic of Germany, German Democratic Republic
1974	138	Bangladesh, Grenada, Guinea-Bissau
1975	144	Cape Verde, Comoros, Mozambique, Papua New Guinea, Sao Tome and Principe, Suriname
1976	147	Angola, Samoa, Seychelles
1977	149	Djibouti, Viet Nam
1978	151	Dominica, Solomon Islands
1979	152	Saint Lucia
1980	154	Saint Vincent and the Grenadines, Zimbabwe
1981	157	Antigua and Barbuda, Belize, Vanuatu
1983	158	Saint Kitts and Nevis
1984	159	Brunei Darussalam
1990	159³	Liechtenstein, Namibia

continued

Appendix

Table 1. Growth in UN Membership, 1945 to Present (continued)

Year	Number	Member States
1991	166	Democratic People's Republic of Korea, Estonia, Federated States of Micronesia, Latvia, Lithuania, Marshall Islands, Republic of Korea
1992	179	Armenia, Azerbaijan, Bosnia and Herzegovina,[3] Croatia,[2] Georgia, Kazakhstan, Kyrgyzstan, Moldova, San Marino, Slovenia,[3] Tajikistan, Turkmenistan, Uzbekistan
1993	184	Andorra, Czech Republic, Eritrea, Monaco, Slovak Republic, The former Yugoslav Republic of Macedonia[3]
1994	185	Palau
1999	188	Kiribati, Nauru, Tonga
2000	189	Tuvalu, Serbia and Montenegro[1]
2002	191	Switzerland, Timor-Leste

continued

Notes:

[1] The Socialist Federal Republic of Yugoslavia was an original Member of the United Nations, the Charter having been signed on its behalf on 26 June 1945 and ratified 19 October 1945, until its dissolution following the establishment and subsequent admission as new members of Bosnia and Herzegovina, the Republic of Croatia, the Republic of Slovenia, The former Yugoslav Republic of Macedonia, and the Federal Republic of Yugoslavia.

The Republic of Bosnia and Herzegovina was admitted as a Member of the United Nations by General Assembly resolution A/RES/46/237 of 22 May 1992.

The Republic of Croatia was admitted as a Member of the United Nations by General Assembly resolution A/RES/46/238 of 22 May 1992.

The Republic of Slovenia was admitted as a Member of the United Nations by General Assembly resolution A/RES/46/236 of 22 May 1992.

By resolution A/RES/47/225 of 8 April 1993, the General Assembly decided to admit as a Member of the United Nations the State being provisionally referred to for all purposes within the United Nations as "The former Yugoslav Republic of Macedonia" pending settlement of the difference that had arisen over its name.

The Federal Republic of Yugoslavia was admitted as a Member of the United Nations by General Assembly resolution A/RES/55/12 of 1 November 2000.

Following the adoption and the promulgation of the Constitutional Charter of Serbia and Montenegro by the Assembly of the Federal Republic of Yugoslavia on 4 February 2003, the name of the State of the Federal Republic of Yugoslavia was changed to Serbia and Montenegro.

[2] The total remains the same because from 21 January 1958 Syria and Egypt continued as a single member (United Arab Republic).

[3] The Federal Republic of Germany and the German Democratic Republic were admitted to membership in the United Nations on 18 September 1973. Through the accession of the German Democratic Republic to the Federal Republic of Germany, effective from 3 October 1990, the two German States have united to form one sovereign State.

Source: http://www.un.org/Overview/growth.htm

Table 2. Trusts and NSGTs, 1945–1999

Administering Power/Authority	Territory	Status	Year
Australia	Cocos (Keeling) Islands	Change in Status	1984
	Papua	Independence as Papua New Guinea	1975
	Nauru *Trust Territory*	Independence	1968
	New Guinea *Trust Territory*	Independence as Papua New Guinea	1975
Belgium	Belgian Congo	Independence as Congo Leopoldville, then Zaire (Now Democratic Republic of the Congo)	1960
	Ruanda-Urundi *Trust Territory*	Independence as Burundi	1962
		Independence as Rwanda	1962
Denmark	Greenland	Change in Status	1954
France	French Equatorial Africa	Independence as Chad	1960
		Independence as Gabon	1960
	(Middle Congo)	Independence as Congo (Brazzaville) (Now Republic of the Congo)	1960
	(Ubangi Shari)	Independence as Central African Republic	1960
	French Establishments in India	Change in Status	1947

continued

Appendix

Table 2. Trusts and NSGTs, 1945–1999 (continued)

Administering Power/Authority	Territory	Status	Year
	French Establishments in Oceania	Change in Status	1947
	French Guiana	Change in Status	1947
	French Somaliland	Independence as Djibouti	1977
	French West Africa	Independence as Dahomey (Now Benin)	1960
	(French Guinea)	Independence as Guinea	1958
	(French Sudan)	Independence as Mali	1960
		Independence as Ivory Coast	1960
		Independence as Mauritania	1960
	(Niger Colony)	Independence as Niger	1960
		Independence as Senegal	1960
		Independence as Upper Volta (Now Burkina-Faso)	1960
	Guadeloupe and Dependencies	Change in Status	1947
	Indo-China	Independence as Cambodia	1953
		Independence as Laos	1949
		Independence as Viet Nam	1945
	Madagascar and Dependencies	Independence as Madagascar	1960
		Independence as Comoros	1975
	Martinique	Change in Status	1947
	Morocco	Independence	1956
	New Caledonia [1] and Dependencies	Change in Status	1947
	New Hebrides (Under Anglo-French Condominium)	Independence as Vanuatu	1980
	Reunion	Change in Status	1947

continued

Table 2. Trusts and NSGTs, 1945–1999 (continued)

Administering Power/Authority	Territory	Status	Year
	St. Pierre and Miquelon	Change in Status	1947
	Tunisia	Independence	1956
	Cameroons *Trust Territory*	Independence as Cameroon	1960
	French Togoland *Trust Territory*	Independence as Togo	1960
Italy	Somaliland *Trust Territory*	Independence as Somalia (joined with British Somaliland)	1960
Netherlands	Netherlands Indies	Independence as Indonesia	1949
	Netherlands New Guinea	Joined with Indonesia as Irian Jaya	1963
	Netherlands Antilles	Change in Status	1951
	Surinam	Change in Status	1951
		Independence as Suriname	1975
New Zealand	Cook Islands	Change in Status	1965
	Niue Island	Change in Status	1974
	Western Samoa *Trust Territory*	Independence as Samoa	1962
Portugal	Angola, including the enclave of Cabinda	Independence	1975
	Cape Verde Archipelago	Independence as Cape Verde	1975
	Goa and Dependencies	Change in Status	1961
	Portuguese Guinea	Independence as Guinea Bissau	1974
	Macau and Dependencies	Change in Status	1972
	Mozambique	Independence	1975
	Sao João Batista de Ajuda	Change in Status	1961

continued

Appendix

Table 2. Trusts and NSGTs, 1945–1999 (continued)

Administering Power/Authority	Territory	Status	Year
	Sao Tome and Principe	Independence	1975
	East Timor[2]	Independence as Timor Leste	2002
South Africa	South West Africa	General Assembly terminated South Africa's mandate	1966
		Independence as Namibia	1990
Spain	Fernando Póo and Rí Muni	Independence as Equatorial Guinea	1968
	Ifni	Change in Status	1969
United Kingdom	Aden Colony and Protectorate	Independence as South Yemen	1967
	Bahamas	Independence	1973
	Barbados	Independence	1966
	Basutoland	Independence as Lesotho	1966
	Bechuanaland Protectorate	Independence as Botswana	1966
	British Guiana	Independence as Guyana	1966
	British Honduras	Independence as Belize	1981
	British Somaliland	Independence as Somalia (joined with Italian Somaliland)	1960
	Brunei	Independence (Now Brunei Darussalam)	1984
	Cyprus	Independence	1960
	Fiji	Independence	1970
	Gambia	Independence as The Gambia	1965
	Gilbert and Ellice Islands Colony	Independence as Kiribati	1979
		Independence as Tuvalu	1978

continued

Table 2. Trusts and NSGTs, 1945–1999 (continued)

Administering Power/Authority	Territory	Status	Year
	Gold Coast Colony and Protectorate	Independence as Ghana	1957
	Hong Kong	Change in Status	1972
	Jamaica	Independence	1962
	Kenya	Independence	1963
	Leeward Islands		
	(Antigua)	Independence as Antigua and Barbuda	1981
	(St. Kitts- Nevis- Anguilla)	Independence as St. Kitts and Nevis (separated from Anguilla)	1983
	Malayan Union	Independence as Federation of Malaya (Now Malaysia[3])	1957
	Malta	Independence	1964
	Mauritius	Independence	1968
	Nigeria	Independence	1960
	North Borneo[3]	Change in status	1963
	Northern Rhodesia	Independence as Zambia	1964
	Nyasaland	Independence as Malawi	1964
	Sarawak[3]	Change in status	1963
	Seychelles	Independence	1976
	Sierra Leone	Independence	1961
	Singapore[3]	Independence	1965
	Solomon Islands	Independence	1978
	Southern Rhodesia	Independence as Zimbabwe	1980
	Swaziland	Independence	1968
	Trinidad and Tobago	Independence	1962
	Uganda	Independence	1962
	Windward Islands		

continued

Appendix 159

Table 2. Trusts and NSGTs, 1945–1999 (continued)

Administering Power/Authority	Territory	Status	Year
	(Dominica)	Independence as Dominica	1978
	(Grenada)	Independence as Grenada	1974
	(St. Lucia)	Independence as St. Lucia	1979
	(St. Vincent)	Independence as St. Vincent and the Grenadines	1979
	Zanzibar	Independence[4] as United Republic of Tanganyika and Zanzibar (Now Republic of Tanzania)	1963
	Cameroons *Trust Territory*	Northern Cameroons joined with Nigeria	1961
		Southern Cameroons joined with Cameroon	1961
	Togoland *Trust Territory*	Joined Gold Coast to form Ghana	1957
	Tanganyka *Trust Territory*	Independence[4] as United Republic of Tanganyika and Zanzibar after joining with Zanzibar (Now Republic of Tanzania)	1963
United States	Alaska	Change in Status	1959
	Hawaii	Change in Status	1959
	Panama Canal Zone	Change in Status	1947
	Puerto Rico	Change in Status	1952
	Pacific Islands *Trust Territory*	Change in Status as Federated Sates of Micronesia	1990
		Change in Status as Republic of the Marshall Island	1990

continued

Table 2. Trusts and NSGTs, 1945–1999 (continued)

Administering Power/Authority	Territory	Status	Year
		Change in Status as Northern Mariana Islands	1990
		Change in Status as Palau	1994

Notes:

[1] In 1986 the General Assembly determined that New Caledonia was a Non-Self-Governing Territory.

[2] Initially administered by Portugal. Under Indonesian control between 1975 and 1999. East Timor attained independence in May 2002 and joined the United Nations in September 2002 as Timor Leste.

[3] In 1963, the Federation of Malaya became Malaysia, following the admission to the new federation of Singapore, Sabah (North Borneo) and Sarawak. Singapore became independent 1965.

[4] Following the ratification in 1964 of Articles of Union between Tanganyika and Zanzibar, the United Republic of Tanganyika and Zanzibar was formed and later changed its name to the United Republic of Tanzania.

Source: http://www.un.org/Depts/dpi/decoloniZahon/trust2.htm

```
                progress  ⟷  evolution
                    ↗                ↘
      advancement     autonomy          higher civilization
                      political independence
                      freedom
                      sovereignty
                    ↘                ↗
                modernity  ⟷  development
```

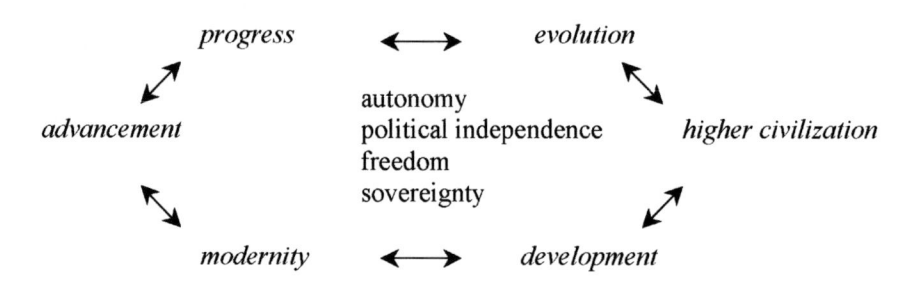

Figure 1. Associational Cluster for Political Independence, Freedom, Autonomy, and Sovereignty

Appendix 161

CHAPTER FIVE

native ↔ *uneducated*

underdeveloped ↗ ↘ *incompetent*

↗ political dependence ↘
lack of sovereignty

lack of civilization ↘ ↗ *simplistic civilization*

primitive ↔ *backward*

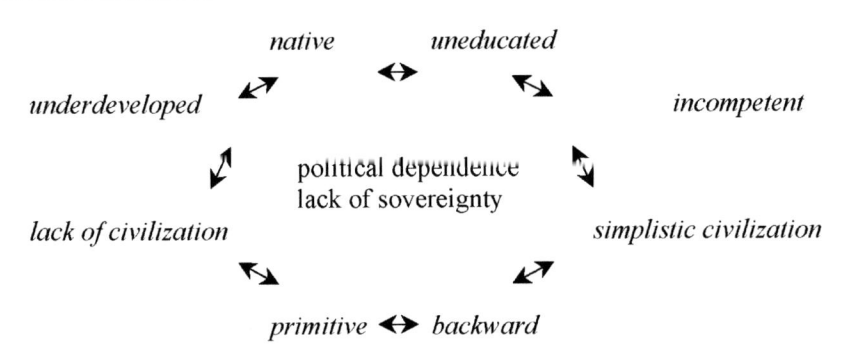

Figure-2. Associational Cluster for Political Dependence and Lack of Sovereignty

ability to make decisions for self

↗ autonomy ↘
maturity — political independence — *growth*
↘ freedom ↗
sovereignty

responsibility, including responsibility for self

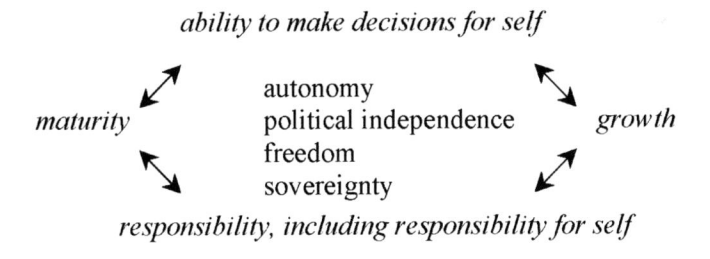

Figure 3. Second Associational Cluster of Political Independence, Freedom, Autonomy and Sovereignty

↔
immaturity *dependency*
↗ ↘
wards political dependence *children*
lack of sovereignty
↘ ↗

lack of responsibility, including responsibility for self

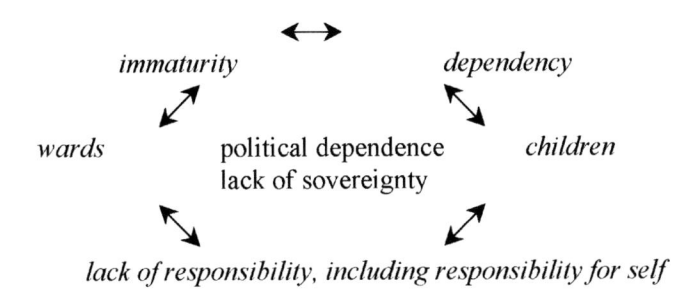

Figure 4. Second Associational Cluster of Political Dependence and Lack of Sovereignty

not advanced, progressed, evolved, developed

not self-governing ↗ ↘ *lower level of culture*

backwardness

↖ ↗

uneducated

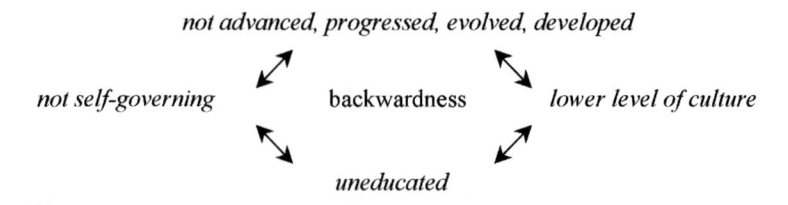

Figure 5. A "Colonialist" Anti-Colonialist Discourse

lack of development, ↔ *independence*
lack of independence   *leads to development*

↕ backwardness ↕

colonialism leads to backwardness,
lack of development

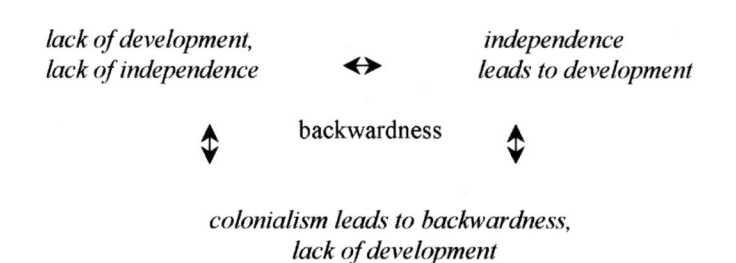

Figure 6. An "Alternative" Anti-Colonialist Discourse

Table 1. Agon Analysis of Political Independence and Political Dependence

Political Independence-Autonomy-Freedom-Sovereignty		Political Dependence-Lack of Sovereignty
Advancement, Development, Modernity, Progress, Evolution	vs	Backward, Underdeveloped Primitive, Native, Incompetent, Uneducated
Higher civilization		Lack of civilization/simplistic civilization

Appendix

Table 2. Second Agon Analysis of Political Independence and Political Dependence

Political Independence-Autonomy-Freedom-Sovereignty	Political Dependence-Lack of Sovereignty
vs	
Maturity, growth	Immaturity, children
Ability to make decisions for self	Wards, dependency
Responsibility (for self)	Lack of responsibility (for self)

Table 3. Political Status, Linear Progression, and Kinship

Key Terms/symbols	Cluster 1: Status in Linear Progression	Cluster 2: Kinship
Political Independence, Autonomy, Freedom, Sovereignty	Advanced	Maturity
	Developed	Growth
	Modern	Ability to make decisions for self
	Progressed	Responsibility (for self)
	Evolved	
	Higher Civilization	
Political Dependence Lack of Sovereignty	Backward	Immaturity
	Underdeveloped	Children
	Primitive	Wards
	Native	Dependency
	Incompetent	Lack of responsibility for self
	Uneducated	
	Lack of civilization/simplistic civilization	

Table 4. Identities, Relationships and Knowledges in the Anti-Colonialist Response

	Identity Distinctions	Relationships	Knowledge
N1	"Advanced" administering authorities versus "backwards" dependent territories	Tutelage required for progress and independence.	Primitive, uncivilized dependent territories require help in modernizing.
N2	"Advanced" administering authorities versus "backwards" dependent territories	Independence required for progress; tutelage not required.	Dependent territories are backwards because of colonialism.
N3	Rejection of categories of "backwards" and "advanced"	Immediate independence required.	Dependent territories are not backwards; no progress required.

*N=Narrative

CHAPTER SIX

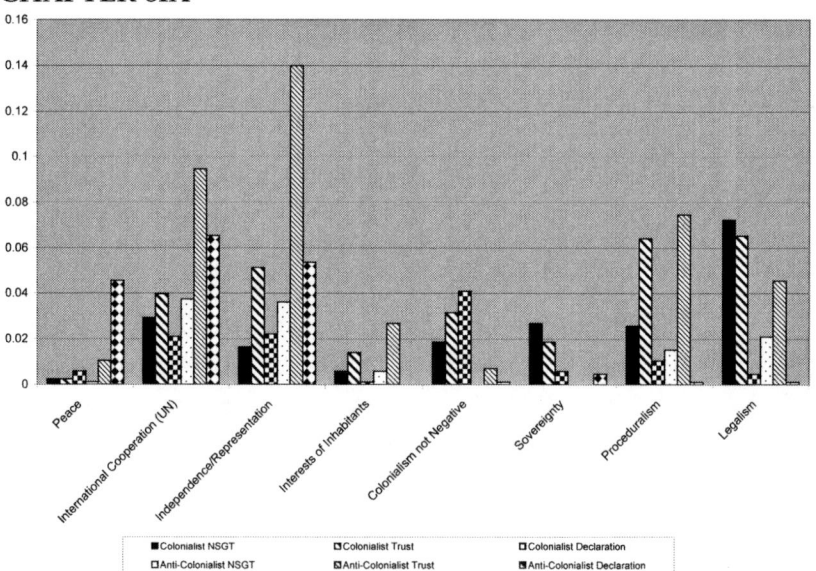

Notes:

[1] This is based on a total of 74 meetings examined, with 20 of those being on NSGTs, 34 being on Trusts, and 20 being on the Declaration.

[2] Percentages are calculated for the total number of appeals across all years of debate in order to control for the different length of time spent on Trusts versus NSGTs versus the Declaration.

Chart 1. Prevalence of Appeals in Debates on NSGTs, Trusts, and the Declaration, by Political Position (%)

Appendix

Table 1. Main Organs of the United Nations

Organ	Membership	Major Functions
Security Council (SC)	11[1] members, including 5 permanent members consisting of US, UK, France, China, USSR and 6 temporary members	Maintain peace and security, act on behalf of GA in situations requiring prompt action, submit reports to GA, revoke and restore membership privileges, deal with all trust territories designated as "strategic," shall have assistance from other UN members as required, shall have assistance from ESC as required, may help enforce decisions of ICJ.
General Assembly (GA)	All members of UN	It could consider and discuss, principles, initiate studies and receive reports, make recommendations,[2] may refer matters to the SC, agree to accept and carry out decisions of SC, approve the budget, oversee the TC with respect to "non-strategic trusts," responsible for the ESC, responsible for overseeing international economic and social cooperation as laid out in Chapter IX. UN members, who assume responsibility for the administration of NSGTs, must help promote the interest of these peoples, assist them in their development (Chapter XI).
Economic and Social Council (ESC)	A number of members elected by GA	Make/undertake studies with respect of economic, social, cultural, educational, health and other matters, generally under GA

continued

Table 1. Main Organs of the United Nations (continued)

Organ	Membership	Major Functions
Trusteeship Council (TC)	Include UN members who administer trusts plus as many non-administering members as required so that each constitutes 1/2 of the Council.	Will operate under authority of GA to oversee the (non-strategic) trust territories.
International Court of Justice (ICJ)		Principle judicial organ of UN
Secretariat	Consists of Secretary-General (appointed by GA upon recommendation of SC) and staff	Will act in capacity of chief administrative officer in meetings of GA, SC, ESC, TC

[1] This was changed in 1963 to 15 members, though the number of permanent members remained 5.

[2] Except on an issue the Security Council is considering, as per Article 12

Notes

NOTES TO CHAPTER ONE

1. For example, world-systems theorists argue for a much earlier dating of the development of the world economy, as well as the continuing relevance of territorial forms of political power. See (Arrighi 1994).
2. I am not using the term "non-European" in any simple, given sense. What counted as "Europe" at any particular moment moved in tandem with countless other historical, cultural and political factors. For more on this, see (Delanty 1995). Given the complexities of what may have counted as Europe and non-Europe in a particular historical moment, I also assume such complexities when I use concepts such as "west," "non-west," and modernity.
3. Of course, such a construction of the body as a metaphor for disorder may not always be oppressive but also liberating, or something else, depending on the context. In this work, however, I am focusing on conditions in which such a construction is positioned in opposition to and below the putative state of order.
4. I do not want to imply here that mechanical philosophy invented the rational/irrational hierarchy out of whole cloth. This hierarchy actually has a long history in traditions claimed by contemporary western thought. For example, in Aristotle's theory of natural slavery, he argues that the distinction between a natural slave and a rational man (who may incidentally be enslaved) is based on a distinction between "rational" and "irrational" souls. A rational man is a fully developed human male in whom the rational triumphs over the irrational, and so possesses the capacity for deliberation or moral choice. According to Aristotle, natural slaves do not possess these qualities, and neither do women and children (Pagden 1995).
5. I am fully aware of the problems of reading "the past" in terms of our needs and investments of the present, as well as how this critique has been applied to the sort of reading of Descartes and of Cartesian philosophy being developed here (for example, see Newman 2002). Following Newman's argument, I fully allow for the possibility of the complexity of the

context in which Descartes wrote as well as multiple readings of Descartes (Newman 2002). I further allow for historically variable realizations of the meaning of Cartesianism. Nevertheless, this complexity does not negate the possibility of a particular kind of reading, as described in the section above, becoming available to the numerous political projects cited above.
6. However, the sort of Weberian interpretation of Cartesianism that is provided here by Turner as largely associated with Protestantism, has been discredited as overly Anglo and Nordic-based, and as ignoring the earlier and perhaps more important influence of Cartesianism among Catholic as well as Jewish capitalists in places like France and the early German states (Moses 2003).
7. Joan Scott discusses how, in this fashion, gender has historically been a metaphor for the articulation of power. Likewise, she argues, other such marked groups (by race, or class or the like) may also signal power relationships (Scott 1988).
8. Interestingly, while not using the terminology above, Jeffery Alexander also speaks of the contemporary "binary discourse of civil society," in which oppositions such as rational-irrational, active-passive, and reasonable-unreasonable serve to distinguish bodies that belong in civil society from those that do not (1992).
9. Though from the other side, Stephanie Coontz argues that the patriarchal family is itself based on the model of a "miniature monarchy" in which the "husband king" enjoys authority over his dependents (Coontz 2005).
10. Regarding the differential recognition given by the *Jus Gentilis* to different categories of humanity, some authors emphasize that some Asian peoples were initially given a higher level of recognition than others. For example, Watson argues that in addition to those Asian territories identified by Grovogui above, European commanders dealt with particularly Hindu authorities much as European rulers dealt with each other—at least until the nineteenth century, when relations deteriorated and these others began to be explicitly treated as inferior (1984).
11. I do not mean to imply with this shift that hierarchical gender relations are simply done away with. As many feminist historians have pointed out, gender hierarchies were redefined and solidified in new ways in the late 18th and 19th centuries in Europe (de Groot 2000; Hunt 1992).
12. Other scholars have also argued that in the 1800s, the language of colonization for the sake of progress and civilization intensified (Itandala 2001).
13. There were various indexes which listed these records and what they contained, including an online index, a *Journal of the General Assembly*, and an *Index to Proceedings* (formerly, *Disposition of Agenda Items*). However, I found that such indexes often left out material I was interested in and the most reliable method was to actually go through the Table of Contents of the actual records themselves.
14. Guba and Lincoln use critical theory as an umbrella term here, denoting neo-Marxism, feminism, and materialism, as well as poststructuralism and postmodernism (Denzin and Lincoln 1998c).
15. Guba and Lincoln also agree that critical and constructivist approaches are commensurable (Denzin and Lincoln 1998c).

Notes to Chapter One

16. The term "good reasons" is also akin to Kenneth Burke's term "appeals." Beginning with the notion (that Fisher eventually adopts) that the central goal of communication is identification, Burke argues that human communication involves three elements: speaker, speech and appeal to the spoken-to person. He sees the appeal, or the rhetorical use of language, as the essence of communication, where language functions as a symbolic means of inducing cooperation in beings that by nature respond to symbols (Donahue and Procter 1997).
17. These authors write about discourse in general. Here, I apply their discussion to the specific case of narrative discourse.
18. Underlying the notion that the works of different rhetors contain "associational clusters" as well as that symbols/terms may have different meanings for different rhetors is the idea that the meaning of language is not transparent or fixed but rather contextual, shifting and interpretive. Speakers may employ the same terminology but with varying definitions of that terminology as well as with varying intent. Cluster-agon analysis, then, moves beyond more traditional methods—particularly more quantitative methods of discourse/textual analysis. For example, the popular content analysis method may be defined as "a quantitatively oriented technique by which standardized measurements are applied to metrically defined units and these are used to characterize and compare documents (Manning and Cullum-Swan in Denzin and Lincoln 1998a: 248)." While such a method may be useful in counting the frequency of particular symbols/terms within the debates, it nevertheless would have less utility in exploring the meaning of particular terms for particular speakers or a particular speaker's worldview.
19. I am speaking of groupings in regard to the issue of decolonization. Groupings were of course situational and shifted based on the issue under consideration. Furthermore, regarding these particular groupings, this division already had a history. Even before the formation of the UN, during WWII, while anti-colonialist groups prioritized issues of decolonization, racism and territorial conquest, the priority for the Allies was sovereignty. This division lasted through numerous meetings regarding the structure of the United Nations and ultimately became an important organizing principle in the Charter, where the anti-colonialist interests of one group were supported to a limited extent through the Trust system but thwarted through the Non Self-Governing Territories (NSGTs) system (Lauren 1998). With regard to the different discourses that are explored here, then, it must be remembered that the membership and goals of the two central groups within the debate had largely already solidified by 1945. As newly independent territories joined the UN, they tended to join the anti-colonialist group.
20. I do not intend to imply unproblematically with these terms that the United States was somehow a colonialist power or that the Soviet Union was not a colonialist power. In what follows, I will argue that while *both* perpetuated hierarchical constructions of space and identity, as did the European colonialist powers, the particular discourse of colonialism produced within the United Nations did not allow for a ready recognition of these practices as colonialist practices. Hence, although on occasion Soviet bloc countries especially

targeted what they termed the colonialist practices of the United States and vice versa, both the United States and the Soviet Union were allowed to position themselves as "outside" of the history of colonialism. While at times, it was recognized that the United States was indeed a colonialist power, it was nevertheless positioned as a "good" power compared to other "bad" powers.

NOTES TO CHAPTER TWO

1. I use the term sui generis here to distinguish nation-states in the non-European world from the European, for as Partha Chatterjee puts it, in the former, we see the historical fusion of the national question with the colonial question (Chatterjee 1986).
2. For example, such a transnational colonialist identity was certainly evident in the League of Nations Covenant.
3. Not all anti-colonial groups supported this Trusteeship System. Many thought it a patronizing suggestion, comparable to the League of Nations mandate system.
4. We must understand this coalition in the context of a centuries-long colonial history in which coalitions between African and Asian peoples were important tactics of resistance (Hall 1997b; Prashad 2001).
5. Scholars of anti-colonialist, nationalist movements often describe the period between World Wars I and II as a period of intensification in which these movements experienced a growing sense of "us" versus "them" regarding the colonialist West. This radicalism is argued to have intensified further with the war experiences of colonial subjects in WW II and especially with the "radical moment" from 1944–1952 in which they saw a weakening of imperial control, as well as a growing intellectual crisis of imperialism, among other developments (Furedi 1994).
6. Abdulgani, Roeslan. (1955). "Foreword" in *Asia-Africa Speaks from Bandung*. Ministry of Foreign Affairs, Republic of Indonesia.
7. Both members of this emerging entity of Asia-Africa and observers have alternatively termed it "Asia-Africa," "Afro-Asia," and "Africa-Asia." For purposes of simplicity, I will use the first designation.
8. The contexts for the three conferences of course had some important dissimilarities. While Bandung was the first gathering of independent Asian and African states on such a global level, the radical Cairo Conference was somewhat marred by tensions such as western suspicions of excessive Soviet influence; and finally, Accra was convened to explore the particular situation of Africa within the larger collectivity of Asia-Africa. Cairo was also the only conference where most of the delegates came from non-governmental organizations, as opposed to Bandung and Accra, where delegates represented independent governments (Legum 1958; Lloyd 1959).
9. Speakers also used the feminine noun "sisters," but this was rare. Even Mrs. R. Nehru, a rare female delegate at the Cairo Conference, began her address during the Opening Session to "Brothers and Sisters" but soon settled on just "brothers."

Notes to Chapter Three

10. In the debates on NSGTs and Trusts, the Asia-Africa argument especially emphasizes this notion of the *moral*, while the focus on *brotherhood* emerges especially in the debates in the final year on the Declaration. Since I examine the debates on the Declaration in a separate chapter, here I will focus on the argument for the *moral* and leave the discussion of *brotherhood* to the chapter on the Declaration.
11. The socialists of *L'Observateur* (later *Le Nouveau Observateur*) had in mind parallels between their own search for a "Third Way" between capitalism and Stalinism and the wave of national liberation movements. (See Encyclopedia of Marxism, www.Marxists.org and www.homme-moderne.org/societe/demo/sauvy/ 3mondes.html).
12. In contrast to these specific territories, I have singled out the issues of South West Africa and the Union of South Africa as one of the big four issues for the sheer amount of time spent on the latter.
13. That these appeals should emerge in the arguments of colonialist speakers as they negotiate with Asia-Africa is not surprising. The first two of these are fundamentally associated with the development of "the west" in Weber's Eurocentric argument (see *Economy and Society, Vols 1 and 2* (1956), and *General Economic History* (1927)), for example, while the very development and meaning of the second two rely on the rational-irrational distinction between imperial/colonial western powers and their "others (Theodoropoulos 1988)."
14. In terms of this contention around the very meaning of the Charter itself, we may understand the UN Charter here as a boundary object. Boundary objects arise "over time from durable cooperation among communities of practice . . . [and are] both plastic enough to adapt to local needs and constraints of the several parties employing them and robust enough to maintain a common identity across sites (Bowker and Star, 2000)." We may say thus that while the boundary object of the Charter allowed colonialist and anticolonialist groups to come together, it also enabled very different constructions for each community of practice of the purpose and significance of that object. Of course, the conflicts inherent in these different interpretations came to make themselves felt within the debates. However, it is perhaps the plasticity of the meaning of the Charter that enabled these radically different groups to come together to form an international community in the first place.

NOTES TO CHAPTER THREE

1. Dutch Guiana is also known as Surinam and the Dutch West Indies are also termed the Netherlands Antilles.
2. This term has been used to describe a group of political changes concerning democracy occurring "close together in time in different countries." An important example is the post-war "wave of democracy (Markoff 1996)."
3. Nevertheless, the resolution on the cessation of information on these territories on the part of the Netherlands passed, and the Dutch West Indies and Dutch Guiana were represented as being granted "self-rule" within

the Tripartite Kingdom of the Netherlands. (Dutch Guiana gained political independence in 1975. Hence, today, the Kingdom of the Netherlands consists of mainland European Netherlands, Aruba and the Dutch West Indies). What self-rule meant was "control over internal affairs," while the Netherlands still controlled defense, foreign affairs, citizenship and extradition. This shift has often been presented as "the end of the colonial relationship." And yet, the Netherlands still "represents" these other territories—for example, in the United Nations and in the European Union. The West Indies and Aruba are not considered part of the EU but rather, have the status of OCTs (overseas countries and territories). Since citizenship is controlled by the Kingdom, however, citizens from all three are considered EU citizens.

4. He argues that the idea of Europe first emerged in classical antiquity, transformed gradually in the Middle Ages from a geographical notion—originally linked to the idea of the Hellenic Occident—into a cultural idea subordinated to the idea of Christendom. It consolidated in the 15th c and eventually became focused more on Europe instead of Christianity. Then, it became enclosed in western Europe. Here, the division between Europe and the Orient was reflected in an internal division within Europe, and the eastern frontier was the determining factor in the shaping of the idea of Europe as the "West." With the opening of the western frontier following the re-conquest of Spain and the colonization of the Americas after 1492, there was a broader and more hegemonic notion of the "West" which provided the basis for European identity. Eventually, it came to rest on the universalistic notion of civilization, constructed in opposition to the Orient and the conquest of nature (Delanty 1995).

5. Arrighi (1994), for example, points out that because the U.S. does not have a history of settler colonialism, its imperialist practices have sometimes been invisible. He points out, however, that the absence of territorialism "abroad" does not negate the remarkable "internal territorialism" displayed by the U.S., in which Manifest Destiny incorporated huge tracts of contiguous land that decimated the local population and replaced it with a rapidly increasing immigrant population.

6. Here, I refer to the forced removal from their lands of about 3000 Meru tribesmen by the administering authority, the UK, of the trust territory of Tanganika. The lands were awarded to 13 white European settlers.

7. No natural geographical borders distinguished Russia from Asia, rendering it European and again, no such borders distinguished it from Europe, rendering it Asian. Hence, before the 18th c, its allegiance was not necessarily to either (Bassin 1991).

8. Interestingly, while it continued to westernize and Europeanize itself, and as it extended its rule in European fashion over territories around it, the various Eastern Europeans Russia conquered were particularly difficult to dominate because they saw themselves as more European and thus more advanced than Russia (Spzorluk 1997).

NOTES TO CHAPTER FOUR

1. See the previous chapter.
2. These territories were also periodically imaged as irrational or feminine, but the image of childhood was used most often in these debates.
3. In philosophy, the term ontology may be used to indicate "that part of metaphysics that specifies the most fundamental categories of existence, the elementary substances or structures out of which the world is made. Ontology will thus analyze the most general and abstract concepts or distinctions that underlie every more specific description of any phenomenon in the world, e.g. time, space, matter, process, cause and effect, system (Heylighen, 1995)." I use the term "ontological difference" here to indicate deeply held assumptions of difference regarding these "most fundamental categories of existence, the elementary substances or structures" between territories or peoples in different territories.
4. One could collapse all of these into more moderate and more extreme versions of the same response. However, following the Tischer, et al (2000) approach to discourse as simultaneously constitutive of identities, relationships between them and knowledge about them, I have chosen to explore each particular response along these three dimensions, distinguishing between them accordingly.
5. Similar to the historical significance of kinship politics for the colonial narrative produced within the arguments examined in the United Nations General Assembly, according to Mary Louise Pratt, these counterarguments also have an important history in the tradition of anticolonial argument (Pratt 2004).
6. The equation of "brotherhood" with "equality" in this context may seem somewhat problematic—particularly as many of these anti-colonialist speakers represented cultures where the institution of brotherhood was hierarchical. Nevertheless, the meaning of language is contextual and situational. In this discursive space, in opposition to the paternalistic kinship politics of colonialist powers, anti-colonialist speakers repeatedly and consistently equated brotherhood with equality and so advanced a preference for fraternal kinship relations.

NOTES TO CHAPTER FIVE

1. Specifically, it indicated an extension of a part of traditional international law governing modes of acquisition, transfer and loss of legal title over territory. It implied the emergence of set of legal obligations for those countries still enjoying sovereignty over colonial territories, and these obligations made it incumbent on those states to enable people in the colonial territories freely to choose whether to opt for independent statehood or association or integration with an existing state (Cassese 1995).
2. However, as pointed out in Chapter 4, this critique was not consistent. Rather, many anti-colonialists distinguished between "good" versus "bad"

colonialists in debates on NSGTs and Trusts, focusing on traditional European colonial powers and turning a blind eye to the practices of the USSR and the United States. In this final year, newly independent countries as well as others that sought to curry the favor of particular powers engaged in a similar activity. Ghana, for example, distinguished between "good" colonialist powers such as France and UK versus "bad" ones such as Portugal and Spain. The United States itself pointed to the USSR as the "worst colonizer" while the USSR returned the gesture.
3. Rajagopal argues that even before the United Nations, with its notion of "sacred trust," the League of Nations provided the mediating role in the transition between colonialism and development. In the process, the League helped to manage anti-colonial resistance (Rajagopal 2003).
4. Organizations such as the FAO, WHO, and ILO, for example, all offered such assistance to member states in their various areas of expertise if requested by those states.
5. A more subtle and convincing version of this argument is that development emerged more out of a "complex process of dealing with, suppressing, and co-opting Third World resistance that stretched out over decades (Rajagopal, 2003). Though in this study, I am more interested in focusing specifically on Asia-Africa's negotiations with the ideology of development.
6. According to Escobar (1995) for a number of years after WWII, the US's primary concern was economic recovery in Europe, and it only turned its focus on the "Third World" after 1949.

NOTES TO CHAPTER SIX

1. The initial republican challenge to the king's authority (in France) was also made in this language of brotherhood (Hunt 1992).
2. I see all of these as *moving metaphors*, the signification of which shift according to the social, cultural, and political conditions of their emergence (Lewis and Wigen 1997).
3. Various authors point out the role of such a temporal identity discourse historically in the colonial construction of sexual, racial and cultural hierarchy (Winant 2001: 29–30; McClintock 1995; Gilroy 1993).
4. These authors argue that the term "nation-state" did not really come into use until after World War II (see Kelly and Kaplan 2004).
5. Of course, in contrast to the totalizing aims of the state, Homi Bhabha reminds us of the inevitably hybrid nature of such ideological spaces (Bhabha 1994).
6. I do not want to suggest, however, that women's movements in decolonizing states necessarily accepted or did not resist these constructions. For example, Mrinalini Sinha shows how in the 1920s and 30s, such movements in India fought against such moves (Sinha 2000).

Bibliography

Abbott, Andrew. 1997. "Of Time and Space: The Contemporary Relevance of the Chicago School." *Social Forces* 75:1149–1182.

Adams, Julia. 2005. "The Rule of the Father: Patriarchy and Patrimonialism in Early Modern Europe." in *Max Weber's Economy and Society: A Critical Companion*, edited by C. Camic, P. Gorski, and D. Trubek. Stanford, CA: Stanford University Press.

Adas, Michael. 2004. "Contested Hegemony: The Great War and the Afro-Asian Assault on the Civilizing Mission Ideology." in *Decolonization: Perspectives from Now and Then*, edited by P. Duara. New York: Routledge.

Agnew, John. 1999. "Mapping Political Power Beyond State Boundaries: Territory, Identity and Movement in World Politics." *Millennium: Journal of International Studies* 28:499–521.

Aldrich, Robert. 1996. *Greater France: A History of French Overseas Expansion*. New York: St. Martin's Press.

Alexander, Jeffery C. 1992. "Citizen and Enemy as Symbolic Classification: On the Polarizing Discourse of Civil Society." Pp. 298–308 in *Cultivating Differences: Symbolic Boundaries and the Making of Inequality*, edited by M. Lamont and M. Fournier. Chicago: University of Chicago Press.

Alexander, M. Jacqui. 1994. "NOT JUST (ANY)BODY CAN BE A CITIZEN: The Politics of Law, Sexuality and Postcoloniality in Trinidad and Tobago and the Bahamas." *Feminist Review* 48:4–23.

Alonso, Ana Maria. 1992. "Gender, Power and Historical Memory: Discourses of Serrano Resistance." Pp. 404–425 in *Feminists Theorize the Political*, edited by J. Butler and J. W. Scott. New York: Routledge.

———. 1994. "The Politics of Space, Time and Substance: State Formation, Nationalism and Ethnicity." *Annual Review of Anthropology* 23:379–405.

Anderson, Benedict. 1991. *Imagined Communities: Reflections on the Origins and Spread of Nationalism*. London: Verso.

Anderson, Perry. 1974. *Lineages of the Absolutist State*. London: Humanities Press.

Appadurai, Arjun. 1994. "Disjuncture and Difference in the Global Cultural Economy." Pp. 324–339 in *Colonial Discourse and Postcolonial Theory*, edited by P. Williams and L. Chrisman. New York: Columbia University Press.
Aries, Philip. 1962. *Centuries of Childhood: A Social History of Family Life*. New York: Alfred A. Knopf.
Arrighi, Giovanni. 1994. *The Long Twentieth Century: Money, Power and the Origin of Our Times*. London: Verso.
Arter, David. 1999. *Scandinavian Politics Today*. Manchester: Manchester University Press.
Asian Relations Organization. 1955. *Asia and Africa in the Modern World*. Bombay, India: Asia Publishing House.
Augstein, Hannah Franziska. 1996. "Introduction." in *Race: The Origins of an Idea, 1760–1850*, edited by H. F. Augstein. Bristol, England: Thoemmes Press.
Bacchetta, Paola. 1999. "When the (Hindu) Nation Exiles Its Queers." *Social Text* 17.
Balibar, Etienne. 1996. "The Nation Form: History and Ideology." Pp. 132–149 in *Becoming National*, edited by G. Eley and R. Suny. Oxford: Oxford University Press.
Barlow, Tani, Ed. 1997. *Formations of Colonial Modernity: Modernity in East Asia*. Durham: Duke University Press.
Bassin, Mark. 1991. "Russia Between Europe and Asia: The Ideological Construction of Geographical Space." *Slavic Review* 50:1–17.
Bell, P. M. H. 2001. *The World Since 1945: An International History*. New York: Oxford University Press.
Bennett, Tony. 1995. *The Birth of the Museum*. London: Routledge.
Berezin, Mabel. 1999. "Political Belonging: Emotion, Nation and Identity in Fascist Italy." Pp. 355–377 in *State/Culture: State-Formation After the Cultural Turn*, edited by G. Steinmetz. Ithaca: Cornell University Press.
Berger, Mark T. 2004. "After the Third World? History, destiny and the fate of Third Worldism." *Third World Quarterly* 25:9–39.
Berman, Morris. 1989. *Coming to Our Senses: Body and Spirit in the Hidden History of the West*. New York: Bantam Books.
Berthold, Carol A. 1976. "Kenneth Burke's Cluster-Agon Method: Its Development and an Application." *Central States Speech Journal* 27:302–309.
Bhabha, Homi K. 1994a. "The Commitment to Theory." Pp. 19–39 in *The Location of Culture*. New York: Routledge.
———. 1994b. "'Race,' time and the revision of modernity." Pp. 236–256 in *The Location of Culture*. New York: Routledge.
Blackwood, Evelyn. 2005. "Gender Transgression in Colonial and Postcolonial Indonesia." *Journal of Asian Studies* 64:849–879.
Boellstorff, Tom. 2006. "Gay and lesbian Indonesians and the idea of the nation." *Social Analysis* 51.
Boli, John and George M. Thomas, Eds. 1999. *Constructing World Culture: International Organizations Since 1875*. Stanford: Stanford University Press.
Bourdieu, Pierre. 1977. *Outline of a Theory of Practice*. Cambridge: Cambridge University Press.

———. 1984. *Distinction: A Social Critique of the Judgment of Taste.* Cambridge, Massachusetts: Harvard University Press.
Bowker, Geoffrey C. and Susan Leigh Star. 2000. "Categorical Work and Boundary Infrastructures: Enriching Theories of Classification." Pp. 285–318 in *Sorting Things Out: Classification and its Consequences.* Cambridge: MIT Press.
Brunschwig, H. 1978. "French Expansion and Local Reactions in Black Africa in the Time of Imperialism (1880–1914)." Pp. 116–140 in *Expansion and Reaction*, edited by H. L. Wessling. Leiden: Leiden University Press.
Brzezinksi, Zbigniew, K. 1967. *The Soviet Bloc: Unity and Conflict.* Cambridge, MA: Harvard University Press.
Burke, Kenneth. 1973. *The Philosophy of Literary Form.* Berkeley: University of California Press.
———. 1984. *Attitudes Toward History.* Berkeley: University of California Press.
Cabral, Amilcar. 1994. "National Liberation and Culture." Pp. 53–65 in *Colonial Discourse and Post-colonial Theory*, edited by P. Williams and L. Chrisman. New York: Columbia University Press.
Cano, Gabriela. 1998. "The *Porfiriato* and the Mexican Revolution: Constructions of Feminism and Nationalism." Pp. 106–120 in *Nation, Empire, Colony: Historicizing Gender and Race*, edited by R. R. Pierson and N. Chaudhuri. Bloomington: Indiana University Press.
Cassese, Antonio. 1995. *Self-determination of Peoples: A Legal Appraisal.* Cambridge: Cambridge University Press.
Caulfield, Richard A. 1997. *Greenlanders, Whales, and Whaling: Sustainability and Self-Determination in the Arctic.* Hanover and London: University Press of New England.
Cerwonka, Allaine. 1999. "Constructed Geographies: Redefining National Identity and Geography in a Shifting International Landscape." *International Politics* 36:335–355.
Chabbott, Colette. 1999. "Development INGOS." Pp. 222–248 in *Constructing World Culture: International Nongovernmental Organizations since 1875*, edited by J. Boli and G. M. Thomas. Stanford, CA: Stanford University Press.
Chatterjee, Partha. 1986. *Nationalist Thought and the Colonial World.* Oxford: Oxford University Press.
———. 1993. *The Nation and Its Fragments.* Oxford: Oxford University Press.
Chilton, Paul and Mikhail Ilyin. 1993. "Metaphor in Political Discourse: The Case of the 'common European house'." *Discourse and Society* 4:7–31.
Christopher, A. J. 1984. *Colonial Africa.* London and Canberra: Croom Helm Ltd.
Collins, Patricia Hill. 2000. "It's All in the Family: Intersections of Gender, Race and Nation." Pp. 156–176 in *Decentering the Center: Philosophy for a Multicultural, Postcolonial and Feminist World*, edited by U. Narayan and S. Harding. Bloomington, IN: Indiana University Press.
Colwill, Elizabeth. 1998. "Sex, Savagery, and Slavery in the Shaping of the French Body Politic." Pp. 198–223 in *From the Royal to the Republican Body: Incorporating the Political in Seventeenth- and Eighteenth-Century France,*

edited by S. E. Melzer and K. Norberg. Berkeley: University of California Press.
Conklin, Alice and Ian Fletcher, Eds. 1999. *European Imperialism, 1830–1930: Climax and Contradiction*. Boston: Houghton Mifflin Company.
Connell, R.W. 2000. *The Men and the Boys*. Berkeley: University of California Press.
Coontz, Stephanie. 2004. "The World Historical Transformation of Marriage." *Journal of Marriage and Family* 66:974–979.
———. 2005. *Marriage, A History: From Obedience to Intimacy or How Love Conquered Marriage*. New York: Viking.
Cooper, Frederick. 1996. *Decolonization and African Society: The labor question in French and British Africa*. Cambridge: Cambridge University Press.
Cooper, Frederick and Randall Packard, Eds. 1997. *International Development and the Social Sciences: Essays on the History and Politics of Knowledge*. Berkeley: University of California Press.
Cox, Kevin. 2002. *Political Geography: Territory, State, and Society*. Oxford: Blackwell.
de Groot, Joanna. 1998. "Coexisting and Conflicting Identities: Women and Nationalisms in Twentieth-Century Iran." in *Nation, Empire, Colony: Historicizing Gender and Race*, edited by R. R. Pierson and N. Chaudhuri. Bloomington: Indiana University Press.
———. 2000. "'Sex' and 'Race': The Construction of Language and Image in the Nineteenth Century." Pp. 37–60 in *Cultures of Empire*, edited by C. Hall. Manchester: Manchester University Press.
Delaney, Carol. 1995. "Father State, Motherland, and the Birth of Modern Turkey." Pp. 177–200 in *Naturalizing Power: Essays in Feminist Cultural Analysis*, edited by S. Yanagisako and C. Delaney. New York: Routledge.
Delanty, Gerard. 1995. *Inventing Europe: Idea, Identity, Reality*. New York: St. Martin's Press.
Democracy of Content, Movement for a. 1954. "'Most Secret' Politics in Togoland: The British Government's Attempt to Annex Togoland to the Gold Coast." New York.
Deng, Francis M. 1993. "Africa and the New World Dis-Order." *Brookings Review* 11.
Denzin, Norman K. and Yvonna S. Lincoln. 1998a. "Collecting and Interpreting Qualitative Materials." Thousand Oaks: Sage.
———. 1998b. "The Landscape of Qualitative Research: Theories and Issues." Thousand Oaks: Sage.
———. 1998c. "Strategies of Qualitative Inquiry." Thousand Oaks: Sage.
Diallo, Mahamadou. 2001. "The 'Literature of Empire' and the African Environment." Pp. 105–126 in *Images of Africa: Stereotypes and Realities*, edited by D. Mengara. Trenton, NJ: Africa World Press, Inc.
Donahue, Ray T and Michael H. Prosser. 1997. *Diplomatic Discourse: International Conflict at the United Nations: Addresses and Analysis*, Edited by E. Mahoney. London: Ablex Publishing Corporation.

Doty, Roxanne Lynn. 1996. *Imperial Encounters: The Politics of Representation in North-South Relations*, vol. 5, Edited by D. C. a. M. J. Shapiro. Minneapolis: University of Minnesota Press.

Duara, Prasenjit. 2001. "The Discourse of Civilization and Pan-Asianism." *Journal of World History* 12:99–130.

———. Ed. 2004. *Decolonization: Perspectives from Now and Then*. New York: Routledge.

Dyer, Richard. 1997. "The Matter of Whiteness." in *White*. London: Routledge.

Edney, Matthew H. 2003. "Bringing India to Hand: Mapping an Empire, Denying Space." Pp. 65–78 in *The Global Eighteenth Century*, edited by F. A. Nussbaum. Baltimore, MD: Johns Hopkins University Press.

El-Ayouty, Yassin. 1971. *The United Nations and Decolonization: The Role of Afro-Asia*. The Hague, Netherlands: Martinus Nijhoff.

Elias, Norbert. 2000. *The Civilizing Process: Sociogenetic and Psychogenetic Investigations*. Translated by E. Jephcott. Oxford: Blackwell Publishers.

Enloe, Cynthia. 1989. *Bananas, Beaches and Bases: Making Feminist Sense of International Politics*. Berkeley: University of California Press.

Escobar, Arturo. 1995. *Encountering Development: The Making and Unmaking of the Third World*. Princeton: Princeton University Press.

Eva, Fabrizio. 1999. "International Boundaries, Geopolitics and the (Post)Modern Territorial Discourse: The Functional Fiction." Pp. 32–52 in *Boundaries, Territory and Postmodernity*, edited by D. Newman. London: Frank Cass.

Fabian, Johannes. 1983. *Time and the Other: How Anthropology Makes its Object*. New York: Columbia University Press.

Felstiner, Mary Lowenthal. 1983. "Family Metaphors: The Language of an Independence Revolution." *Comparative Studies in Society and History* 25:154–180.

Finkelstein, David. 2003. "Imperial Self-Representation: Constructions of Empire in *Blackwood's Magazine*, 1880–1900." Pp. 95–108 in *Imperial Co-Histories: National Identities and the British and Colonial Press*, edited by J. Codell. London: Associated University Press.

Finnemore, Martha. 1996. *National Interests in International Society*. Ithaca: Cornell University Press.

———. 1998. "International Norm Dynamics and Political Change." *International Organization* 52:887–917.

Fisher, Walter R. 1987. *Human Communication as Narration: Toward a Philosophy of Reason, Value and Action*. Columbia, South Carolina: University of South Carolina Press.

Foss, Sonja K. 1989. *Rhetorical Criticism: Exploration and Practice*. Prospect Heights, Illinois: Waveland Press, Inc.

Foucault, Michel. 1977. *Discipline and Punish: The Birth of the Prison*. New York: Vintage Books.

———. 1978. *The History of Sexuality: An Introduction*, vol. 1. Translated by R. Hurley. New York: Random House.

———. 1988a. "The Political Technology of Individuals." Pp. 145–162 in *Technologies of the Self: A Seminar with Michel Foucault*, edited by L. H. Martin, H. Gutman, and P. H. Hutton. Amherst: University of Massachusetts Press.

———. 1988b. "Technologies of the Self." Pp. 16–49 in *Technologies of the Self: A Seminar with Michel Foucault*, edited by L. H. Martin, H. Gutman, and P. H. Hutton. Amherst: University of Massachusetts Press.

Franklin, Sarah and Susan McKinnon. 2001. "Relative Values: Reconfiguring Kinship Studies." Pp. 1–28 in *Relative Values: Reconfiguring Kinship Studies*, edited by S. Franklin and S. McKinnon. Durham, NC: Duke University Press.

Furedi, Frank. 1994. *Colonial Wars and the Politics of Third World Nationalism*. London: I.B. Tauris Publishers.

Ganguly-Scrase, Ruchira and Roberta Julian. 1997. "The Gendering of Identity: Minority Women in Comparative Perspective." *Asian and Pacific Migration Journal* 6:415–438.

Giddens, Anthony. 1990. *The Consequences of Modernity*. Stanford, California: Stanford University Press.

Gieryn, Thomas F. 2000. "A Space for Place in Sociology." *Annual Review of Sociology* 26:463–496.

Gilroy, Paul. 1993. *The Black Atlantic: Modernity and Double Consciousness*. Cambridge, MA: Harvard University Press.

Goldberg, David Theo. 2002. *The Racial State*. Malden, MA: Blackwell.

Goslinga, Cornelis Ch. 1990. *The Dutch in the Caribbean and in Surinam, 1971/5–1942*. Assen/Maastricht, The Netherlands: Van Gorcum.

Gosnell, Jonathan. 2001. "Mediterranean Waterways, Extended Borders and Colonial Mappings: French Images of North Africa." Pp. 159–174 in *Images of Africa*, edited by D. M. Mengara. Trenton, NJ: Africa World Press.

Gottdiener, M. 1993. "A Marx for Our Time: Henri Lefebvre and The Production of Space." *Sociological Theory* 11:129–134.

Gottman, Jean. 1975. "The Evolution of the Concept of Territory." *Social Science Information* 14:29–47.

Greenhalgh, Susan. 1994. "Controlling Births and Bodies in Village China." *American Ethnologist* 21:3–30.

Gregory, Derek and John Urry. 1985. *Social Relations and Spatial Structures*. New York: St. Martin's Press.

Grewal, Inderpal. 1998. "On the New Global Feminism and the Family of Nations: Dilemmas of Transnational Feminist Practice." Pp. 501–532 in *Talking Visions: Multicultural Feminism in a Transnational Age*, edited by E. Shohat. New York: MIT Press.

Grimal, Henri. 1978. *Decolonization: the British, French, Dutch and Belgian Empires, 1919–1963*. Translated by S. D. Vox. Boulder, CO: Westview Press.

Grosfoguel, Ramon. 2003. *Colonial Subjects: Puerto Ricans in a Global Perspective*. Berkeley: University of California Press.

Grovogui, Siba N'Zatioula. 1988. "Conflicting Selves in International Law: An Analysis of Colonialism and Decolonization in Namibia." Doctor of Philosophy Thesis, Political Science, University of Wisconsin, Madison, Madison, Wisconsin.

———. 1996. *Sovereigns, Quasi Sovereigns, and Africans: Race and Self-Determination in International Law*, vol. 3, Edited by D. Campbell a. M. J. Shapiro. Minneapolis: University of Minnesota Press.

Bibliography

Hall, Catherine. 1999. "An Imperial Man in Australasia and the West Indies." Pp. 100–110 in *European Imperialism, 1830–1930: Climax and Contradiction*, edited by A. Conklin and I. Fletcher. Boston: Houghton Mifflin Company.
———. 2002. *Civilizing Subjects: Metropole and Colony in the English Imagination, 1830–1867*. Chicago: University of Chicago Press.
Hall, Catherine, Keith McClelland, and Jane Rendall. 2000. *Defining the Victorian Nation: Class, Race, Gender and the British Reform Act of 1867*. Cambridge: Cambridge University Press.
Hall, Stuart. 1997a. "The Local and the Global: Globalization and Ethnicity." Pp. 19–39 in *Culture, Globalization and the World-System: Contemporary Conditions for the Representation of Identity*, edited by A. D. King. Minneapolis: University of Minnesota Press.
———. 1997b. "Old and New Identities, Old and New Ethnicities." Pp. 41–68 in *Culture, Globalization and the World-System*, edited by A. D. King. Minneapolis: University of Minnesota Press.
Haraway, Donna. 1988. "Situated Knowledges: The Science Question in Feminism and the Privilege of the Partial Perspective." *Feminist Studies* 14:575–600.
Haraway, Donna and Thyrza Nichols Goodeve. 2000. *How Like a Leaf*. New York: Routledge.
Harding, Sandra. 2000. "Gender, Development and Post-Enlightenment Philosophies of Science." Pp. 240–261 in *Decentering the Center*, edited by U. Narayan and S. Harding. Bloomington: Indiana University Press.
Harvey, David. 2000. *Spaces of Hope*. Berkeley: University of California Press.
Heng, Geraldine. 1997. "'A Great Way to Fly': Nationalism, the State, and the Varieties of Third-World Feminism." Pp. 30–45 in *Feminist Genealogies, Colonial Legacies, Democratic Futures*, edited by M. J. Alexander and C. T. Mohanty. New York: Routledge.
Hevia, James L. 2001. "World Heritage, National Culture and the Restoration of Chengde." *positions* 9.
Hoad, Neville. 1999. "Between the White Man's Burden and the White Man's Disease: Tracking Lesbian and Gay Human Rights in Southern Africa." *Gay and Lesbian Quarterly* 5:559–584.
Hobsbawn, E.J. 1990. *Nations and Nationalism Since 1780: Programme, Myth, and Reality*. Cambridge: Cambridge University Press.
Hobsbawn, Eric and Terence Ranger, Eds. 1983. *The Invention of Tradition*. Cambridge: Cambridge University Press.
Holliday, Ruth and John Hassard, Eds. 2001. *Contested Bodies*. London: Routledge.
Horkheimer, Max and Theodor W. Adorno. 1973. *Dialectic of Enlightenment*. London: Allen Lane.
Hovet Jr, Thomas. 1960. *Bloc Politics in the United Nations*. Cambridge, MA: Harvard University Press.
Hunt, Lynn. 1992. *The Family Romance of the French Revolution*. Berkeley: University of California Press.
Itandala, A. 2001. "European Images of Africa from Early Times to the Eighteenth Century." Pp. 61–81 in *Images of Africa: Stereotypes and Realities*, edited by D. Mengara. Trenton, NJ: Africa World Press, Inc.

Janussen, Jakob. 1999, "The Constitution, a 150 Years: The Community of the Realm Viewed from a Greenland Aspect", Folketinget's commemorative volume on the occasion of the Constitution's 150th anniversary on 5 June 1999. Retrieved.

Johansson, S. Ryan. 1991. "'Implicit' Policy and Fertility During Development." *Population and Development Review* 17:377–414.

Johnson, Mark. 1987. *The Body in the Mind: The Bodily Basis of Meaning, Imagination and Reason*. Chicago: University of Chicago Press.

Kandiyoti, Deniz. 1994. "Identity and Its Discontents: Women and the Nation." Pp. 376–391 in *Colonial Discourse and Postcolonial Theory: A Reader*, edited by P. Williams and L. Chrisman. New York: Columbia University Press.

Kaplan, Caren, Norma Alarcon, and Minoo Moallem, Eds. 1999. *Between Woman and Nation*. Durham, NC: Duke University Press.

Kelly, J. D. and M. Kaplan. 2004. "'My Ambition is Much Higher than Independence'." in *Decolonization: Perspectives from Now and Then*, edited by P. Duara. New York: Routledge.

Kim-Puri, H. and J. 2005. "Conceptualizing Gender-Sexuality-State-Nation." *Gender and Society* 19:137–159.

King, Anthony D. 1997. "The Times and Spaces of Modernity (Or Who Needs Postmodernism?)." Pp. 108–123 in *Global Modernities*, edited by M. Featherstone, Scott Lash and Roland Robertson. London: Sage Publications.

Korang, Kwaku Larbi. 2004. *Writing Ghana, Imagining Africa: Nation and African Modernity*, Edited by T. Falola. Rochester: University of Rochester Press.

Korzeniewicz, Roberto Patricio, Angela Stach, Vrushali Patil, and Timothy Patrick Moran. 2004. "Measuring National Income: A Critical Assessment." *Comparative Studies in Society and History* 46.

Larvie, Sean Patrick. 1999. "Queerness and the Specter of Brazilian National Ruin." *Gay and Lesbian Quarterly* 5:527–558.

Lauren, Paul Gordon. 1998. *The Evolution of International Human Rights*. Philadelphia: University of Pennsylvania Press.

Lefebvre, Henri. 1991. *The Production of Space*. Translated by D. Nicholson-Smith. Oxford: Blackwell.

Legum, Colin. 1958. *Bandung, Cairo and Accra: A Report on the First Conference of Independent African States*: The Africa Bureau.

Lentin, Alana. 2004. *Racism and Anti-Racism in Europe*. London: Pluto Press.

———. 2005. "Replacing 'race', historicizing 'culture' in multiculturalism." *Patterns of Prejudice* 39:379–96.

Lewis, Martin W. and Karen E. Wigen. 1997. *The Myth of Continents: A Critique of Metageography*. Berkeley: University of California Press.

Lloyd, William Bross. 1959. "The Significance of the Bandung, Cairo and Accra Conferences." *Race Relations Journal* 26:135–144.

Lopez, Maria Milagros. 1998. "No Body is an Island: Reproduction and Modernization in Puerto Rico." Pp. 193–202 in *Talking Visions: Multicultural Feminism in a Transnational Age*, edited by E. Shohat. Cambridge, MA: MIT Press.

Lowenthal, David. 1998. *The Heritage Crusade and the Spoils of History*. Cambridge: Cambridge University Press.

Bibliography

Lyon, Peter. 1984. "The Emergence of the Third World." Pp. 229–238 in *The Expansion of International Society*, edited by H. Bull and A. Watson. Oxford: Clarendon Press.

Lyotard, J-F. 1984. *The Postmodern Condition*. Translated by G. Bennington and B. Massumi. Minneapolis: University of Minnesota Press.

Malley, Robert. 1996. "When South Met North: On the Origins of Third Worldism." Pp. 17–33 in *The Call from Algeria: Third Worldism, Revolution and the Turn to Islam*, edited by R. Malley. Oxford: Clarendon Press.

Mani, Lata. 1987. "Contentious Traditions: The Debate on SATI in Colonial India." *Cultural Critique* 7:119–156.

Markoff, John. 1996. *Waves of Democracy: Social Movements and Political Change*. Thousand Oaks, CA: Pine Forge Press.

Marx, Anthony W. 1998. *Making Race and Nation: A Comparison of the United States, South Africa and Brazil*. Cambridge: Cambridge University Press.

Matias, Albert. 1999. "On Boundaries, Territory and Postmodernity: An International Relations Perspective." Pp. 53–68 in *Boundaries, Territory and Postmodernity*, edited by D. Newman. London: Frank Cass.

Mayer, Tamar. 2000. *Gender Ironies of Nationalism: Sexing the Nation*. New York: Routledge.

McClintock, Anne. 1995. *Imperial Leather: Race, Gender and Sexuality in the Colonial Conquest*. New York: Routledge.

McMichael, Philip. 2000. *Development and Social Change*. Thousand Oaks, CA: Pine Forge Press.

Melucci, Alberto. 1995. "The Process of Collective Identity." Pp. 41–63 in *Social Movements and Culture*, vol. 4, *Social Movements, Protest and Contention*, edited by H. Johnston and B. Klandermans. Minneapolis: University of Minnesota Press.

Mengara, Daniel M, Ed. 2001. *Images of Africa*. Trenton, NJ: Africa World Press.

Merrick, Jeffrey. 1998. "The Body Politics of French Absolutism." Pp. 11–31 in *From the Royal to the Republican Body: Incorporating the Political in Seventeenth- and Eighteenth-Century France*, edited by S. E. Melzer and K. Norberg. Berkeley: University of California Press.

Meyer, John W. 1999. "The Changing Cultural Content of the Nation-State: A World Society Perspective." in *State/Culture: State Formation After the Cultural Turn*, edited by G. Steinmetz. Ithaca: Cornell University Press.

Meyer, John W., John Boli, George M. Thomas and Francisco O. Ramirez. 1997. "World Society and the Nation-State." *American Journal of Sociology* 103:144–181.

Meyer, John W., Richard Rubinson, Francisco O. Ramirez, and John Boli-Bennett. 1976. "The World Educational Revolution, 1950–1970." *Sociology of Education* 50:242–258.

Moghadam, Valentine. 1994. "Introduction: Women and Identity Politics in Theoretical and Cultural Perspective." Pp. 4–26 in *Identity Politics And Women: Cultural Reassertions and Feminisms in International Perspective*, edited by V. Moghadam. Boulder: Westview Press.

Montalvo-Barbot, Alfredo. 1997. *Political Conflict and Constitutional Change in Puerto Rico, 1898–1952*. Lanham: University Press of America, Inc.

Moon, Seungsook. 2005. *Militarized Modernity and Gendered Citizenship in South Korea*. Durham: Duke University Press.
Mortimer, Robert A. 1984. *The Third World Coalition in International Politics*. Boulder and London: Westview Press.
Moses, Claire. 2003. "Protestant Individualism." Personal Communication, edited by V. Patil. College Park.
Mosse, George L. 1985. *Nationalism and Sexuality: Respectability and Abnormal Sexuality in Modern Europe*. New York: Howard Fertig.
Nandy, Ashis. 1987. *Traditions, Tyranny and Utopias*. Delhi: Oxford University Press.
———. 1988. *The Intimate Enemy: Loss and Recovery of Self under Colonialism*. Delhi: Oxford University Press.
Narayan, Uma. 1997. *Dislocating Cultures: Identities, Traditions and Third-World Feminism*. New York: Routledge.
Newman, Jane O. 2002. "The Present and Our Past: Simone de Beauvoir, Descartes, and Presentism in the Historiography of Feminism." Pp. 141–173 in *Women's Studies on Its Own: A Next Wave Reader in Institutional Change*, edited by R. Wiegman. Durham: Duke University Press.
Nicholson, Philip Yale. 1999. *Who Do We Think We Are? Race and Nation in the Modern World*. London: M.E. Sharpe.
Nugent, Paul. 2002. *Smugglers, Secessionists and Loyal Citizens on the Ghana-Togo Frontier: The Lie of the Borderlands Since 1914*. Athens, OH: Ohio University Press.
Nussbaum, Felicity A, Ed. 2003. *The Global Eighteenth Century*. Baltimore: The Johns Hopkins University Press.
Obadele, Imari Abubakari. 1996. *The New International Law Regime and United States Foreign Policy*. Baton Route, LA: Malcolm Generation, Inc.
Orlando, Valerie. 2001. "Transposing the Political and the Aesthetic: Eugene Fromentin's Contributions to Oriental Stereotypes of North Africa." Pp. 175–191 in *Images of Africa: Stereotypes and Realities*, edited by D. Mengara. Trenton, NJ: Africa World Press, Inc.
Paasi, Anssi. 1999. "Boundaries as Social Processes: Territoriality in the World of Flows." Pp. 69–88 in *Boundaries, Territory and Postmodernity*, edited by D. Newman. London: Frank Cass.
Pagden, Anthony. 1995. *Lords of all the World: Ideologies of Empire in Spain, Britain, and France c. 1500-c.1800*. New Haven and London: Yale University Press.
Painter, David S. 1999. *The Cold War: An International History*, Edited by Evans E. and R. Henig. London and New York: Routledge.
Papanek, Hanna. 1994. "The Ideal Woman and the Ideal Society: Control and Autonomy in the Construction of Identity." in *Identity Politics and Women: Cultural Reassertions and Feminisms in International Perspective*, edited by V. Moghadam. Boulder: Westview Press.
Parrott, Bruce. 1997. "Analyzing the Transformation of the Soviet Union in Comparative Perspective." Pp. 3–29 in *The End of Empire? The Transformation*

of the USSR in Comparative Perspective, vol. 9, The International Politics of Eurasia, edited by K. Dawisha and B. Parrott. London: M. E. Sharpe.
Pateman, Carole. 1988. The Sexual Contract. Cambridge: Polity Press.
Patterson, Charles. 2002. Eternal Treblinka: Our Treatment of Animals and the Holocaust. New York: Lantern Books.
Pedler, Sir Frederick. 1975. "British Planning and Private Enterprise in Colonial Africa." Pp. 95–126 in Colonialism in Africa, 1870–1960. Cambridge: Cambridge University Press.
Perry, Steven. 1983. "Rhetorical Functions of the Infestation Metaphor in Hitler's Rhetoric." Central States Speech Journal 34:229–235.
Pierson, Ruth Roach and Nupur Chaudhuri, Eds. 1998. Nation, Empire, Colony: Historicizing Gender and Race. Bloomington, IN: Indiana University Press.
Prashad, Vijay. 2001. Everybody Was Kung Fu Fighting: Afro-Asian Connections and the Myth of Cultural Purity. Boston: Beacon Press.
Pratt, Mary Louise. 2002. "Modernity and Periphery: Toward a Global and Relational Analysis." Pp. 21–48 in Beyond Dichotomies: Histories, Identities, Cultures and the Challenge of Globalization, edited by E. Mudimbe-Boyi. Albany, NY: State University of New York Press, Albany.
———. 2004. "The Anticolonial Past." Modern Language Quarterly 65:443–456.
Prott, Lyndel V. 1991. "Argumentation in International Law." Argumentation 5:299–310.
Puri, Jyoti. 2004. Encountering Nationalism. Malden, MA: Blackwell Publishing.
Rajagopal, Balakrishnan. 2003. International Law from Below: Development, Social Movements, and Third World Resistance. Cambridge: Cambridge University Press.
Ramamurthy, Anandi. 2003. Imperial Persuaders: Images of Africa and Asia in British Advertising. Manchester: Manchester University Press.
Reus-Smit, Christian. 2001. "Human Rights and the Social Construction of Sovereignty." Review of International Studies 27:519–538.
Rist, Gilbert. 2002. The History of Development. London: Zed Books.
Roberts, Dorothy. 1997. Killing the Black Body: Race, Reproduction and the Meaning of Liberty. New York: Pantheon Books.
Robertson, Roland. 1997. "Glocalization: Time-Space and Homogeneity-Heterogeneity." Pp. 25–44 in Global Modernities, edited by M. Featherstone, Scott Lash and Roland Robertson. London: Sage Publications.
Ruggie, John Gerard. 1993. "Territoriality and Beyond: Problematizing Modernity in International Relations." International Organization 47:139–174.
Sartori, Andrew. 2005. "The Resonance of 'Culture': Framing a Problem in Global Concept-History." Comparative Studies in Society and History 47:676–699.
Schneider, David. 1980. American Kinship: A Cultural Account. Chicago: University of Chicago Press.
Scott, Joan Wallach. 1988. Gender and the Politics of History. New York: Columbia University Press.

Sewell, James P. 1975. *UNESCO and World Politics*. Princeton: Princeton University Press.
Shapiro, Michael J. 1999. "Triumphalist Geographies." Pp. 159–174 in *Spaces of Culture: City, Nation and World*, edited by M. Featherstone and S. Lash. London: Sage Publications.
Shlapentokh, Vladimir. 2001. *A Normal Totalitarian Society: How the Soviet Union Functioned and How It Collapsed*. London: M. E.Sharpe.
Sinha, Mrinalini. 1995. *Colonial Masculinity: The 'manly Englishman' and the 'effeminate Bengali' in the late nineteenth century*. New Delhi, IN: Raj Press.
———. 2000. "Refashioning Mother India: Feminism and Nationalism in Late Colonial India." *Feminist Studies* 26:623–644.
Sluglett, Peter. 2005. "Colonialism, the Ottomans, the Qajars, and the Struggle for Independence." Pp. 248–268 in *A Companion to the History of the Middle East*, edited by Y. M. Choueiri. Malden, MA: Blackwell Publishing.
Soja, Edward W. 1989. *Postmodern Geographies: The Reassertion of Space in Critical Social Theory*. New York: Verso.
Spruyt, Henry. 1994. *The Sovereign State and Its Competitors: An Analysis of Systems Change*. Princeton: Princeton University Press.
Staum, Martin S. 2003. *Labeling People: French Scholars on Society, Race and Empire, 1815–1848*. London: McGill-Queen's University Press.
Stephan, Nancy Leys. 2000. "Race, Gender, Science and Citizenship." Pp. 61–86 in *Cultures of Empire*, edited by C. Hall. Manchester: Manchester University Press.
Strang, David. 1991. "Anomaly and commonplace in European Political Expansion: Realist and Institutional Accounts." *International Organization* 45:143–162.
Szporluk, Roman. 1997. "The Fall of the Tsarist Empire and the USSR: The Russian Question and Imperial Overextension." Pp. 65–93 in *The End of Empire? The Transformation of the USSR in Comparative Perspective*, vol. 9, *The International Politics of Eurasia*, edited by K. Dawisha and B. Parrott. London: M. E. Sharpe.
Taylor, Peter J. 1994. "The State as Container: Territoriality in the Modern World-System." *Progress in Human Geography* 18:151–162.
Teitelbaum, Michael S. and Jay M. Winter. 1985. "Demography and International Politics: 1870–1945 and Demography and Internal Politics, 1870–1945." Pp. 13–62 in *The Fear of Population Decline*: Academic Press.
Theodoropoulos, Christos. 1988. *Colonialism and General International Law: The Contemporary Theory of National Sovereignty and Self-Determination*. Benin City, Nigeria: New Horizon Publishing House.
Thomas, George M. and John W. Meyer. 1984. "The Expansion of the State." *Annual Review of Sociology* 10:461–482.
Thompson, Virginia and Richard Aldoff. 1975. "French Economic Policy in Tropical Africa." Pp. 127–164 in *Colonialism in Africa: 1870–1960*, edited by P. Duignan and L. H. Gann. Cambridge: Cambridge University Press.
Titscher, Stefan, Michael Meyer, Ruth Wodak, and Eva Vetter. 2000. "Two Approaches to Critical Discourse Analysis." Pp. 144–170 in *Methods of Text and Discourse Analysis*, edited by S. Titscher, M. Meyer, R. Wodak, and E. Vetter. London: Sage Publications.

Todorov, Tzvetan. 1993. *On Human Diversity: Nationalism, Racism, and Exoticism in French Thought*. Translated by C. Porter. Cambridge, MA: Harvard University Press.
Turner, Bryan. 1992. "The Rationalization of the Body: Reflections on Modernity and Discipline and The Body Politic: The Secularization of Sovereign Bodies." Pp. 115-159 in *Max Weber: History to Modernity*. New York: Routledge.
———. 1996. *Body and Society*. London: Sage Publications.
———. 1997. "What Is the Sociology of the Body?" *Body and Society* 3:103-107.
United Nations. 1946. *Yearbook of the United Nations*, Edited by Office of Public Information. New York: United Nations.
———. 1947. *Yearbook of the United Nations*, Edited by Office of Public Information. New York: United Nations.
———. 1948. *Yearbook of the United Nations*, Edited by Office of Public Information. New York: United Nations.
———. 1949. *Yearbook of the United Nations*, Edited by Office of Public Information. New York: United Nations.
———. 1950. *Yearbook of the United Nations*, Edited by Office of Public Information. New York: United Nations.
———. 1951. *Yearbook of the United Nations*, Edited by Office of Public Information. New York: United Nations.
———. 1952. *Yearbook of the United Nations*, Edited by Office of Public Information. New York: United Nations.
———. 1953. *Yearbook of the United Nations*, Edited by Office of Public Information. New York: United Nations.
———. 1955. *Yearbook of the United Nations*, Edited by Office of Public Information. New York: United Nations.
———. 1957. *Yearbook of the United Nations*, Edited by Office of Public Information. New York: United Nations.
———. 1959. *Yearbook of the United Nations*, Edited by Office of Public Information. New York: United Nations.
———. 1960. *Yearbook of the United Nations*, Edited by Office of Public Information. New York: United Nations.
United Nations. 2003. "United Nations Documentation: Research Guide," Retrieved May 31, 2003 (http://www.un.org/Depts/dhl/resguide/).
Valderama, Ferdinand. 1995. *A History of UNESCO*. Paris: UNESCO Publishing.
Wallerstein, Immanuel. 1996. *Open the Social Sciences*. Stanford: Stanford University Press.
Watson, Adam. 1984. "European International Society and its Expansion." Pp. 13-33 in *The Expansion of International Society*, edited by H. Bull and A. Watson. Oxford: Clarendon Press.
Wells, Clare. 1987. *The UN, UNESCO and the Politics of Knowledge*. London: Macmillan Press.
Wesseling, H. L. 1997. *Imperialism and Colonialism: Essays on the History of European Expansion*. Westport, CT: Greenwood Press.

Winant, Howard. 2001. *The World is a Ghetto: Race and Democracy Since World War II*. New York: Basic Books.
Witz, Anne. 2000. "Whose Body Matters? Feminist Sociology and the Corporal Turn in Sociology and Feminism." *Body and Society* 6:1–24.
Wolf, Eric. 1982. *Europe and the People Without History*. Berkeley: University of California Press.
Yanagisako, Sylvia and Carol Delaney. 2001. "Naturalizing Power." Pp. 1–24 in *Naturalizing Power: Essays in Feminist Cultural Analysis*, edited by S. Yanagisako and C. Delaney. New York: Routledge.
Yuval-Davis, Nira. 1994. "Identity Politics and Women's Ethnicity." Pp. 408–424 in *Identity Politics and Women: Cultural Reassertions and Feminisms in International Perspective*. Boulder: Westview Press.
———. 1997. *Gender and Nation*. London: Sage Publications.
Zanger, Abby. 1998. "Lim(b)i-nal Images: 'Betwixt and Between' Louis XIV's Martial and Marital Bodies." Pp. 32–63 in *From the Royal to the Republican Body: Incorporating the Political in Seventeenth- and Eighteenth-Century France*, edited by S. E. Melzer and K. Norberg. Berkeley: University of California Press.

Index

A
Absolute authority, 3, 20, 21, 23 29, 30, 137
Absolute monarchies, 21
Administering authorities, 46, 56, 57, 58, 60, 61, 65, 66, 70, 73, 89, 96, 97, 98, 102, 103, 104, 106, 108, 110, 111, 120, 125, 126
Administrative unions, 60, 61, 62
Afghanistan, 27, 92
Africa, 2, 13, 14, 27, 29, 47–53, 66, 78–79, 82, 92, 93, 118, 121, 128, 129, 134, 135, 138, 141, 146
   North Africa, 25–26, 52
   southern Africa, 27, 146
   South West Africa, 60, 61, 62, 64, 98, 99, 171
   Union of South Africa, 60, 61, 62, 64, 98, 106, 171
African-Asian People's Solidarity Organization (AAPSO), 49
African Personality, 50
Alexander VI, Pope, 21
Algeria, 25–26, 52
All-Ewe Conference, 87, 89–90; *see also* Ghana
Allies, 28, 42, 44, 169
Alptekin, Isa Yusuf, 84
American exceptionalism, 80
American Revolution, 7, 81
Americas, 2, 21, 36–37, 129, 172
Anachronistic space, 9; *see also* space, politics of
Animism, 49
Anti-colonialist discourse, 37, 75, 104–105, 111, 145

Anti-colonialist states, 31, 40, 70, 147; *see also* Asia-Africa
Anti-colonialist view, definition of, 36–37
Anti-colonial movements, 29; *see also* Asia-Africa
Anti-slavery movements, 29
Appeals, in argument, 34–37, 55, 57–64, 73, 76, 81, 91–92, 95, 105, 117, 169, 171; *see also* good reasons
Argentina, 36, 117, 23
Ariès, Philip, 23
Asia, 2, 14, 47–53, 66, 78–79, 85, 117–118, 129, 141, 172
   East Asia, 141
   South Asia, 13
   Southeast Asia, 26
Asia-Africa, 36, 39, 41, 46–55, 65–66, 69–94, 114, 116–118, 124, 125, 134, 170, 171;
   see also anti-colonialist states; anti-colonial movements
   and Denmark, 72, 76–78, 82–83
   and Ghana, 86–93
   and global political context, 46–49
   and Netherlands, 72–73
   and Soviet Union, 83–86
   and United States, 72, 73, 74–76, 81
   as collective identity, 50–55, 78
   as voting bloc, 78
Asian Relations Organization, 48
Atiogbe, I. K., 89–90
Atlantic Charter, 42
Auger, Pierre, 131
Australia, 26, 76, 97, 119, 120
Azerbaijan, 84

189

B

Bandung Conference, 49–52, 70, 78, 84–85
Belgium, 25, 59–60, 99, 103, 106
Berlin Conference, 27
Biblical chronology, 9
Biological determinism, 25
Body, *see* embodiment politics; kinship politics
    as metaphor of association, 17–19
    as nature metaphor, 19
    body politic, 18
Bourbon absolutism, 16
Brazil, 58, 60, 98
Britain, 21, 23, 25, 26–27, 29, 47, 100
    British colonial discourse, 26–27; *see also* embodiment politics
    British colonies, 19
    Colonial Development Act, 27
    Colonial Office, 27
    Commonwealth, 47, 88, 103
British Togoland, *see* Ghana
Brotherhood, 4, 41, 50, 52, 54, 113–115, 120–121, 123, 124, 135, 139, 141, 146, 171, 173, 174; *see also* kinship politics; masculinity, politics of Buddhism, 49
Burke, Kenneth, 34, 36, 169

C

Cabral, Amílcar, 134
Cameroons, 52, 62
Capitulation regime, 23
Caribbean, 26
Cartesianism, 10, 168
Ceylon, 49–50, 54, 118–119
Childhood, politics of, 23–24, 26, 102, 173; *see also* kinship politics
Chile, 19, 77
China, 21, 27, 54, 60–61, 116, 127
Christianity, 8, 11, 18, 21, 49, 172
Civilization, 8, 14, 15, 19, 23–28, 30, 53, 79, 85, 92, 97–99, 102, 105–107, 109, 111, 118–119, 121, 131, 140, 168, 172
    Asian civilization, 53
    imperial civilization, 53
    unilinear theories of, 23
Classical patriarchal family, 20
Classic patriarchy, 3
Classification, politics of 9, 11, 13, 24–25
    and Enlightenment, 15
    and League of Nations Mandates System, 29

Cold War, 47, 49, 54, 96, 108
Collective identity, 37, 46, 63, 78, 82, 134
Colombia, 97
Colonialist discourse, 2–3, 17, 26, 29, 99, 103, 106, 110
    British, 14, 27
    French, 25
Colonialist view, definition of, 36–37
Colonial protectorate, 23
Committee on Information (from Non Self-Governing Territories), 56, 101
Communist bloc, 69
Conference of Independent African States, 49
Congo (Brazzaville), 122
Contract philosophers, 11–12
Convention People's Party (CPP), 88
Costa Rica, 74
Counterinsurgency politics, 29
Crimea, 84
Cuba, 61, 76

D

Danquah, Joseph B., 87–88
Declaration of the United Nations, 42
Declaration on the Granting of Independence to Colonial Countries and Peoples (Declaration), 3, 31, 110, 111, 113, 114, 116, 117, 122, 171; *see also* legal decolonization
Decolonization, *see* legal decolonization
Denmark, 61, 70, 72–73, 76–78, 82–83, 86, 88, 98, 99
Denmark and the incorporation of Greenland, 76–78, 82–83
Dependent territories in United Nations Charter, 44–47
Descartes, Rene, 10, 12, 19, 167, 168
Development, stages of, 24, 29, 140; *see also* underdevelopment
Development assistance, 115, 123, 125, 128–129
Differential personhood, 2–3, 9, 17, 35, 112
Differential subjectivity, *see* differential personhood
Disembodied individual, 11–12; *see also* political individual; universal individual
Doctrine of four humors, 18
Dominican republic, 74

Index

Draft Declaration on the Rights of Nations, *see* sovereignty

E

Eastern bloc countries, 54
Eastern New Guinea, 119–120
Economic and Social Council (ECOSOC), 127, 129–130
Egypt, 27, 48, 61, 128, 131
Eisenhower, Dwight, 80
Embodiment politics, 2–3, 5, 9, 12–18, 24, 30, 46, 64, 112; *see also* body; family; feminization; racialization
Enlightenment, 15, 23, 102, 138
Ethiopia, 92
Europe, 7, 8, 14, 20, 21, 24, 47, 79, 85, 86, 117, 118, 127, 128, 129, 138, 139–140, 141, 167, 168, 172, 174
   idea of/collective identity of, 8, 79, 85, 138, 140, 167, 172
   eastern and central Europe, 86, 172
   medieval Europe, 7
   western Europe, 8, 20, 85, 86, 172
European colonialist powers, 36, 79, 86, 169
European colonial project, 15, 19
Evolution, concept of, 27, 64, 97, 99, 102, 104, 105, 120

F

Family, *see* embodiment politics; kinship politics; brotherhood
   as metaphor of association, 17–19
   as nature metaphor, 19
   classical patriarchal, 20
   idea of childhood, 23
   Roman family, 21
   transformation in structure and relationships, 23
Fanon, Franz, 53
Far East, 128–129
Fascism, 46
Feminization, 13–14, 25; *see also* embodiment politics
Feudalism, 22
Filmer, Robert, 21
First Afro-Asian People's Solidarity Conference, 49
Fisher, Walter, 34
Food and Agriculture Organization (FAO), 125
Fourth Committee, 89–90, 101

France, 18, 23, 25–26, 29, 47, 64, 106, 168, 174
   colonial discourse, 25
   colonial policy, 26
   French civilizing mission, 25
   French Community, 47
   French Revolution, 7, 18, 25, 55
   French Union, 47
   Third Republic, 25
   Togoland, 87, 89, 93; *see also* Ghana

G

Gabon, 122
Germany, 25
Gettysburg Address, 80
Ghana, 51, 54, 71, 86–87, 89, 91–94, 100–101, 121, 174
Giddens, Anthony, 139
Gold Coast, *see* Ghana
Good reasons, 34–35, 37, 169; *see also* appeals
Greenland, 70, 71, 72, 73, 76–78, 82–83, 88, 98
Grotius, Hugo, 18, 21
Group of 77 (G-77), 54
Guatemala, 37, 75, 92
Guinea, 122

H

Haiti, 105, 128
Hawaiian Islands, 72
Hegel, Georg Wilhelm Friedrich, 24
Henry, Patrick, 81
Hierarchy of masculinities, 13; *see also* embodiment politics; feminization; racialization
Hingitaq 53 (Thrown out in 53), 83
Hottentots, 15
Huk rebels, 29
Human rights, 31, 43, 44, 57, 114, 126

I

Iceland, 81, 119
Idil-Ural, 84
India, 13, 14, 26–27, 49, 53, 54, 57, 61, 64, 65, 75, 91–93, 106–107, 118, 119, 121, 128, 174
Indian Council of World Affairs, 48
Indonesia, 48, 49, 52, 170
Indonesian President Susilo Banbang Yudhoyono, 48

International Bank for Reconstruction and Development, *see* World Bank
International Committee on Monuments, Artistic and Historical Sites, and Archeological Excavations, 130
International community, 2–4, 5, 16, 17, 29, 30, 31, 39, 54, 55, 58, 63, 66, 80, 99, 102, 106, 112, 113–115, 120, 124, 135, 137, 147, 148, 171
  definition of, 3–4
  anti-colonialist redefinition of,115, 120, 135, 147
  in argument in the UNGA, 54, 55, 58, 63–66, 99, 102, 106
  in formal colonial era, 3, 4, 5, 16–30
International cooperation, 55, 57, 58, 59, 60, 61, 62, 63, 66, 73, 117
International law, 17, 18, 21–23, 27, 43, 44, 55, 74, 113, 118, 173
  and 'harsher' legitimations of colonial rule, 21–23, 113, 118
  and 'softer' legitimations of colonial rule, 23–25, 27–30; *see also* League of Nations Mandates System; United Nations Charter
  jus cogens, 113
  jus gentiles, 21, 168
International relations, 4, 114
  and metaphor of brotherhood, 4, 114
  and metaphor of parent-child, 4
International society, 8
International Study Centre for the Presentation and Restoration of Cultural Property, 131
International Trade Organization (ITO), 125, 142
Iran, 51, 54, 108, 119, 120,124
Iraq, 29, 48, 54, 60, 118, 128
Iron Curtain, 84
Israel, 116

J
Jamaica, 27
Japan, 21, 54
Jordan, 48, 52, 121, 123; *see also* Transjordan

K
Khrushchev, Nikita S., 116
Kinship politics, 2–3, 5, 16, 17, 19, 20, 29, 30, 35, 37, 38, 40, 41, 46, 47, 52, 55, 63, 65, 66, 69, 86, 94, 95, 96, 97, 104, 111, 114, 115, 141, 173
  and anti-colonialist politics in the UNGA, 37–38, 41, 52, 69, 86, 94, 111, 114, 115, 141, 173
  and colonial rule, 19–20, 29, 30, 37, 38, 46, 69, 95, 96–97, 104, 111
  and 'harsher' legitimations of colonial rule, 20–23, 24, 29, 30, 95, 137
  and 'softer' legitimations of colonial rule, 3, 20, 23–24, 25–29, 30, 95, 96, 104
  impact on international law, 21–23, 27–29; *see also* League of Nations Mandates System; United Nations Charter; Declaration on the Granting of Independence to Colonial Countries and Peoples theory of, 17–19
Ku Klux Klan, 79

L
Laos, 119
Latin America, 79, 128–129, 141
League of Arab States, 48
League of Arab States, Covenant of, 48
League of Nations, 28–29, 44, 45, 107, 118, 170, 174
League of Nations Mandates System, 28–29, 118
Lebanon, 29, 48, 52, 54, 77, 120, 127, 130
Legal decolonization, 2–3, 5, 16, 17, 29, 30, 31, 32, 39, 40, 44, 45, 65, 96, 102, 108, 110, 111, 113, 116, 123, 135, 137, 143
Liberia, 54, 73, 76, 81, 119
Libya, 52, 54
Lincoln, Abraham, 81
Linear progression, 99–112, 117, 119, 120, 122, 124, 139, 143; *see also* time, politics of and anti-colonialist argument in UNGA, 104–110, 111, 112
  and colonialist argument in UNGA, 99–104, 110–111, 112, 117, 119
  and lack of sovereignty, 122–124
  and status of underdevelopment, 122–124, 143
Locke, John, 15
Lockean theory of property rights, 15

Index

Louis XIV, 16

M
Mali, 81, 118
Manifest destiny, 79, 86, 172
Marx, Karl, 17
Masculinity, politics of, *see* brotherhood; feminization; racialization; hierarchy of masculinities; embodiment politics; kinship politics
Mau Mau rebels, 29
Mechanical philosophy, 10, 167
Medieval system of rule, 6
Mexico, 37, 60, 128
Middle East, 26, 129
Mill, James, 26
Mill, John Stuart, 16
Minh, Ho Chi, 53
Modernity, 1, 7, 9, 10, 12, 18, 30, 53, 86, 97–102, 103, 114, 115, 119, 125, 139–141, 144, 145, 146, 167
  and Eurocentrism, 139–141
  and politics of gender and sexuality, 145–146
  and time, 9, 119, 139–141
Monroe Doctrine, 83
Morant Bay rebellion, 27
Morocco, 25, 52

N
Nagy, Imre, 85
Nation-state system, 2, 5, 114, 116, 124, 125, 132, 133, 135; *see also* international law; sovereignty
  and European colonialism, 2, 5, 8–9
  as cultural system, 132–133, 135
Nature metaphors, 17–19, 118
Nazism, 46
Nehru, Jawaharlal, 53, 54
Nepal, 50
Netherlands, Kingdom of, 21, 47, 62, 64, 70, 72–73, 76, 78–79, 81, 86, 171–172
  Dutch Guiana, 70, 72–73, 171–172
  Dutch West Indies, 70, 72–73, 171–172
New medievalism, 8
Nigeria, 52, 79
Nkrumah, Kwame, 51, 53, 54, 88–89
Non-aligned movement, 54
Non Self-Governing Territories (NSGTs), 29, 31, 32, 37, 44–46, 55–62, 65– 66, 69–70, 71, 73, 77, 98–101, 110–111, 113, 117, 126, 169, 171, 174
  in UN Charter, 42–46
  as debated in UNGA, 55–60, 62–66
North Atlantic Treaty Organization (NATO), 83
North-Caucasia, 84
North Vietnam, 54

O
Overseas départements, 47

P
Pacific, the, 26, 29
Pakistan, 49, 54
Palestine, 29
Panama, 65
Panoptical time, 9; *see also* time, politics of
Papal bulls, 21
Party for the Independence of Guinea Bissau and Cape Verde (PAIGC), 134
Paternalism, *see* kinship politics
Patriarchal family, *see* classical patriarchal family
Peru, 36
Philippines, 29, 54, 57, 58, 61, 76, 90–92, 128
Poland, 81
Political individual, 11; *see also* disembodied individual; universal individual
Portugal, 21, 47, 117, 174
Postcolonial international community, 4, 135
Postcolonial states, 4, 40, 135, 143
Progress, *see* linear progression
Pro-slavery plantocracy, 27
Puerto Rico, 70–76, 80, 82

R
Racialization, 1, 13–14; *see also* embodiment politics; feminization; hierarchy of masculinities; sexualization
  dark continent, 49
  mysterious East, 49
  racial science, 25
Rationalization, politics of, 1, 3, 11; *see also* embodiment politics
Resistance, 38, 39–40, 52, 66–67, 72, 80, 87, 114, 138, 147, 170, 174; *see also*, brotherhood
Roman Empire, 21

Roman family, 21

S
Sacred trust, 28, 45, 90, 102, 111, 74
Saint Domingue, 26
Saudi Arabia, 48, 119, 120
Sauvy, Alfred, 54
Schamyl, Said, 84
Scientific racism, 27; *see also* racialization
Sexualization, 1; *see also* feminization; racialization
Siam, 21
Sieyes, Emmanuel Joseph, 55
Smith, Adam, 24
Social, Humanitarian, and Cultural Committee (Third Committee), 129
Somalia, 52
South Africa, Union of, 60, 61, 62, 64, 98, 106, 171
South West Africa, 60, 61, 62, 64, 98, 99, 171
Sovereignty, 7, 22–23, 42–44, 48, 55, 58, 59, 60, 62, 63, 64, 66, 72, 73, 76, 85, 95–99, 101, 102, 106, 109, 130, 169, 173
  and colonial rule, 22–23
  and kinship politics, 99–102
  concept of, 7
  in anti-colonialist argument, 42, 48, 106
  in UN Charter, 42–44, 169
  in UNGA debates, 55, 58–60, 62–64, 66, 73, 76, 96–99, 101, 102, 106, 109, 130
Soviet Union, 36, 47, 49, 60, 61, 82, 85–86, 169–170; *see also* USSR
Soviet Utopia, 86
Space, politics of, 2, 5–10, 14, 16, 17, 29, 30, 37, 39, 66, 69, 71, 95, 112, 114, 127, 133, 135, 138–141, 143–145, 148, 169, 174
Spain, 19, 21, 172, 174
Special United Nations Fund for Economic Development (SUNFED), 128–129
Sudan, 54, 92
Sudan, medieval kingdom of, 87
Syria, 29, 48

T
Thailand, 52, 63
Third World, 29, 47, 49, 54, 55, 80, 82, 127, 174
  as identity and movement, 49
  coinage of term, 54–55
Time, politics of, 138; *see also* linear progression; modernity
  and anti-colonialism, 114–115, 120–122, 124, 135, 139–141
  and colonialism, 9, 119–120, 138–141
  time concepts, 139
Togoland, British, *see* Ghana
Togoland Congress (TC), 88–90, 93
Togolander movements, 71
Togoland, French, 87, 89, 93
Togoland, German protectorate of, 88
Togoland Union, 87
Transjordan, 29, 48
Transnational collective identity, 63
Treaty of Westphalia, *see* sovereignty
Trust Territories (Trusts)
  in UN Charter, 42–46
  as debated in UNGA, 60–66
Tunisia, 25
Turkestan, 84
Turkey, 21, 54, 118

U
Ukrainian Soviet Socialist Republic, 61
Underdevelopment, 2, 50, 146; *see also* development, stages of
United Arab Republic, 54, 81, 109–110, 118
United Gold Coast Convention, 87
United Nations, as international organization, 30–32
  Institutionalization of development in, 125–132
  Trusteeship System, 29, 44, 45, 62, 64, 65, 92, 93, 100, 105, 107, 110, 118, 125, 126, 170; *see also* Non Self-Governing Territories; Trust Territories
  UN Charter, 43–44
  UN Charter, in UNGA debates, 63–65
  UN Educational, Scientific, and Cultural Organization (UNESCO), 125, 129–131, 133–135
  UN General Assembly (UNGA), 31–32
  UN system, 124–125
United States, 25, 29, 36, 47, 54, 57, 59, 70, 72–76, 78, 79–83, 85–86, 100–101, 116, 128, 142, 169–170, 174
  and Asia-Africa, 78–83, 169–170

Index

and Puerto Rico, 74–76, 80–82
United Soviet Socialist Republics (USSR), 54, 69, 70, 72, 80, 82, 83–85, 92, 93, 105, 116, 174; *see also* Soviet Union
   and Asia-Africa, 84–86, 169–170
   republics of, 70, 84–85
   satellites of, 70, 84–85
Universal Declaration of Human Rights (UDHR), 57
Universal individual, 12; *see also* disembodied individual; political individual
Uruguay, 61, 92
Utilitarian political theories, 18

V
Vassalages, 23

Venezuela, 92, 98, 100

W
Washington, George, 81
Weber, Max, 11, 168, 171
World Bank, 54, 125, 128–129, 142
World economy, 6, 167
World Health Organization (WHO), 125
World polity, 81–82; *see also* world society
World society, 6, 132–133; *see also* world polity
World War I, 28, 53, 55, 88, 117
World War II, 42, 48, 55, 73, 81, 86, 132, 133, 147, 174

Y
Yemen, 48
Yugoslavia, 119